The International Reader

Interdisciplinary Perspectives on Current Events and Global Issues

First Edition

Edited by Kathryn LaFever
Miami University

cognella
SAN DIEGO

Bassim Hamadeh, CEO and Publisher

Jennifer Codner, Senior Field Acquisitions Editor

Michelle Piehl, Senior Project Editor

Alia Bales, Production Editor

Jess Estrella, Senior Graphic Designer

Trey Soto, Licensing Coordinator

Natalie Piccotti, Director of Marketing

Kassie Graves, Vice President of Editorial

Jamie Giganti, Director of Academic Publishing

cognella | ACADEMIC PUBLISHING

3970 Sorrento Valley Blvd., Ste. 500, San Diego, CA 9212

Contents

Chapter 6   Latin America   223

Introduction

THIS ANTHOLOGY PRESENTS INSIGHTS INTO MAJOR world regions and an array of complex international and interdisciplinary topics and current events. As the world turns, the international community is voicing intensifying concerns about topics this book addresses, including but not limited to climate change mitigation and adaptation, environmental degradation, pandemics, urbanization, and rising wealth and income disparities.

The scope of some of these issues can be international, national, regional, or local. In our increasingly interconnected and interdependent world, issues like terrorism and fragile states can have far-reaching impacts, threatening state, regional, and global security. Conversely, events and issues may occur exclusively in one place, often in highly contextualized and regionally specific ways. While issues or events may be discussed in the context of one region, they often manifest variously and simultaneously in different parts of the world. For example, issues such as rising sea levels or deforestation impact multiple global regions. A food security issue in one place may be similar to or distinct from food security issues elsewhere. This book sets out not to simplify but to recomplicate the issues and sets of questions they pose. Further, it problematizes attempts to arrive at a "silver bullet" or "one-size-fits-all" policy or solution.

This book is organized into chapters on each of the six major world regions: Africa, Asia, Europe, Latin America, the Middle East, and Oceania. Each chapter commences with a map and a list of the names of countries in the region and contains an introduction and readings corresponding to each region.

A **world region** refers to a territory that includes a group of countries and is defined by its homogeneous characteristics. Regions are human constructions, and there is no consensus on how to define each global region. For instance, some countries, like Turkey, can be understood as belonging to multiple regions or even none at all. Some regions may overlap, and the ways that regions are conceptualized shift and evolve over time. Further, the global regions discussed in this text do not include all of the countries of the world; notably, the United States and Canada fall out of the scope of this edition. Which countries to include in a region or the common characteristics of each can be a contentious issue, since regions are delineated to serve a variety of functions and expectations.

The content of this book represents knowledge and expertise from multiple disciplines. This anthology cultivates interdisciplinary approaches, encouraging questions, discussions, and analyses that integrate a range of disciplines and fields of study. Beyond reporting on international current events, this anthology seeks to inform and encourage readers to step out of their comfort zone, develop a healthy skepticism, press their thinking and perspectives, and make informed decisions as global citizens. Hopefully, readers will be inclined to follow closely, think deeply, and build continuously on their knowledge of these and related international and interdisciplinary topics.

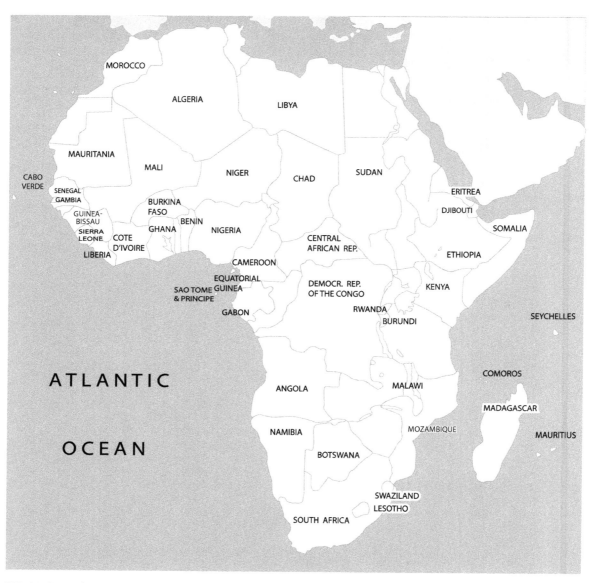

Chapter I

Africa

List of countries included in the world region of Africa:

- Algeria
- Angola
- Benin
- Botswana
- Burkina Faso
- Burundi
- Cabo Verde
- Cameroon
- Central African Republic (CAR)
- Chad
- Comoros
- Côte d'Ivoire
- Democratic Republic of the Congo (DRC)
- Djibouti
- Equatorial Guinea
- Eritrea
- Eswatini (formerly Swaziland)
- Ethiopia
- Gabon
- Gambia
- Ghana
- Guinea
- Guinea-Bissau
- Kenya
- Lesotho
- Liberia
- Libya
- Madagascar
- Malawi
- Mali
- Mauritania
- Mauritius
- Morocco
- Mozambique
- Namibia
- Niger
- Nigeria
- Republic of the Congo
- Rwanda
- São Tomé and Principe
- Senegal
- Seychelles
- Sierra Leone
- Somalia
- South Africa
- South Sudan
- Sudan
- Tanzania
- Togo
- Tunisia
- Uganda
- Zambia
- Zimbabwe

Introduction

This book discusses the vast and varied continent of Africa, minus Egypt, as a major world region. While much research tends to focus on Africa as a single global region, there are several reasons why this approach is problematic. For one thing, this approach reinforces the current tendency in much of the non-African world to erroneously conceptualize the African continent as one country. Further, facts and statistics on Africa are often provided in terms of its subregions, the two major ones being **North Africa** and **sub-Saharan Africa**. Of the 54 states, in general, 8 are in North Africa and 46 in sub-Saharan Africa. There are considerable cross-country and -regional variations among and between African subregions, which pose challenges to compiling, analyzing, and evaluating data on the whole African region. Moreover, North Africa may be classified as a part of the transcontinental Greater Middle East, a region often referred to as the **Middle East and North Africa** (**MENA**). In general, while North Africa is considered to share more similarities with the Middle East than sub-Saharan Africa, statistical data on the Middle East does not necessarily include North Africa. While this chapter discusses Africa as a singular major world region, in future editions of this text, it—as well as other world regions—may be conceptualized differently.

There is no consensus on the number of states in Africa, but what is a **state**? In general there are six characteristics that make a state a state (country). A state must have land and a human population. A state must have a government and the capacity to enter diplomatic, trade, and similar relations with other states. A state must be sovereign, meaning it has political autonomy and is recognized as a state by other states. The continent of Africa is home to the oldest and youngest countries in the world. Egypt, which began around 3100 B.C.E. and is considered the oldest country in the world, whereas South Sudan became independent of Sudan in 2011. The African continent is generally considered home to 54 states and two *de facto* independent but disputed states (Somaliland and the Saharan Arab Democratic Republic) that have limited international recognition. Africa also contains nine dependencies, or territories administered by non-African countries (for more information on dependencies, please see the Latin America chapter).

Demography is an important aspect of researching world regions and their issues. **Demography**, the study of the statistical data on human populations, looks at the overall size, distribution, and composition of a population. The standard demographic segments include but are not limited to age, ethnicity, race, religion, gender, education, and income.

In terms of demographics, Africa has a population of over 1.34 billion, accounting for nearly 17% of the world's population (United Nations, 2019b). Based on its population, Africa is the second-largest major world region after Asia. Africa is the world's youngest region, with a median age of about 20 years old. In fact, more than 40% of its population is under the age of 15. Further, unlike many world regions, Africa is not immediately facing an aging population or precipitously declining fertility rates. African fertility rates (live births per woman) have fallen from about 6.6% in 1955 to 4.4% in 2020. During the same time, infant and child mortality fell significantly as life expectancy increased by nearly 20 years, to around age 64 (Worldometer, 2020). With a population increase of 2% per year, Africa's population has more than doubled in the past 30 years and is expected to triple again by 2099 (Cohen & de Bassompierre, 2019). In particular, the population of Nigeria, currently one of the most populous countries on earth, is expected to increase eight-fold within the next two or three generations. By around 2050, Nigeria, a country about the size of Texas, is expected to be the third largest country by population, after China and India (World Population Review, 2019; Cohen & de Bassompierre, 2019).

Africa's Geographical Features

Among its distinctive geographical characteristics, Africa is a continent and region of astonishing size. In terms of total land mass, Africa is the second largest continent in the world after Asia. Covering approximately 30,380,560 square kilometers, Africa occupies about one fifth of Earth's total land surface. It stretches 5,000 miles (over 8,046 square kilometers) from north to south and 4,600 miles (over 7,400 square kilometers) from east to west. To put its vast size into perspective, consider that Africa is more than three times larger than Canada, the Sahara Desert is equal to the size of China, and the Democratic Republic of the Congo is about three times the size of Texas. Yet, despite its enormity, the *region* of Africa, at 11.73 million square miles, is smaller than the largest world *region* (not continent), Asia, which encompasses approximately 14.585 million square miles.

Among the region's unique geographical features, Africa is a plateau continent, generally about 3,000 feet above sea level. Africa contains multiple vast deserts, including coastal deserts as well as the Kalahari Desert in southern Africa and the Sahara Desert in northern Africa. It includes the Great Rift Valley in eastern Africa, comprised of 6,000 miles of fissures in the Earth's crust between Mozambique and Syria. Some of its valleys are 20 to 60 miles wide and filled with elongated lakes, home to unique species and ecosystems. Moreover, Africa is the only continent centered on the equator. In 2020, Burkina Faso was the hottest country on Earth, and six of the top 10 hottest countries on the planet were in Africa (Hottest Countries in the World, 2020). While all maps contain some distortion, Africa's equatorial symmetry generally makes it appear much smaller compared to other land masses than it actually is. For instance, most maps are two-dimensional and therefore do not compensate for the three-dimensional curve of the earth. So the size of Africa is distorted due to its equatorial symmetry. An oft-sighted fact is that while Africa may appear to be about the same size as Greenland, Africa is in fact fourteen times larger.

Many of the region's geographical features—including impenetrable jungles, vast deserts, awe-inspiring mountains, and precipitous escarpments—pose formidable topographical barriers to global and regional trade. The immensity and overall elevation of Africa compounds movement and trade across and within it. Further, this global region faces significant sea and waterway transportation and trade issues, despite bordering several major bodies of water—including the Atlantic Ocean as well as the Mediterranean, Red, and Indian Seas. The region of Africa has nearly 19,000 miles (30,500 kilometers) of coastline, yet it suffers from few natural inlets and bays, as well as underdeveloped commercial ports. Further, while Africa contains seven major rivers, including the Nile (the longest in the world), many rivers are not entirely navigable or accessible year-round by sea. Moreover, Africa contains 16 landlocked countries, which do not have direct sea or ocean access and must cross another country to reach a coastline.

Africa's Commodities and Resource-Dependent Economies

A **commodity** is a physical substance, an article of trade or commerce, that can be bought and sold. There are three major categories of commodities: agriculture, energy, and metals. Africa has tremendous natural resource wealth. It produces and exports a range of raw materials and manufactured goods, including cacao, cotton, coffee, tea, tobacco, clothing and textiles, and livestock, as well as fish, peanut, and wood products. In fact, Africa has some of the world's greatest reserves of valuable commodities, including fossil fuels and rare earth minerals. Resource-rich Africa contains about 30% of the world's mineral reserves, including the world's largest reserves of cobalt, diamonds, platinum, and uranium. It is home to 90% of the world's chromium and platinum and 40% of the world's gold. Africa contains about 12% of the world's oil and 8% of the world's natural gas reserves (UN Environment Program, n.d.). Why is this region the most impoverished on the planet?

Africa's natural resources have long been exploited. The Europeans postponed the First World War by concentrating efforts on colonizing Africa and capitalizing on its resources, which fueled the European industrial revolution. Today, Africa consumes little of its own resources and exports most of its raw materials. This arrangement benefits foreign economies far more than Africa's. Further, Africa loses an estimated $195 billion, annually, of its natural capital through illicit financial flows. There is tremendous loss of natural resources and raw materials through illegal extractive industries and logging as well as unregulated fishing and the illegal wildlife trade. Unabated economic exploitation and environmental degradation have contributed to the destabilization of Africa's economies and the depletion of its natural resources (UN Environment Program, n.d.). Further, the exploitation of Africa's raw materials helps to arm and fuel militant groups and keep corrupt leaders in power. In 2017, Africa was home to 15 of the top 25 most corrupt countries in the world (Transparency International, 2018).

The **resource curse** (resource trap or paradox of plenty) refers to a plight found mostly but not exclusively in Africa. The paradox is that a natural resource ends up being more of a curse than a blessing for the majority of the population. It starts with the discovery and export of a nonrenewable natural resource like oil or minerals. While little or no economic growth or quality of life develops from the sale of this valuable commodity relative to the broad distribution of the population, it creates an economic boon for those in power. The country's corrupt, authoritarian regime accumulates unconscionable wealth, skimming billions of dollars they receive illicitly and deposit clandestinely into offshore accounts. Typically, the kleptocratic government maintains its grip on resources for decades, sustaining dynastic families while running the country into the ground and depriving generations of their peoples opportunities for a prosperous future. Simultaneously, the majority of citizens experience staggering poverty and inequality, existing in a fragile, violent state, often as internally displaced persons in need of humanitarian aid caught between armed conflicts.

The terms **resource-dependent economy** or commodity-dependent economy are often used interchangeably. These terms can refer to a country or its economy that relies on export revenue. In general, a resource-dependent economy refers to a country that receives 60% or more of its revenue from commodity exports. The majority of these states are in sub-Saharan Africa (International Monetary Fund, 2019).

To what extent is a resource-dependent economy dependent? The International Monetary Fund (2019) estimates that in 35 countries, 90% of their economies depend on commodity exports. Similarly, the United Nations (2019a) finds that the economies of 89% of sub-Sahara are developing and resource-dependent countries, where commodities represent more than 60% of the value of their total merchandise exports. Coke-Hamilton (2019) finds that 13% of developed countries, 64% of developing countries, and 85% of the least-developed countries have resource-dependent economies. The economies of most developing nations depend on exporting their own commodities. In some resource-dependent economies, a single product accounts for three-fourths of all export revenue (Coke-Hamilton, 2019).

The poorest countries, relying on a single or limited number of commodities, are those less likely to absorb the economic shocks of declining real prices in commodities as well as the inevitable volatile swings and boom-and-bust cycles of the global commodities market. In other words, compared with diversified, service-based, and less commodity-based economies, global commodity price fluctuations tend to disproportionately impact resource-dependent countries.

More specifically, resource-dependent countries are prone to experience the negative economic repercussions (impacted by demand) of price volatility, oversaturated markets, and the economic stagnation associated with less domestic and global demand for commodities.

How can resource-dependent economies support sustained and inclusive growth to break the cycles of underdevelopment? It may seem logical for such countries to produce more of that commodity. Yet, increasing production often forces people to work more and in more detrimental conditions. Not only does this approach risk straining natural resources and compromising sustainable development, but it often produces diminishing—or fewer and lower—returns. Solutions often center on diversifying the economy and exports of resource-dependent countries. Among other things, these approaches can serve to reduce the dependency on one or a limited number of commodity exports, and increase the value of exports (Coke-Hamilton, 2019).

Agricultural Development in Africa

Africa's agriculture is the primary source of its own food and income, providing approximately 60% of all jobs in the region, 30–60% of the GDP, and about 30% of the value of exports (Diop, 2016). Although the majority (65%) of the world's arable land is in Africa, this region utilizes only about 38% of its total land area for agriculture. In other words, approximately 50 to 74 million additional acres of Africa's arable land that could be developed for agricultural production lie fallow. In particular, sub-Sahara, which is home to the majority of the world's impoverished and malnourished people, contains half of the world's arable land, much of which is currently unfarmed. Some of Africa's cultivable land is inaccessible due to the lack of roads and infrastructure as well as its location in forested areas and armed conflict zones (Diop, 2016; FAO, 2018; Goedde et al., 2019). Advances in peacekeeping and state building, as well as climate change resiliency and sustainable farming techniques, are among the critical issues related to growing Africa's vital agricultural economy.

More than 60% of sub-Sahara's population are **smallholder farmers**, referring to those who own small plots of land, usually less than 12 acres. These farmers typically rely on family labor to grow subsistence crops and one or two cash crops, which are crops that are grown for the purpose of selling for a profit (Goedde et al., 2019). Smallholder farmers produce approximately 80% of all food consumed in Africa (and Asia). They must compete on an unlevel playing field in the global marketplace, where they do not enjoy the same privileges as farmers in developed countries who benefit from a host of advantages, including insurance and subsidy programs. Smallholder farmers are among the poorest and most marginalized groups in the world. As the stewards of increasingly scarce natural resources, Africa's smallholder farmers are the vanguard addressing climate change (much of which is caused by developed nations), food security, water sustainability, wildlife conservation, deforestation, and biodiversity loss (African Smallholder Farmers Group, 2013).

African Cocoa

The cacao bean, from which chocolate is made, originated in the neotropical region of Latin America. The Spanish began importing cacao to Europe in 1585, and by the mid-1800s cocoa was being cultivated in Spain and Portugal's tropical colonies in Latin America, Asia, and Africa.

Now most of the world's cocoa comes from Africa. In 2016, six of the top 15 cocoa-producing countries were in sub-Saharan Africa, including the world's largest producer, Côte d'Ivoire. Côte d'Ivoire and Ghana produce cocoa mainly as a commodity crop grown for export. Those two countries combined produce over 60% of all global cocoa. In 2018, Africa produced and exported, mostly to Europe, more than two thirds of the world's cocoa. In 2019, Africa produced 75% of the world's cocoa but made only 2% of the $100 billion annual international chocolate market. In fact, from 1961 until 2016, Africa's share of total cocoa exports grew only 0.9%.

Cocoa farming is labor intensive and unprofitable for Africa's cocoa farmers, who utilize child and slave labor. The $60 billion chocolate industry does not pay its farmers a living wage and largely turns a blind eye to children who are forced to work in African cocoa farms (Fairtrade Foundation, 2020). An estimated two million West African children work or are enslaved on cocoa farms. These children are not adequately fed or educated and are habitually exposed to pesticides and other harmful chemicals (Food Empowerment Project, 2020). Cocoa production is dangerous work, and these children routinely suffer mental and physical abuse, including cuts, bruises, sprains, and musculoskeletal injuries. They wield machetes to cut the cacao pods and are forced to carry bags weighing 100 pounds or more, twice the weight of many of these children.

Conflict and Violence

In 2019, the world was slightly more peaceful than in the previous five years. Yet, nearly two billion people—one quarter of the global population—live in countries where development is impacted by conflict and violence. Conflict and violence are concentrated in pockets of developing nations, mostly in fragile states in sub-Saharan Africa, as well as the Middle East and North Africa, which were the least peaceful areas in the world (World Bank, 2019a; Institute for Economics & Peace, 2019). Conflict and violence cost those countries most impacted the equivalent of 35% GDP (Institute for Economics & Peace, 2019). Many countries have attitudes, institutions, and structures that do not prevent violence from breaking out, making it difficult to escape from a violence trap or vicious cycle of conflict (Institute for Economics & Peace, 2019).

Of the top 20 least peaceful countries in the world, eight are in Africa, more than any world region. While there were improvements in peace in Rwanda, The Gambia, Djibouti, Eswatini, and Somalia, violence increased in ongoing conflicts in Burkina Faso, Zimbabwe, Togo, Sierra Leone, Namibia, and Nigeria. For example, in 2018 there was civil unrest in Zimbabwe, militant attacks in 14 provinces in Burkina Faso, and militant attacks by Boko Haram in northeastern Nigeria. Yet, there was a reduction in ethnic violence in the Gambia, a major peace agreement between warring factions in CAR, and improvements between Eritrea and Ethiopia that have resulted in reduced violence between them. While levels of violent crime, state-based violence, and political instability improved in 2018, overall sub-Saharan Africa was deemed less safe than in 2017, based on an increase in violent demonstrations, terrorism, and incarceration (Institute for Economics & Peace, 2019). The number and intensity of armed conflicts in sub-Saharan Africa have increased in the past few years, affecting about one-third of sub-Saharan African states (International Monetary Fund, 2019).

The African Union, Agenda 2063, and Its Flagship Projects

The **African Union** (**AU**) is a multilateral international governmental organization (IGO), established in 2001 with 55 member states. Based in Addis Ababa, Ethiopia, it works for peace, security, and stability as well as greater unity and solidarity between African peoples and states. This IGO also promotes the political and socioeconomic integration of the African continent.

"Agenda 2063, The Africa We Want," adopted in 2015, is the African Union's long-term, 50-year plan for transforming Africa by the year 2063. Its 14 flagship projects include developing infrastructure, including an integrated high-speed train network, a single African air market between capital cities, and a Pan-African e-network. It includes developing energy and communications infrastructure. Among others, the flagship projects include establishing an integrated electronic all-Africa passport system, removing border restrictions, and implementing other forms of integration for the free movement of Africans within the continent.

One of the African Union's flagship projects is instituting the African Continental Free Trade Area (AfCFTA). It establishes a liberalized free-trade area comprised of all members states of the African Union. The AfCFTA free-trade area includes a single market of 1.3 billion people with a combined GDP of $2.5 trillion, and over $6.7 trillion in combined consumer and business spending (IMF, 2019; Signe, 2018; United Nations, 2019b). The inter-Africa free-trade agreement replaces multiple and overlapping trade agreements that currently exist between many African countries. It has multiple goals, including the integration of

African economies and liberalization of trade through a single continental market for African goods and services, as well as the free movement of business people and investments. The AfCFTA pact is expected to help many African states diversify their commodity-dependent economies and export more high-value exports (United Nations, 2019b). It has the potential to increase sustained export growth as well as boost industrialization and foreign direct investment in African countries. It is expected to increase Africa's industrial exports by more than 50% over 12 years as well as create jobs and entrepreneurial opportunities for its young population (United Nations, 2019b). This treaty, ratified in 2018, created the world's largest free-trade agreement since the formation of the World Trade Organization in 1995.

References

African Smallholder Farmers Group. (2013, July). *Supporting smallholder farmers in Africa: A framework for an enabling environment*. http://www.ruralfinanceandinvestment.org/sites/default/files/ASFG-Framework-Report.pdf

Cohen, M., & de Bassompierre, L. (2019, May 17). How booming population is challenging Africa. *Washington Post*. https://www.washingtonpost.com/business/how-booming-population-is-challenging-africa/2019/05/17/ce642764-7860-11e9-a7bf-c8a43b84ee31_story.html?utm_term=.1f3cbebacc3a

Coke-Hamilton, P. (2019, May 17). *We must help developing countries escape commodity dependence*. World Economic Forum. https://www.weforum.org/agenda/2019/05/why-commodity-dependence-is-bad-news-for-all-of-us/

Diop, M. (2016, January 22). *Foresight Africa 2016: Banking on agriculture for Africa's future*. Brookings Institute. https://www.brookings.edu/blog/africa-in-focus/2016/01/22/foresight-africa-2016-banking-on-agriculture-for-africas-future/

Fairtrade Foundation. (2020). *Cocoa farmers*. https://www.fairtrade.org.uk/Farmers-and-Workers/Cocoa

Food and Agriculture Organization of the United Nations (FAO). (2018). *World food and agriculture: Statistical pocketbook 2018*. http://www.fao.org/3/ca1796en/CA1796EN.pdf

Food Empowerment Project (2020). *Child labor and slavery in the chocolate industry*. https://foodispower.org/human-labor-slavery/slavery-chocolate/

Goedde, L., Ooko-Ombaka, A., & Pais, G. (2019, February). *Winning in Africa's agricultural market*. McKinsey & Company. https://www.mckinsey.com/industries/agriculture/our-insights/winning-in-africas-agricultural-market

Hammill, J. (2019, January 29). The mask slips from the grim reality of Mnangagwa's Zimbabwe. *World Politics Review*. https://www.worldpoliticsreview.com/articles/27301/the-mask-slips-to-reveal-the-grim-reality-of-mnangagwa-s-zimbabwe

Institute for Economics & Peace. (2019, June). *Global Peace Index 2019: Measuring peace in a complex world*. http://visionofhumanity.org/app/uploads/2019/06/GPI-2019-web003.pdf

International Monetary Fund (IMF). (2019, April). Regional economic outlook. *Sub-Saharan Africa: Recovery amid elevated uncertainty*. https://www.imf.org/en/Publications/REO/SSA/Issues/2019/10/01/sreo1019

Pilling, D. (2018, August 13). African economy: The limits of "leapfrogging." *Financial Times*. https://www.ft.com/content/052b0a34-9b1b-11e8-9702-5946bae86e6d

Signe, L. (2018, March 26). African leaders have created the world's largest free-trade area since the WT—here's its potential. *Quartz Africa*. https://qz.com/1238185/africa-creates-worlds-largest-free-trade-area-since-wto-heres-its-potential/

Transparency International. (2018). *Corruption perceptions index 2018*. https://www.transparency.org/cpi2018

UN Environment Program. (n.d.). *Our work in Africa*. https://www.unenvironment.org/regions/africa/our-work-africa

United Nations. (2019a). *State of commodity dependence 2019*. United Nations Conference on Trade and Development. https://unctad.org/en/PublicationsLibrary/ditccom2019d1_en.pdf

United Nations. (2019b). *World economic situation and prospects 2019*. https://unctad.org/en/PublicationsLibrary/wesp2019_en.pdf

Wee, R. Y. (2019, July 18). Most ethnically diverse countries in the world. *World Atlas*. https://www.worldatlas.com/articles/most-ethnically-diverse-countries-in-the-world.html

World Bank. (2019a, April). *Africa's pulse: An analysis of issues shaping Africa's economic future*, Vol. 19. https://openknowledge.worldbank.org/handle/10986/32480

World Bank. (2019b, October 15). *World Bank in Africa: Sub-Saharan Africa's growth is projected to reach 3.1 percent in 2018, and to average 3–6 percent in 2019–20*. https://www.worldbank.org/en/region/afr/overview

World Population Review. (2019). *Africa population 2019*. http://worldpopulationreview.com/continents/africa-population/

Worldometer. (2020). Africa demographics. https://www.worldometers.info/demographics/demographics-of-africa/

Islamist Extremism in East Africa

Abdisaid M. Ali

HIGHLIGHTS

- While Islamist extremism in East Africa is often associated with al Shabaab and Somalia, it has been expanding to varying degrees throughout the region.

- Militant Islamist ideology has emerged only relatively recently in East Africa—imported from the Arab world—challenging long-established norms of tolerance.

- Confronting Islamist extremism with heavy-handed or extrajudicial police actions are likely to backfire by inflaming real or perceived socioeconomic cleavages and exclusionist narratives used by violent extremist groups.

THE RISK OF ISLAMIST EXTREMISM IN East Africa frequently focuses on Somalia and the violent actions of al Shabaab. Yet local adherents to extremist versions of Islam can now be found throughout the region. As a result, tensions both within Muslim communities and between certain Islamist groups and the broader society have been growing in the region in recent years.

These tensions have not emerged suddenly or spontaneously. Rather, they reflect an accumulation of pressure over decades. The genesis of this is largely the externally driven diffusion of Salafist ideology from the Gulf states. Buoyed by the global oil boom and a desire to spread the ultraconservative Wahhabi version of Islam throughout the Muslim world, funding for mosques, madrassas, and Muslim youth and cultural centers began flowing into the region at greater levels in the 1980s and 1990s. Opportunities for East African youth to study in the Arab world steadily expanded. As these youth returned home, they brought with them more rigid and exclusivist interpretations of Islam. The expanding reach of Arab satellite television has reinforced and acculturated these interpretations to a wider audience.

The effect has been the emergence of an increasingly confrontational strain of Islam in East Africa. Salafist teachings, once seen as fringe, became mainstream. The number of Salafist mosques has risen rapidly. In turn, it became increasingly unacceptable to have an open dialogue on the tenets of Islam (see box). Growing intolerance has fostered greater religious polarization.

Over time, these tensions have turned violent. Attacks by militant Islamists against civilians in East Africa (outside of Somalia) rose from just a few in 2010 to roughly 20 per year since then. The vast majority of these have been in Kenya. Most sensational was the days-long 2013 siege of the Westgate shopping complex in Nairobi, where militants caused more than 60 civilian deaths and left hundreds injured. Though al Shabaab claimed responsibility for the attack, experts agree that the attack required support from multiple local, Kenyan sympathizers. Al Shabaab committed an even deadlier attack the following year when Somali and Kenyan members of the group stormed the campus of Kenya's Garissa University and killed 147 students. Al Shabaab has attempted to maximize the potential divisiveness of these attacks by singling out non-Muslims for execution.

Questioning the Nature of Apostasy in Islam

In 2014, Abdisaid Abdi Ismail published a book questioning whether the death penalty for apostasy was just in Islam. In doing so he joined a growing stream of Muslim scholars rejecting the use of Islamic tenets as a political tool to support violent movements. The response in the region was dramatic. He himself was labeled an apostate, received death threats, and was kicked out of hotels in Kenya and Uganda. Some East African clergy called for his book to be burned. Their protests ultimately led to the book being removed from Kenyan bookstands—despite more than 80 percent of Kenyans being Christian and just over 10 percent being Muslim. His experience reveals the extent to which moderate voices and open debate on the teachings of Islam are being suppressed—reinforcing more rigid interpretations of Islam in East Africa.

Local, smaller scale attacks have also increased in regularity. Bus stations, bars, shops, churches, and even moderate mosques and imams have been targeted. Some of these attacks have been attributed to the Muslim Youth Center (MYC), a Nairobi-based group that has lauded Islamic militant activities. MYC, which began using the name al Hijra in 2012, has also supported al Shabaab with fundraising and recruitment and was allegedly linked to the

Westgate attack. In Mombasa, violent street clashes between followers of militant Islamist clerics and the police have erupted on a number of occasions.

In Tanzania, Sheikh Ponda Issa Ponda and his group Jumuiya ya Taasisi za Kiislam ("Community of Muslim Organizations") have been accused of inciting riots and burning churches in Dar es Salaam. Tanzania is also home to the al Shabaab-linked Ansaar Muslim Youth Center.[1]

The U.S. embassy in Uganda has regularly issued warnings of possible attacks since 2014. One of those alerts coincided with Ugandan forces foiling an imminent attack by a Kampala-based terror cell, arresting 19 people and seizing explosives and suicide vests.[2] Most memorably, Uganda suffered twin bombings in July 2010 that killed 76 who had gathered at a restaurant and a rugby club in the capital to watch the World Cup final. Al Shabaab claimed responsibility but in 2016 seven men from Uganda, Tanzania, and Kenya were convicted of carrying out the attack.

Connections between the region and the global jihad movement also appear to be expanding. While Kenya and Tanzania were targets of the al Qaeda-orchestrated U.S. embassy bombings in 1998 and the Mombasa tourist hotel attack in 2002, the region has not been a hotbed of support for global jihadism. However, Tanzanian Defense Minister Hussein Ali Mwinyi has warned that increasing numbers of citizens were joining the Islamic State and al Shabaab.[3] At some point, these East African recruits may also return home, presenting a new security threat.

The rising violence of Islamist extremists has generated a strong response from security actors in East Africa. At times, these operations are conducted indiscriminately, however. The Kenyan government's Operation Usalama Watch, for example, resulted in the incarceration of an estimated 4,000 people, the majority without charge. Largely conducted in regions with sizable Somali Muslim populations, the impression of many in these communities was that they were being unjustly punished for the acts of a handful of extremists.[4] The result may be more support for violent Islamist groups. Interviews with Kenyan-born members of extremist Islamist groups found that 65 percent of respondents pointed to Kenya's counterterrorism policy as the primary factor that motivated them to join their violent campaign.[5]

In short, radical Islamist ideology has been spreading throughout East African communities—bringing with it greater societal polarization and violence. Further escalation is not inevitable, however. The region has a long tradition of inter-religious harmony. Nonetheless, experience demonstrates that Islamist extremist ideology can be very difficult to counter once it takes root in a society. It is vital for East African governments and citizens, therefore, to understand both the external and domestic drivers of these extremist ideologies, so that the process of radicalization can be interrupted before it cements itself within local communities and grows increasingly violent.

The Evolution of Islam in East Africa

Muslims have lived in East Africa for generations. Trade and cultural exchanges between East Africa and the Arab world are centuries old. These links predate European colonization and retain substantial social and economic influence. Precise numbers are not fully known but Muslims seem to comprise between 10 and 15 percent of the population in Kenya and Uganda and some 35–40 percent of the Tanzanian population.

There has never been a uniform Islamic community in East Africa. Rituals, celebrations, and theological interpretations vary across the region. Most East African Muslims subscribe to Sunni interpretations of Islam, though there are also Shi'ia communities and members of the Ahmadiyya sect. Sufism, often described as a "mystical" interpretation of Islam that includes the veneration of saints, is also common. Some Muslim communities have absorbed practices and rituals from traditional African beliefs, including attributing spiritual significance to sacred objects. Despite these differences, religious communities in the region, whether Muslim or non-Muslim, have historically tended to coexist peacefully and overlook differences in theology or religious practice.

This has changed for some communities in recent decades as a result of the growing influence of Salafist ideology. A small but growing number of Muslims have adopted more exclusivist interpretations of their religion, thereby changing their relationship with other Muslims, with other faiths, and with the state. The radical view of a global struggle for Islam is by no means pervasive but it is very much present in a way it was not before.[6]

One channel by which this shift has occurred is through education. Lacking other opportunities for schooling, Muslim families in marginalized areas rely on madrassas, or Islamic schools. Over the last several decades, these madrassas have been the beneficiaries of growing streams of funding from centers of religious education based in Arab countries. In the process, these students have been steadily exposed to the cultural and religious identity of their sponsors.

Opportunities for tertiary education have also expanded. While college degrees in the West continue to be viewed as most prestigious, following the 2001 World Trade Center attacks Western countries raised immigration hurdles. At the same time, scholarship opportunities in the Arab world were ramping up. This trend has continued and has been accelerating since 2010 (see figure). Out of practicality, many East African Muslims turned to these opportunities and became exposed to more fundamentalist versions of Islam.

Another vehicle through which interpretations of Islam in East Africa were shifted was through access to media from the Arab world. The expansion in the number and geographic reach of Arab satellite TV stations in the 1990s and 2000s brought Arab cultural norms to a wider audience in East Africa on a daily basis. This fostered more conservative interpretations of Islam regarding dress, the role of women, and differentiated relationships between Muslims and non-Muslims.

The traction of such ideas is evident in the expanding popularity and influence of extremist clerics. Salafism, which had been a fringe off-shoot of Islam in East Africa in the 1990s, has become common today. A leading proponent in Kenya was the preacher Abou Rogo Mohammed, who for over a decade denigrated non-Muslims, criticized moderate Muslims, and instructed followers to forsake inter-religious dialogue, to abstain from politics, and to boycott elections. In one sermon Rogo deemed an attack on a church that killed 17 people as "just retribution" for Christian encroachment on Muslim lands. Rogo, who was closely affiliated with the militant Islamist group al Hijra and other conservative Islamic schools, separately proclaimed that "in this country we [Muslims] live amongst infidels."[7] Rogo's ideology has persisted since his death in 2012. Tapes and DVDs of his and others' incendiary sermons are still traded throughout the region.

In Tanzania, extremist clerics now aggressively challenge the authority of more moderate Islamic organizations and incite protests and clashes with government bodies under questionable pretenses. Sheikh Ponda has also challenged moderate Islamic groups such as Baraza Kuu la Waislam Tanzania (Bakwata), a quasi-state Islamic body. He and his followers have called for boycotts of state censuses and the removal of education officials whom they claim discriminate against Islamic schools.[8] Ponda's network, which has been active since the 1990s, includes hundreds of mosques and dozens of Islamic schools across

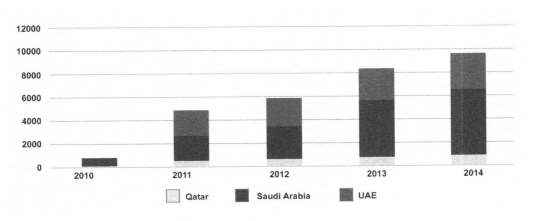

East African Students Enrolled in Gulf State Universities

Source: UNESCO

Tanzania. Extremist interpretations of Islam and notions of a religious divide and persecution by the state have crept into the sermons of other Tanzanian Islamic preachers as well.[9] As in Kenya, such rhetoric has come with an uptick in attacks, including against foreigners and Christian leaders.[10]

External Influences

A major contributing factor to East Africa's shift toward more militant interpretations of Islam is the influence of well-funded foreign Islamist groups. This includes so-called Wahhabi organizations whose sponsorship of educational and religious activities has been fueled by the wealth of Saudi Arabia, Qatar, and other oil-rich Gulf states. Unlike East Africa's historical tradition of infusing religious customs with local traditions, Wahhabism is an extremely conservative interpretation of the Koran. It forbids most aspects of modern education, requires strict dress codes, abides by ancient traditions of social relations, and disregards many basic human rights, particularly for women. While Wahhabism does not on principle denounce other faiths, many Wahhabi preachers do not tolerate other viewpoints. Even other interpretations of Islam, such as Sufism, are considered heretical and offensive to Wahhabis.[11] In effect, the version of Islam that is being imported to East Africa is rooted within a particular Arab cultural identity.[12] This is very different from the Islamic traditions that have evolved in other Muslim countries like Malaysia or Indonesia.

Foreign-sponsored East African Muslim groups have had a presence in East Africa since the mid-20th century, but have expanded significantly since the 1970s.[13] One estimate pegged funding from Saudi Arabia at $1 million per year on Islamic institutions in Zanzibar alone.[14] The aims of the foreign funding are diffuse, going to social centers, madrassas, primary, secondary, and tertiary educational institutions, and to humanitarian and social programs. Many investments are large and multiyear. The Kuwait-based Africa Muslims Agency is a prime example.[15] It has operations across the continent, including in Kenya, Malawi, Madagascar, Uganda, and Zimbabwe. One such operation involves a 33-year agreement signed in 1998 with the Zanzibari government to operate a university that has so far produced over 1,200 graduates.[16]

Not all beneficiaries of these funds are strictly Wahhabi or conservative to begin with. Some schools, social centers, and humanitarian outreach programs mix Wahhabi materials and programs with secular activities to reach a broader audience. In Kenya, the Saudi government has for decades provided financial support and scholarships to the Kisauni College of Islamic Studies in Mombasa, where Abou Rogo Mohammed studied.[17] Likely dozens and potentially hundreds of madrassas and primary and secondary schools in Kenya have been built and underwritten in a similar manner.

Some activities supported by these foreign Islamic groups are laudable. They have sponsored medical care and provided aid during disasters, similar to other faith-based and secular organizations. However, these humanitarian activities are not entirely benign, since many of these Islamic groups will integrate proselytization into all their activities or will require that participants abide by strict, conservative customs to access funds or benefits.[18]

Some groups do have links to militant Islamist organizations. The Saudi-funded Al Haramain Islamic Foundation, for example, which had a large presence in refugee camps and supported many madrassas in East Africa, including some linked to Ansaar Muslim Youth Center, was closed and expelled from Kenya and Tanzania for such links.[19] The Revival of Islamic Heritage Society, a Kuwaiti nongovernmental organization, was likewise found to have been providing financial and material support to al Qaeda-linked organizations, including al Shabaab's predecessor, Al-Itihaad al-Islamiya (AIAI). Notably, AIAI's Somali leaders were largely educated in the Middle East.[20]

Whether universities or bare-bones madrassas, educational institutions have obvious strategic value in shaping the beliefs of youth. Some of these schools do provide valuable instruction in math, sciences, and more. However, they also inculcate a rigid interpretation of Islam that is exclusionary and emphasizes da'wa, or the further proselytization of this brand of Islam. The curriculum also sometimes follows a principle called "Islamization of knowledge" developed in an effort to reconcile fundamentalist Islamic ethics into the disciplines of law, banking, and finance, among others. Over time, students absorb very definitive ideas of what is and what is not Islamic and who is and who is not a Muslim—and are encouraged to actively advance these same views.[21] This is a recipe for confrontation, even if the programs that initially promoted such views did not advocate violence.

This growing influence of extremist Islam in East Africa has mostly been limited to particular neighborhoods, cities, or regions. But those effects have been cumulative and compounding, leading an increasing number of groups in the region to adopt progressively more aggressive and confrontational missions. The growth of networks that may be sympathetic to violent extremism lays the groundwork for the local collaboration that has been seen or suspected in deadly al Shabaab attacks in Kenya, Tanzania, and Uganda.

Socioeconomic Grievances

While the extremist Islamist ideology taking hold in East Africa is imported from elsewhere, exacerbating factors play a role in how meaningfully such ideology resonates upon exposure. For instance, despite terrorists exhibiting varying levels of wealth, education, zealousness, and experience, socioeconomic marginalization fuels the credibility and dispersal of extremist narratives. In East Africa, perceptions of unequal socioeconomic status and some ill-advised state actions have nudged Muslims toward more conservative tendencies and enabled "us versus them" narratives to resonate.

East African Muslims do have legitimate grievances. Youth unemployment in Kenya's Muslim-dominated Coast and North Eastern provinces are 40–50 percent higher than the national average.[22] Rates of primary and secondary school completion and attendance tend to be lower in Muslim counties, probably because there are fewer schools and teachers per student in the two coastal provinces than in other parts of Kenya. Similar patterns can be seen in Tanzania. The youth unemployment rate in the overwhelmingly Muslim island of Zanzibar has been about 17 percent in recent years,[23] almost twice the national average of 9 percent.[24] Also, the primarily Muslim coastal areas often have poorly defined property rights, hindering economic opportunities and paving the way for occasional land seizures by the government or large, non-local businesses.

Public opinion surveys depict a less divisive portrait at national levels. One survey of Kenyans showed that about half of Muslim respondents perceived their living conditions as the same or better than others. In comparison, about two-thirds of Christian respondents felt the same way. Still, this reflects Muslim sentiment that roughly matches the rest of Kenyan society—a perspective that has persisted for a number of years according to earlier survey rounds in 2008 and 2011.[25] In Tanzania, 53 percent of Muslims surveyed perceived their living conditions as the same or better than other Tanzanians. Christians answered identically. Such results likely reflect the long history of harmonious interfaith relations in the region and the continuing resilience of such bonds when viewed at a nationwide level.

The challenge of Islamic extremism is often a more local phenomenon. Perceptions of religious discrimination are higher in particular areas where divisive and exclusionary Islamic narratives have been present and circulating longer, such as Mombasa, Zanzibar, Tanga, and sections of Dar es Salaam and Nairobi. Accordingly, East African Muslims who subscribe to extremist interpretations of Islam remain a small (though vocal) minority. Yet the growth of this minority reflects and perpetuates a steady erosion of East African resilience in the face of the extremist Islamist ideology that has been coursing the region.

Claims that Muslims are deliberately denied economic, educational, and other opportunities relative to their non-Muslim compatriots have become common within the region's Muslim communities, moderate and extremist alike.[26] For many Muslims, particularly youth, such inequality validates the divisive messages of fundamentalist Islamic centers, madrassas, and mosques.

Government Actions That Alienate

East African governments have pursued legal action against various Muslim leaders in recent years in an attempt to isolate suspected extremists. Unfortunately, many of these judicial efforts have failed, further reinforcing a sense that the government is unfairly persecuting Muslims. For instance, when Sheikh Ponda was tried for inciting riots in Tanzania in October 2012, poorly framed charges and a weak investigation led only to a short, suspended sentence. Ponda was later charged again with inciting Muslims in Zanzibar and Morogoro to strike and riot. Yet, after 2 years of litigation he was acquitted for lack of evidence. Even then, prosecutors announced their intent to raise the twice-lost case to Tanzania's High Court. In Kenya, Sheikh Mohammed Dor was charged with incitement after allegations that he intended to fund a coastal separatist group. Prosecutors soon altered the charges, a judge then postponed the trial, and eventually the state dropped its case entirely.

Prominent Muslim leaders in Kenya and Tanzania have also been detained by security agents without charge. Some have been mysteriously assassinated. Allegations of police-sponsored death squads that target radical Muslim leaders have been circulating widely for years. One incident attributed to such a squad is the death of Abou Mohammed Rogo, who was killed in a drive-by shooting in Mombasa in August 2012. In his vehicle were his father and daughter as well as his wife, who was injured. A little over a year later and just weeks after the Westgate mall attack in Nairobi, Rogo's successor Sheikh Ibrahim Ismail and three others were killed in another drive-by shooting. Ismail's successor, Sheikh Abubakar Shariff, known as Makaburi, was killed in April 2014, just 2 days after the police's anti-terror unit linked him to al Hijra attacks in Mombasa the previous month.

Muslims for Human Rights, a Kenyan advocacy group, has claimed that police and prosecutors may be turning to extrajudicial measures due to their inability to conduct proper investigations or prosecutions of suspected Islamic extremists. That narrative has only strengthened over time. Human Rights Watch reported that, from 2014 to 2016, Kenyan security forces "forcibly disappeared" at least 34 people during counterterrorism operations in Nairobi and the northeast, and in at least 11 cases dead bodies were found of people who had recently been arrested by government authorities. One of Kenya's top investigative journalists has claimed that the numbers were even higher, saying that he has uncovered 1,500 extrajudicial killings of citizens by the police since 2009.[27]

Similar charges have unfolded in Tanzania. In October 2012, Sheikh Farid Hadi Ahmed, the head of the Uamsho Islamic group, which advocates for an autonomous Zanzibar under Islamic law, went missing. Uamsho leaders called for the police to investigate. Supporters launched demonstrations, some deadly. Ahmed reappeared after 4 days and claimed that he had been abducted by police officers. He was promptly arrested by police and held without bail for months under a provision of the National Security Act. A judge ultimately dismissed several district-level charges against Ahmed since prosecutors failed to furnish any evidence against him. However, charges of incitement and conspiratorial involvement in his own kidnapping remained in place. Prosecutors then blocked Ahmed's ability to file for bail or even to enter a plea. After taking his case to Tanzania's High Court, Ahmed was eventually granted bail in 2014 after 17 months in jail. Six months later, he was rearrested on terrorism charges.

Beyond the specifics of this or other cases, the lack of transparency and pattern of haphazard arrests, bail policies, and prosecutions have made many Muslims suspicious of political leaders and state institutions. Combined with a sense that they have been economically marginalized, many are increasingly disinclined to work through existing governance structures in order to right perceived wrongs. As a result, extremist and exclusivist Islamic narratives can seem more compelling.

Reversing the Spread of Extremism

This review has shown that the drivers of Islamist extremism in East Africa are both external and internal. A framework for redressing this threat, therefore, will require a series of actions on both levels.

Counter External Influences and Emphasize Domestic Traditions of Tolerance

Destabilizing, exclusivist Islamist narratives—a relatively recent import—have begun to erode a long history of tolerance in East Africa. Governments and civil society groups need to counter these by capitalizing on and strengthening the region's much longer history of religious diversity and tolerance. This will take genuine and patient engagement on behalf of political leaders as well as indirect efforts to support more interreligious dialogue that yields constructive and tangible benefits for participants.

As part of reinforcing indigenous, tolerant traditions, governments will have to address funding by foreign, fundamentalist Islamic entities. This will require adopting transparent and consistent means to regulate the funding sources, sectarian rhetoric, and militant leanings of religious groups. Groups that promote violence or open confrontation should clearly be banned and prosecuted. In addition, funding for social services should be separated from proselytization. However, blanket criminalization of conservative Islamic groups should be avoided as this will likely spur more support for violent movements. Rather, a policy of tolerance with a clear prohibition against violence and divisiveness should be pursued.

Improve Political Inclusion of Muslim Communities

Political leaders should acknowledge that Muslims have some legitimate claims of marginalization, whether by design or neglect. This alone will send a powerful message to Muslim constituencies and may spark a sense of trust in collaboration and reform. Leaders should also expand engagement with Muslim communities, including those that may have experienced some radicalization but have not advocated violence.

When security improved in Kenya's northeast in the latter half of 2015 it was credited to the regional coordinator Mohamud Ali Saleh, a former ambassador to Saudi Arabia who had been named to the post after the Garissa University attack. The subsequent reduction in terrorism observed in this region stemmed not from more robust enforcement but rather as a result of Saleh's skills as an interlocutor between the government and local communities. This resulted in improved community policing and intelligence tip-offs.

Invest in Citizens Economically and Institutionally

Socioeconomic inequalities must be transparently addressed so they are minimized as legitimate grievances. Programs should target inequality of education, income, and opportunity, regardless of whether the root cause is truly religious discrimination or in fact a symptom of regional, urban, or rural dynamics. Programs could aim to boost employment levels in Muslim-majority areas.

> *"The situation calls for rebuilding and cultivating East African resilience in the face of radical messages and violent behavior"*

Strengthening and clarifying property codes and land rights would also help. Muslims in coastal East Africa who hold tenuous land rights to their homes and businesses fear exploitation and expropriation by the government or large businesses. Strengthened property rights may ease religious tensions and allow for the growth and political engagement of a successful Muslim middle class.

Education is also key. Muslim-dominated regions of East Africa lag behind in the number and quality of schools and teacher-to-student ratios. Politically, even small, quick improvements to existing facilities in these regions could build goodwill. Longer term, more Muslim youth should be targeted for scholarships to balance the effects from external ideological influences. Such educational opportunities will also enable them to fill subsequent leadership roles in the broader society, facilitating greater integration.

Practice Due Process

Governments must also understand that perceptions matter when countering radical ideology. Individuals who stir others to violence are certainly a threat to stability. However, if the public does not believe that legal processes are being followed, then police actions can further fuel support for radicals and their messages. Adhering to the law reinforces its value in the minds (and actions) of these marginalized communities, both as a source of protection and as a demarcation of illegality.

Governments should thus avoid expansive legal actions that have a weak basis or are likely to fail in court. Instead, they should focus on improving law enforcement procedures, evidence collection, and building prosecutorial capacity. When authorities do not have sufficient grounds to prosecute incendiary Muslim leaders or entities, arrests will only be perceived as harassment and counterproductively burnish extremists' claims of victimization.

Extrajudicial police action must also stop. The government should instead support transparent, credible investigations by independent experts to evaluate claims that Islamic leaders were killed by anyone connected to the state or political leadership. Making these findings public may rebuild some element of trust in the government.

In aggregate, these efforts should not myopically focus on particular individuals who may come and go irrespective of the wider resonance of their views. Instead, they must delegitimize the ideology of violent extremism itself.

Notes

1. "Al Shabaab in Somalia still a threat to peace in spite of decline—UN," defenceWeb, August 14, 2012.

2. "Uganda arrests 19 tied to suspected terror attack plot," *CBC News*, September 14, 2014.

3. "Situation Report: Tanzania: Video Shows Possible New Islamic State Affiliate," Stratfor Web site, May 18, 2016.

4. Ryan Cummings, "Al-Shabaab and the Exploitation of Kenya's Religious Divide," IPI Global Observatory, December 2014.

5. Anneli Botha, "Radicalisation in Kenya: Recruitment to al-Shabaab and the Mombasa Republican Council," ISS Paper 265, September 2014.

6. Terje Østebø, "Islamic Militancy in Africa," *Africa Security Brief* No. 23 (Africa Center for Strategic Studies, November 2012), 4. Chanfi Ahmed, "Networks of Islamic NGOs in Sub-Saharan Africa: Bilal Muslim Mission, African Muslim Agency (Direct Aid), and *al-Haramayn*," *Journal of East African Studies* 3, no. 3 (November 2009), 426–437. Ioannis Gatsiounis, "After Al-Shabaab," *Current Trends in Islamist Ideology* 14 (December 2012).

7. David Ochami, "How fiery cleric Rogo developed, propagated extremism," *The Standard*, September 2, 2012.

8. Anne Robi, "Muslim Clerics Call for New Census Team," *Tanzania Daily News*, June 4, 2012.

9. Ahmed, 430–431. "Muslim clerics warned against hate sermons," *The Citizen*, January 7, 2013.

10. Andre LeSage, *The Rising Terrorist Threat in Tanzania: Domestic Islamist Militancy and Regional Threats*, Strategic Forum No. 288 (Washington, DC: National Defense University Press, September 2014).

11. "Interview: Vali Nasr," PBS "Frontline" Website, available at <http://www.pbs.org/wgbh/pages/frontline/shows/saudi/interviews/nasr.html>.

12. Ben Hubbard, "A Saudi Morals Enforcer Called for a More Liberal Islam. Then the Death Threats Began," *The New York Times*, July 10, 2016.

13. Gatsiounis, 74.

14. Katrina Manson, "Extremism on the rise in Zanzibar," *Financial Times*, December 28, 2012.

15. Ahmed, 427.

16. "Africa Muslim Agency Sets Up College in Zanzibar," Panafrican News Agency, July 26, 1998.

17. *Kenyan Somali Islamist Radicalisation*, Africa Briefing No. 85 (Nairobi/Brussels: International Crisis Group, January 2012), 5, 11.

18. Ahmed, 434–435.

19. Patrick Mayoyo, "Kenya Muslims Say No to US School Funds," *The East African*, February 23, 2004. "Treasury Announces Joint Action with Saudi Arabia Against Four Branches of Al-Haramain In The Fight Against Terrorist Financing," U.S. Department of the Treasury press release, January 22, 2004.

20. "Kuwaiti Charity Designated for Bankrolling al Qaida Network," U.S. Department of the Treasury press release, June 13, 2008.

21. Joseph Krauss and Megan Lindow, "Islamic Universities Spread through Africa," *Chronicle of Higher Education* 52, no. 44 (July 2007), 33–37.

22. *Kenya's Youth Employment Challenge*, UNDP Discussion Paper (New York: United Nations Development Programme, January 2013), 64.

23. Issa Yussuf, "Zanzibar Pushes to Curb Unemployment," *Tanzania Daily News*, November 24, 2014.

24. *Tanzania Mainland Integrated Labour Force Survey 2014: Analytical Report*, Tanzania National Bureau of Statistics (2015), 83.

25. See *"Economy: Personal Economic Conditions:* Your living conditions vs. others," under *Afrobarometer Round 5 (2010–2012): Kenya* and *Afrobarometer Round 4 (2008–2009): Kenya*, Afrobarometer: Online Analysis.

26. Liat Shetret, Matthew Schwartz, and Danielle Cotter, *Mapping Perceptions of Violent Extremism: Pilot Study of Community Attitudes in Kenya and Somaliland* (New York: Center on Global Counterterrorism Cooperation, 2013).

27. Mohammed Ali and Seamus Mirodan, "Killing Kenya: *People & Power* investigates allegations that Kenya's police are involved in extra judicial killings," Al Jazeera, September 23, 2015.

Plunder of Africa's Resources
Time for an Audit

Pusch Commey

An audit of African resources is long overdue and a proper geological survey and mapping is a matter of urgency. After all, if you can't measure it, you can't control it, argues **Pusch Commey** as he revisits the ever-vexing issue of why Africa remains largely poor amidst plenty.

THE VALUE OF AFRICA'S NATURAL RESOURCES, in the trillions of dollars, dwarfs other sources of capital such as remittances and aid. Yet sub-Saharan Africa remains the poorest in the world. Just how do estimates that Africa has 10% of the world's known reserves of oil, 40% of its gold, plenty of ferro alloys, coal and diamonds, as well as 80–90% of the chromium and platinum group metals, not equate to the broad reality on the ground, while by and large these resources remain as catalysts for wars and conflict fuelled by greed?

Over 20 years after the execution of environmental activist Ken Saro-Wiwa, for his work in the oil-rich Niger Delta, 70% of Nigerians still live in incomprehensible poverty while oil companies continue to make stupendous profits. Equatorial Guinea, which has a major oil deal with a mega American oil company, got to keep a mere 12% of the oil revenues in the first year of its contract, according to a report on the CBS news programme *60 Minutes*—a share so low it would have been scandalous even at the height of colonial oil pillage.

Sub-Saharan Africa is also the most profitable investment destination. It offers, according to the World Bank's Global Development Finance report, "the highest returns on foreign direct investment of any region in the world". Africa is poor because its investors and its creditors are so incredibly rich.

Predation or the rule of the jungle lies at the heart of every anti-colonial struggle in history, before and after the Boston Tea Party when the USA got rid of the suffocating tentacles of Britain. In modern times the international rule of law becomes a weapon. It comes in the form of "free trade" and countless skewed trade agreements, informed by power relations. The vilification of Zimbabwean President Robert Mugabe, a vehement defender of his country and Africa's natural resources, whose country has been under sanctions for some years now, is illuminated by historical perspectives.

Once contextualised with Ronald Reagan and Margaret Thatcher's resolute opposition to sanctions during South Africa's apartheid era, the picture becomes clearer. The argument against sanctions then was that they would hurt black people most. But why that's not the case with blacks in Zimbabwe, begs the question.

Zimbabwe's President Robert Mugabe, a staunch defender of his country and Africa's natural resources

The elder statesman has seen it all however and shared his rich experiences for posterity. Back in May 2013 for example, when he spoke at the Conference of Intelligence and Security Services of Africa (CISSA) in Harare, he called for the beneficiation of natural resources to increase value and to support industrialisation.

He said: "It is time for Africa to be proactive in using her resources for her developmental objectives, bearing in mind that African resources have, hitherto, been predominantly foreign-owned and exploited with little benefit to Africans."

The conference, which ran under the theme "The Nexus between Africa's Natural Resources, Development and Security", originated at a time when Zimbabwe's implementation of resource nationalism through land reforms was so derided by the West and Zimbabwe's former colonizer—Britain. CISSA was mooted in the wake of Zimbabwe's interception of a plane-load of mercenaries who were on their way to Malabo, Equatorial Guinea, to depose the government of President Teodoro Obiang Nguema Mbasogo on 7 March 2001 in the wake of the discovery of massive oil reserves off the Gulf of Guinea.

This made everyone in intelligence services in Africa rethink closer co-operation and culminated in the formation of CISSA in Abuja, Nigeria, on 26 August 2004. CISSA's aims and objectives include assisting the African Union and specifically the Peace and Security Commission to effectively deal with security challenges confronting the continent. Mugabe proffered then that, "If we arrest the scourge of conflicts, a bright future for Africa becomes a reality as the necessary tranquil environment will then obtain. Consequently, Africa will be fully capable of exploiting her own resources for developmental purposes."

It is estimated that Africa loses $18 billion per annum through conflicts, often backed by the same people who further gain from arms sales and the exploration of natural resources in conflict zones.

History and Winning the Future

There is always plenty of talk and outcry about good governance, transparency and accountability (or the lack of it) in Africa. All of which are extremely important. But so is African unity, underpinned by a strong pan-African philosophy. An *African-centred education,* curriculum and books should permeate the educational system, so that African children don't fall into the same traps of their pre- and immediately post-independent Africa.

Lack of proper statistics and information and bad business contracts should be a thing of the past. Good contracts should be designed that allow for contingent events, and must be founded on a well designed tax system. How Western countries deal with their resources should be a template. What is good for the goose is also good for the gander.

The issue of contractual expertise is fundamental, preferably both in a colonial and an African language. And there is no reason why the transcripts and outcome of deliberations on contractual agreements can't be posted online, or videotaped for all to see on YouTube. There is also no reason why a nation's audited accounts can't have the same treatment. After all, corruption and dark deeds thrive in dark places.

Treaties and contracts are old colonial tricks working in tandem with force and coercion. During the scramble for Africa, Ethiopia in the 19th century was wise enough to have an Amharic version of the Treaty of Wuchale, a co-operation agreement signed with Italy.

Strangely the Italian version made Ethiopia a protectorate of Italy, completely different from the Amharic version. The Italians then decided to enforce their version. The ensuing war to colonise Ethiopia resulted in a crushing defeat of Italy at the battle of Adwa (1895–96). Italy subsequently had to pay indemnities to Ethiopia.

The war was won because Emperor Menelik II understood the importance of having his language version of contracts and most decisively he convinced all the rival princes (Ras) to unite under his leadership. They contributed 100,000 troops to defeat the invaders. It is a great argument for African unity.

In modern times wars will be fought with superior knowledge and technology, both economically and militarily. Is there any doubt as to where Africa's resources should be invested? And what will be the use of resources if African nations cannot utilise them and trade them amongst one another, and be able to control the price. What lessons Africa could learn from a desert now called Dubai, a marvel destination achieved by organisation, resolve, and proper investment of its resources. The biblical story goes that Peter was able to walk on water when Jesus told him to do so. But when he saw the boisterous winds he was afraid, and he began to doubt. And when he began to doubt he began to sink. Whether you are a Christian or not, the story illustrates the disproportionate value of confidence in everything Africa does. With confidence comes self-respect, and respect for one another which in turn lessens or even quells the need for conflict. Many long-oppressed Africans do not have confidence in themselves and this becomes a self-fulfilling prophesy. The institutions left in place by the colonialists, such as the British Commonwealth and Francophone arrangements, were designed to perpetuate self-serving interests and subjugation. Therefore dismantling neo-colonialism and the neo-colonial mentality, is another war that must be fought and won by all Africans, that in turn will go a long way in curtailing the so-called resources curse.

Reading 1.3

Multidimensional Poverty in Sub-Saharan Africa

Kathryn LaFever

W HILE POVERTY IS A PERVASIVE GLOBAL issue, it is associated in particular with sub-Saharan Africa, where in 2015 more extreme poor lived than the rest of the world combined. While sub-Saharan poverty levels vary widely, from 15% in Gabon to 92% in South Sudan, overall the region is home to the highest rates of global poverty, 27 of the world's 28 poorest countries, and the world majority (two-thirds) of extremely poor humanity (World Bank, 2018a; Horton, 2019). Since 1990, poverty has been declining in all global regions except sub-Saharan Africa. During this time, compared to most world regions, sub-Sahara's unrelenting poverty has been exacerbated by weak economic growth, negative economic shocks, high levels of armed conflict or violence, pandemics, low health and education spending, and inadequate private sector development, as well as a precarious dependence on natural resources and commodity exports (United Nations Development Program (UNDP), 2019; World Bank, 2018a). Since 1990, one billion fewer people in the world are living in extreme poverty, yet in sub-Saharan Africa the absolute numbers of people living in poverty are escalating (UNDP, 2019). The region is the home of 14 of the 18 countries where the number of extreme poor are rising as the standard of living is declining for the poorest 40% of its population (World Bank, 2018a). By 2030, sub-Saharan Africa is expected to be home to 87 to 90% of the global poor and more than 400 million people living in extreme poverty (Kharas et al., 2018; World Bank, 2018a, UNDP, 2019). This essay explores some of the multidimensional aspects of poverty in the context of the sub-Saharan region.

While there is no international consensus on how to define poverty, the term generally refers to **income poverty,** or a lack of money to meet basic needs for food, clothing, and housing. It can also refer to a lack of income or an income level below a certain threshold.

Poverty is often understood in absolute or relative terms. **Absolute poverty** refers to a fixed, universal monetary measure of poverty. It corresponds to living at or below the **international**

poverty line, $1.90 per day (based on 2011 purchasing power parity in U.S. dollars), established by the World Bank in 2015 to categorize the number of people living in extreme poverty around the world (Aguilar et al., 2019). A person surviving on less than $1.90 per day lives in extreme poverty, which, in 2018, was the state of approximately 767 million people, or about 10% of the global population. In contrast, the first sustainable development goal defines extreme poverty as the condition of a daily per capita consumption or income of less than $1.25 per day (Sustainable Development Goals Knowledge Platform, 2019). Further, the typical monetary threshold for moderate poverty is $3.20 per day, upper-middle-income is $5.50 per day in lower and middle-income countries, and $15 per day for the middle class (World Bank, 2018a, 2018b). Between 1990 and 2015, extreme poverty rates rapidly declined globally. In fact, sub-Saharan absolute or extreme poverty fell from 36% in 1990 to 8.6% in 2018 (UNDP, 2019). Yet, this decline is due primarily to the expansion of the population, which found 85% of sub-Saharans earning less than $5.50 per day (Aguilar et al., 2019). Further, considering sub-Sahara's growing population, the region currently represents in absolute terms the largest proportion of the world's extremely poor people, an economically vulnerable demographic that continues to rise (Wadhwa, 2018).

Relative poverty equates with societal poverty. It can indicate a substandard quality of life, meaning one's economic distribution, status, or opportunity is below what average people enjoy in a society. It refers to not having enough money to maintain an average standard of living, as well as consumption or income level, in a particular community context, so people are poor relative to the consumption levels in their communities. Many countries have established their own (relative) national poverty lines. Compared to other global regions, overall sub-Saharan Africa has the highest absolute and relative poverty rates (World Bank, 2018a).

In most world regions, even full-time paid employment is no guarantee of earning enough to escape poverty. Among the types or measures of poverty, **working poverty** refers to workers with a paying job or jobs who do not earn a living wage. The working poor are impoverished because they are not paid enough remuneration to meet their basic needs or maintain a decent standard of living. Globally in 2019, there are approximately 300 million working poor, living on less than $1.90 per day. In 2018 in sub-Saharan Africa, 38%, or more than one-third, of the population is considered to be the working poor (Sustainable Development Goals Knowledge Platform, 2019). In sub-Saharan Africa, women as well as young people, aged 15 to 24, each comprise about one-third of the working poor and those living in extreme poverty (Gammarano, 2019). While sub-Sahara's working poverty rate has steadily declined since 2000, its decline has been more sluggish compared to most global regions (Gammarano, 2019).

The **feminization of poverty** typically refers to the fact that globally more women than men are poor and living in impoverished conditions, and the majority of women are affected by poverty. There are higher poverty rates among women than men; women comprise about 50% of the world's population but 62.3% of impoverished people ages 15 and above (World Bank, 2018a). In fact, adult women heads of households (with children and nonearners), are disproportionately represented among the poor in Latin America and sub-Saharan Africa (World Bank, 2018a).

A closely related concept, **the feminization of the causes of poverty** refers to a wide range of overlapping, cumulative, and resilient legal and social disadvantages that limit women's survival and equitable access to economic and financial resources (Medeiros & Costa, 2008). For example, compared to men, impoverished women suffer disproportionately from bias, prejudice, and discrimination as well as inadequate health care, nutrition, education, legal protection, and work. Further, while no place in the world experiences gender equality, sub-Saharan Africa has the highest maternal mortality rates and lowest education rates for women, as well as less access than men to the workforce, less political power, and less protection from violence (UNDP, 2019). For example, local laws and customs constrain women's mobility, prohibiting work outside of the home or in certain professions. In some countries, it is illegal for women to get an education, passport, medical treatment, or a job without permission of their male guardian. Further, women tend to have less formal educational access and opportunities, reflected in the fact that globally about two-thirds of those who are illiterate are women (World Bank, 2018a). In fact, according to the "Gender Gap Report 2020," in terms of education attainment, seven out of eight countries that have yet to close more than 20% of their gender gaps in educational attainment are the sub-Saharan nations of Togo, Angola, Mali, Benin, Guinea, Congo, and Chad (World Economic Forum, 2020). Further, particularly in poor households, financial resources are inequitably distributed between men and women. Especially in the poorest countries, compared to men, women and children have disproportionately less access to resources and basic services (World Bank, 2018a). Women often lack agency, including decision-making rights regarding the use of family income and access to that income (World Bank, 2018a). In addition, particularly in impoverished countries, women of peak productive and reproductive age (20–34) often lose their earning potential due to responsibilities traditionally associated with women, such as unpaid domestic and caregiver work, which reinforce women's deprivations and exclusions (UNDP, 2019). For example, many women do not have money for their own health care (UNDP, 2019). As the World Bank (2018a) explains, "The gender gap in poverty rates is largest during the reproductive years when care and domestic responsibilities, which are socially assigned to women, overlap and conflict with productive activities" (p. 6). Moreover, pronounced gender gaps in property ownership account for 20 million fewer women than men owning housing in sub-Saharan Africa, where women are likely to be landless if not destitute due to discriminatory land ownership and inheritance laws

(Gandhi, 2018). Relatedly, women typically are income and asset poor; they do not own assets and therefore cannot access the collateral required for loans and banking services. The 2019 United Nations Development Program (UNDP) report laments that these norms, gaps, and vulnerabilities are invisible or "are not directly observable, so they are often overlooked and not systematically studied" (p. 161).

Painting in broad strokes, multiple complex factors have contributed to poverty in sub-Saharan Africa. For example, a range of geographical features, including sub-Sahara's vast size, numerous landlocked countries, thick jungles, vast mountain ranges, (seasonally) unnavigable rivers, and lack of seaports contribute to its lack of trade and consequential levels of poverty. The sociocultural, political, and economic strife caused by centuries of European imperialism and colonialism continues to manifest in myriad forms, including but not limited to sub-Saharan armed conflicts, political border issues, racist and sexist legal systems, land ownership inequities, and poverty. Further, public health issues, such as HIV/AIDS, Ebola, malaria, bubonic plague, and an appalling array of tropical diseases, have had a profound effect on the economies of a region increasingly prone to natural disasters and the effects of climate change. Despite being resource rich, poverty is endemic in this region where more vulnerable single-market and commodity-dependent economies exist than anyplace on earth. Another scourge is the resource curse, in which an abundant resource is more of a curse than a blessing. Typically, the resource is an extractive industry that produces economic gains (and often short-term spikes in gross domestic product statistics) and tremendous wealth for relatively few people. But such commodity exports rarely benefit the majority of the population and have proven to be inadequate in reducing poverty (World Bank, 2018a). Under corrupt political leadership, numerous sub-Saharan African governments have demonstrated blatant disregard for the well-being of their populations. Such governments have spent decades, among other things, indefensibly looting their countries, squandering resources and foreign aid, propping up weak institutions, obstructing liberal democracy, and maintaining indifference toward their destitute populations. In 2015, sub-Saharan Africa was home to 54% of the world's fragile states and states experiencing armed conflicts, and in 2019 to six of the top ten fragile states (World Bank, 2018a; Fund for Peace, 2019).

International governmental organizations increasingly regard poverty as a multidimensional concept (World Bank, 2018a, 2018b), meaning that impoverished people simultaneously experience a host of entrenched and life-threatening deprivations. In other words, poverty is not just an economic condition; it is often the direct result of the systemic lack of resources, capabilities, and freedoms measured by a range of social, political, and cultural indicators (Medeiros & Costa, 2008). Income poverty is only one aspect of being destitute. Poverty is indicated by basic measures of well-being, such as access to safe drinking water, sanitation, medical care, reproductive health, electricity, decent work, social benefits, education, and protections from violence (World Bank, 2018a). The World Bank (2018a) describes multiple, overlapping, and cumulative deprivations as components of poverty, explaining, "Poverty encompasses a shortfall in income and consumption, but also low educational achievement, poor health and nutritional outcomes, lack of access to basic services, and a hazardous living environment" (p. xi). In 2013, 44.9% of the population of sub-Saharan Africa lived in absolute poverty, whereas 64.3% were multidimensionally deprived (World Bank, 2018a). Currently, compared to people in other global regions, sub-Saharans suffer the greatest average number of poverty indicators, or the most overlapping Multidimensional Poverty Index (MPI) deprivations, including the lack of education and infrastructure (World Bank, 2018a; UNDP, 2019). Being impoverished is not just defined by lack of income or adequate consumption but by access to measures of well-being, a combination of factors that underscore the challenges of ending sub-Saharan poverty.

The Multidimensional Poverty Index (MPI), designed by the United Nations Development Program (UNDP), uses microdata from household surveys to assess the level of poverty of a given population. Based on education, health, and standard of living indicators, the figures are aggregated; a larger statistic indicates more extreme poverty. One of the qualities of the MPI is that it considers past, present, and future inequities. For example, access to broadband, social protection systems, and tertiary education can help to alleviate poverty and prevent its future entrenchment of inequalities. In addition, even though cash benefit coverage is considered essential to reduce and prevent poverty in many world regions, such modern social protection systems do not exist for 87% of sub-Saharan Africans (Sustainable Development Goals Knowledge Platform, 2019). In another example, despite sub-Saharan Africa's recent and considerable progress in expanding primary education, particularly among its poorest 20%, the region has the highest rates of children who do not attend school and lags behind other world regions in providing tertiary education, particularly to women (UNDP, 2019).

While understandings of poverty continue to evolve and paint a more comprehensive and complex picture, certain issues stand out with relative clarity. The range of economic, cultural, historical, geographical, and political circumstances, often so distinct from those found in other global regions, find sub-Saharan Africa a devastatingly poor world region. While the first sustainable development goal, ending extreme poverty by 2030, will focus on this region, it is unclear whose or what targets, policies, or models—such as Beijing and Northern European models that have helped countries to substantially reduce poverty—will prove most effective in the context of short- or long-term solutions to end poverty in sub-Sahara Africa. Highly contextualized solutions, arrived at mutually by all stakeholders, including women, will likely prove the best approaches. To ensure that poverty is alleviated through sustainable and equitable development (namely that it benefits the poor) governments need to make enduring investments—for example, in infrastructure and human capital—in sub-Saharan Africa. To accelerate poverty reduction as well as eliminate absolute and relative poverty in sub-Saharan Africa, investment in human development seems critical, particularly in terms of generating positive health and education outcomes as well as gender-inclusive growth and prosperity (UNDP, 2019). Compared to the populations of other world regions, Africa is the youngest. It should be an economic dividend that the majority of its population is of prime working age. Yet, with the pronounced lack of quality jobs and earnings, young people are among the nearly 35% of Africa's population currently living in extreme poverty. Africa is working toward a future of economic progress and sustainable development based on inclusive prosperity distributed across the population, not concentrated in the hands of a relative few. An African proverb holds, "If you wish to move mountains tomorrow, you must start by lifting stones today." Whether moving pebbles, mountains, or something in between, sub-Saharan Africa is demonstrating collective action and a willingness to do the requisite heavy lifting to alleviate poverty for its mutual, sustained benefit.

References

Aguilar, R. A. C., Jolliffe, D. M., Fujs, T., Lakner, C., & Prydz, E. B. (2019, October 3). 85% of Africans live on less than $5.50 per day. *World Bank Data Blog*. https://blogs.worldbank.org/opendata/85-africans-live-less-550-day

Fund for Peace. (2019, April 10). *Fragile states index 2019*. https://fundforpeace.org/wp-content/uploads/2019/04/9511904-fragilestatesindex.pdf

Gammarano, R. (2019, April). *Spotlight on work statistics, No. 6. The working poor: Or how a job is no guarantee of decent living conditions*. International Labor Organization. https://ilo.org/wcmsp5/groups/public/---dgreports/---stat/documents/publication/wcms_696387.pdf

Gandhi, D. (2018, September 14). *Africa in focus figures of the week: Female property ownership in sub-Saharan Africa*. Brookings Institute. https://www.brookings.edu/blog/africa-in-focus/2018/09/14/figures-of-the-week-female-property-ownership-in-sub-saharan-africa/

Horton, R. (2019, July 27). Offline: Global health's indifference to poverty must end. *The Lancet, 394*, p. 286. https://www.thelancet.com/action/showPdf?pii=S0140-6736%2819%2931710-6

Kharas, H., Hamel, K., & Hofer, M. (2018, June 19). *The start of a new poverty narrative*. Brookings Institute. https://www.brookings.edu/blog/future-development/2018/06/19/the-start-of-a-new-poverty-narrative/

Medeiros, M., & Costa, J. (2008, July). *What do we mean by "feminization of poverty"?* International Poverty Centre, no. 58. https://ipcig.org/pub/IPCOnePager58.pdf

Sustainable Development Goals Knowledge Platform. (2019). *Progress of goal 1 in 2019*. https://sustainabledevelopment.un.org/sdg

United Nations (2019). *World economic situation and prospects 2019*. https://unctad.org/en/PublicationsLibrary/wesp2019_en.pdf

United Nations Development Program (UNDP). (2019). *Human development report 2019: Beyond income, beyond averages, beyond today—Inequalities in human development in the 21st century*. http://hdr.undp.org/sites/default/files/hdr2019.pdf

Wadhwa, D. (2018, September 19). The number of extremely poor people continues to rise in Sub-Saharan Africa. *World Bank Data Blog*. https://blogs.worldbank.org/opendata/number-extremely-poor-people-continues-rise-sub-saharan-africa

World Bank. (2018a). *Poverty and shared prosperity 2018: Piecing together the poverty puzzle*. https://openknowledge.worldbank.org/bitstream/handle/10986/30418/9781464813306.pdf

World Bank. (2018b). *Riding the wave: An East Asian miracle for the 21st century. World Bank East Asia and Pacific Regional Report*. http://documents.worldbank.org/curated/en/770241511445721465/pdf/121613-REVISED-PUBLIC-211145cmp-eProof.pdf

World Economic Forum (2020). *Global gender gap report 2020*. https://www.weforum.org/reports/gender-gap-2020-report-100-years-pay-equality

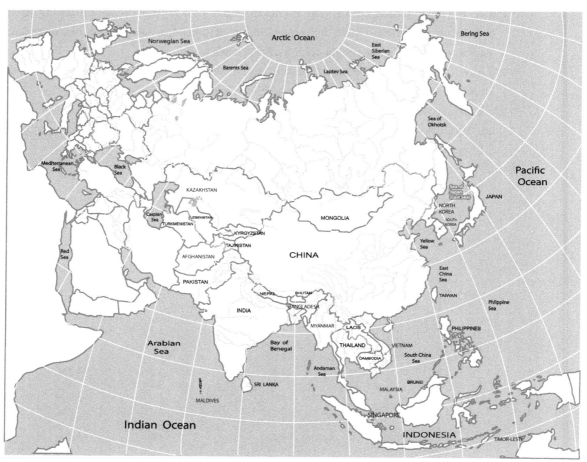

FIG. 2.1: Copyright © 2010 Depositphotos/jelen80.

Chapter II

Asia

List of countries included in the world region of Asia:

- Afghanistan
- Bangladesh
- Bhutan
- Brunei Darussalam
- Cambodia
- China
- India
- Indonesia
- Japan
- Kazakhstan
- Kyrgyzstan
- Laos
- Malaysia
- Maldives
- Mongolia
- Myanmar
- Nepal
- North Korea
- Pakistan
- Philippines
- Singapore
- South Korea
- Sri Lanka
- Taiwan
- Tajikistan
- Thailand
- Timor-Leste
- Turkmenistan
- Uzbekistan
- Vietnam

Introduction

Asia is both a region and continent. It dominates the Central and Eastern portions of the Eurasian landmass, located mostly in the Eastern and Northern Hemispheres. The region of Asia is comprised of 30 countries in the subregions of East Asia, Southeast Asia, South Asia, and Central Asia (some sources include the subregion of West Asia, another name for the Middle East, the world region discussed in Chapter 5). East Asia is about 11.8 million square kilometers, or 4.5 million square miles. Southeast Asia is approximately 4.54 million square kilometers, or 1.755 million square miles. South Asia is about 5.13 million square kilometers, or 1.98 million square miles. Central Asia is just over 4 million square kilometers, or 1.54 million square miles. Based on this delineation, Asia is the largest world region in terms of area. Asia covers an area of 25.47 million square kilometers, or 9.83 million square miles.

In terms of Asia's geography, it includes the highest point on Earth, Mount Everest, in Nepal, at 8.848 kilometers, or 29,029 feet high. Asia also includes the Tibetan Pateau, the largest and highest plateau in the world. It is called the "Rooftop of the World" and averages over 5,000 meters, or 16,000 feet above sea level. Asia is bordered by the Arctic, Indian, and Pacific Oceans. The Bay of Bengal, on the Indian Ocean, is the largest bay in the world. Nine of the world's top 10 container ports are in Asia, and seven of those are in China (World Shipping Council, 2020).

Asia is the largest region in terms of population. Asia includes about 4.36 billion, or over half of the world's 7.8 billion total population (Worldometer, 2020). Asia includes the two most populous countries, China and India. China is the most populated country on Earth with over 1.4 billion people. Based on the size of its population, India is the world's largest democracy. In 2020, six out of the world's top 10 most densely populated cities are located in Asia (Shanghai, Beijing, Karachi, Mumbai, Guangzhou, and Delhi). Yet, the largest urban area in Asia is Tokyo, Japan.

Nearly 2,300 languages are spoken in Asia. The main languages spoken in Asia, in descending order, are Chinese, Hindi, English, and Russian. The Chinese language is the most pervasive, yet Russian is widely spoken in Central Asia. Asia is also home to the oldest language in the world, Tamil, which has existed for around 5,000 years.

China's Belt and Road Initiative (BRI)

Among the most significant recent events in the region of Asia, in 2013, Xi Jinping became president of China and initiated his signature project, the **Belt and Road Initiative (BRI)**. Initially, the project was called the "New Silk Road," since it retraced much of the land "belt" and maritime "road" of the **Silk Road**, an ancient trade route connecting China and the West. The BRI is one of the most ambitious investment and infrastructure projects in human history. It is a trillion-dollar international network of infrastructure projects along land and sea routes. **Infrastructure** refers to the physical and often complex systems of a country that are often vital to its economic development and prosperity. Infrastructure includes but is not limited to roads, railways, and power plants, as well as electrical, transportation, telecommunication, education, and health care services. The BRI has expanded well beyond its original plan spanning three continents and linking China to Europe, Africa, and the Middle East (Chatzky and McBride, 2019). Now it circumnavigates the planet, including countries in Oceania and Latin America. To what extent will the BRI reshape the current global, economic, and political landscape?

While the BRI promises economic opportunities to member countries, it simultaneously advances many Chinese foreign policy, economic, and security initiatives on a global scale. **Foreign policy** is a state's diplomatic strategy for interacting with other countries, and the BRI is China's major foreign policy project. Another example of Chinese foreign policy is the **One- China policy** through which China has expanded its political and economic influence by insisting that if states want official diplomatic relations and trade advantages with mainland China, they must acknowledge that there is only one Chinese government (People's Republic of China, or PRC) and agree to break formal diplomatic interactions with Taiwan (Republic of China, or ROC).

Foreign policy is often described in terms of hard and soft power. In general, **hard power** refers to foreign policy that explicitly uses or threatens to use sanctions or military force to achieve foreign policy objectives. On the other hand, **soft power** is the term for foreign policy that openly uses subtle and indirect forms of persuasion (such as cultural exchange, propaganda, and "checkbook diplomacy") to curry favor and achieve its desired present and future diplomatic outcomes.

China has exercised soft power in various ways, namely through its economic investment and aid to countries along the BRI. Yet, through the BRI, China has branded itself, in part through the promotion, control, and creation of particular narratives that advance Chinese interests. **Narratives** are stories that can be based in fact, fiction, or a combination of the two. Narratives serve a wide range of purposes, such as the myths that serve to empower or disempower individuals or groups of people. The BRI is woven into Chinese narratives that represent the "Chinese Dream" as well as China's financial power, openness to the world, and desire to foster world peace and prosperity. China's use of soft power to forge strategic alliances and provide alternative foreign policy visions directly challenges the status quo, including the United States as the global superpower. While the BRI places China in the epicenter of the global economy and protects China's security interests, it expands Chinese influence and projects a vision of the future led by China as the global superpower (Hillman, 2018).

As part of the BRI, China has provided billions of dollars in loans to construct a series of commercial, industrial, and military installations from Hong Kong to Iran, increasing China's presence in the East China Sea, South China Sea, Indian Ocean, and Red Sea. For example, the BRI includes a naval thoroughfare of ports and shipping lanes in the Indian Ocean Region (IOR), connecting China with Myanmar, Bangladesh, Sri Lanka, and Pakistan to points beyond. These vantage points provide China with maritime access and other tactical advantages, making it possible for China to rest its crews, station ships, patrol shipping lanes, and guard vessels along approximately 5700 nautical miles of major trillion-dollar trade routes through which most of the world's shipping tonnage flows.

Debt-trap diplomacy refers to foreign policy strategies that impoverish a country in exchange for its land and resources. For example, a country may agree to high-interest loans, corrupt deals, and opaque contracts, often with little or no environmental or social impact assessments. The loans are collateralized by strategically important natural assets, like minerals, land, and ports, with high long-term value. The indebted country becomes mired in unsustainable debt and is then forced to repay the debt with its natural assets, such as land and ports. Such schemes jeopardize the sovereignty of an indebted country, which, among other things, could find itself bending to the will of its creditors and unable to benefit from its economic growth in the short or long term. By 2020, many BRI countries moved into the global recession caused by the COVID-19 pandemic strapped with hefty loans from China and, consequently, unsustainable and financially destabilizing debt levels.

Djibouti, a small BRI country on the Horn of Africa, became enveloped in China's debt-trap diplomacy. This east African country is geostrategic in that it is adjacent to the Bab-el-Mandeb, a strait connecting the Red Sea to the Gulf of Aden, and a major shipping lane between Europe and China through which approximately 4.8 million barrels of oil are transported daily (Martin, 2018). China's state-run banks loaned billions of dollars to Djibouti, which, by 2017, could not repay its debt in cash. Djibouti was forced to relinquish a few key assets to China. Djibouti nationalized one of its major ports, the Doraleh Container Terminal, which became a Chinese-operated port. Further, Djibouti handed over land adjacent to the port, which in 2017 became the first Chinese People's Liberation Army Naval (PLAN) overseas base, located in close proximity (about 8 miles, or 13 kilometers) to Camp Lemonnier; since 2001, it has been the only permanent U.S. military base in Africa. Moreover, cash-strapped Djibouti commissioned China to build the $3.5 billion Djibouti International Free Trade Zone (DIFTZ), the largest in Africa (Dahir, 2018). A **free-trade zone** (FTZ) is a special locale that offers a range of economic trade advantages. For example, it is an area where goods can be manufactured, imported, handled, warehoused, exported, and re-exported without certain customs duties or tariffs. Modeled after China's Shenzhen Special Economic Zone, the DIFTZ is one of fifty FTZs China plans to build along the BRI (Chatzky and McBride, 2019). In Djibouti, China seized opportunities to maneuver into a significant global economic and geographic position, once again utilizing the BRI to deftly tip the balance of power in its favor.

China's Rare Earths

Rare earths include approximately 17 chemical elements found in the Earth's crust. Often called rare earth minerals or rare earth elements, these elements are known for their magnetic, luminescent, and electrochemical properties (King, 2020).

Although there is an impending shortage of rare earths, China has secured or has influence over key mineral and other natural resources globally. With control over 80% of the production and 37% of the reserves of rare earths, China has established a near monopoly of these elements. In 2019, China is home to the largest deposits of many rare earths and has stockpiled significant quantities from around the world. Further, China holds stock and mining rights in rare earth mines around the world. For example, it currently holds 70% of production and 24% of reserves of graphite, which is a highly conductive element used in battery, solar panels, and steel production. Further, China controls over 59% of all global lithium resources. China controls 56% of production and 48% of the world's reserves of vanadium, which is used mainly in the production of batteries. China controls much of the rare earths market and is developing the technology to build semiconductors. If these devices are used in defense systems, the concern is that they could threaten the national security of those countries (*Foreign Policy*, 2019).

Among other things, through its growing international influence, China is forging strategic alliances, challenging the status of the United States as the global superpower, and providing alternative foreign policy visions. It is actively reshaping the future global, economic, and political landscape. By positioning itself at the epicenter of global trade and international rare earths market, China seems poised to achieve its security goals.

Kashmir

Kashmir is an 86,000-square-mile mountainous, Muslim-majority region between India and Pakistan. Kashmir is a **shatterbelt,** or bitterly contested area. Kashmir is also a **flashpoint** area where war could quickly escalate between two nuclear-armed powers, India and Pakistan. How did Kashmir become, "the most dangerous place in the world" (Dorsey, 2019)?

India fought and won its independence from Britain in 1947, the same year that, within Indian territory, the Muslim-majority state of Pakistan was born. During this tumultuous time, many princely border states, including Kashmir, could stay a part of India or join Pakistan. Despite being a Muslim-majority region, Kashmir's Hindu ruler opted to remain a part of India.

Many political maps of Kashmir are inaccurate, representing it only as the northernmost part of India. In fact, Kashmir is divided into three areas, each administered by India and Pakistan as well as Pakistan's powerful ally, China. India controls the southernmost state of Jammu and Kashmir, encompassing about 45 percent of the disputed territory in Kashmir. Pakistan-occupied Kashmir (PoK) is the northernmost area, about 35% of Kashmir. This territory, often called Azad Jammu and Kashmir (AJK), includes the states of Azad Kashmir, Gilgit, and Baltistan. China controls the northeast province of Aksai Chin, comprising about

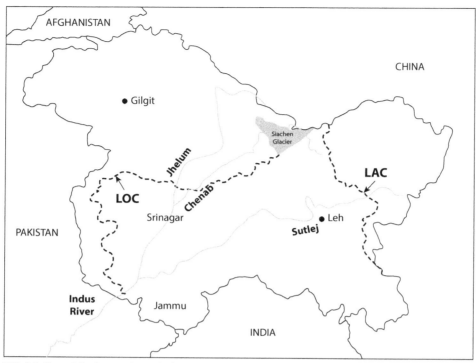

FIG. 2.2: Copyright © 2017 Depositphotos/Lesniewski.

20% of Kashmir (CNN Library, 2019). In particular, both India and Pakistan administer different parts of Kashmir while claiming to have rightful control over all of it.

There have been several wars between India, Pakistan, and China, due in part to control of Kashmir. The India-Pakistan Wars were fought in 1947 and 1965, with a limited war in 1999. These wars erupted from multiple disputes, but mainly control of Kashmir. The war of 1965 ended in a fragile ceasefire, with Indian and Pakistani territories in Kashmir separated by the heavily militarized **Line of Control** (LOC). This 450-mile long de facto border was drawn in 1949 and finally agreed upon in 1972. Further, the Sino-Indian War, between China and India, began and ended in 1962. Among their disputes was control of Chinese-held territory in Kashmir, separated from Jammu and Kashmir by a border called the Line of Actual Control (LAC).

Since 2016, aggressions and retaliations have escalated between India and Pakistan over Kashmir, clear violations of their 1965 cease-fire agreement. Diplomatic relations between India and Pakistan have deteriorated, and violence along their uneasy border has increased. Most of the violence centers on anti-Indian protests and clashes in Indian-administered areas of Kashmir. The violence includes armed and unarmed Islamic militant group attacks in Indian-controlled territory, surgical strikes in Pakistani territory by the Indian military, and cross-border gunfire and skirmishes. Thousands of residents have been displaced, injured, and killed on both sides of the border.

Indian-Controlled Kashmir

By many measures, India has for centuries been a religiously diverse and nonsectarian country, tolerant and welcoming of all religions. Particularly since the end of British rule in 1947, the democratic vision of its modern founding fathers—namely Mahatma Gandhi, B.R. Ambedkar, Jawaharlal Nehru, and Vallabhbhai Patel—made India one of the most pluralistic multicultural, multilinguistic, and multiethnic democratic states the world has ever seen. One indication of India's historic respect for religious plurality is that the Indian Constitution allowed special status to the Muslim-majority peoples of Indian-controlled Kashmir region. For 72 years, Articles 370 and 35A of India's Constitution established Indian-controlled Kashmir as a semiautonomous state and formed the basis of India and Kashmir's relationship.

On August 5, 2019, the ruling Hindu nationalist party (Bharatiya Janata Party, BJP, or Indian People's Party) of the Indian government escalated the already tense political situation in Kashmir by abrogating parts of Articles 370 and 35A of the Indian Constitution, which tightened Indian control over Kashmir and abolished Kashmir's special autonomy. The peoples of Kashmir felt betrayed by India for imposing these sweeping changes. Among other things, revoking these articles meant Indian-held Kashmir no longer had its own constitution, laws, or flag. It became legal for Indians to buy property in Kashmir and live there permanently, which could lead to significant demographic shifts in the region. There are fears that the Kashmiri people could end up becoming displaced, an oppressed minority in their homeland, or victims of cultural or other forms of genocide.

The legal definition of **genocide** is provided in Article II of the United Nation's Convention on the Prevention and Punishment of the Crime of Genocide (United Nations Human Rights, Office of the High Commissioner, 1948). Genocide means causing serious bodily harm or the deliberate killing of people because they are members of an ethnic group or nation. Genocide, which can occur during peace or war, refers to the intentional physical destruction of a group as well as deliberately inflicting on a group conditions intended to bring about the physical destruction, all or in part, of the group. The official definition does not include cultural genocide. However, it does specify that forcibly transferring children of one group to another constitutes genocide (which exemplifies cultural genocide) (Legal Information Institute, n.d.; Office of the UN Special Adviser, n.d.).

Abrogating Articles 370 and 35A fulfills a campaign promise in the 2019 election manifesto of Narendra Modi's BJP party, which pledged to remove Article 370. More significantly, this change in policy and governance is part of the "New India" policy of Indian Prime

Minister Modi. The policy seeks to deepen India's national unity and bring the hope of economic development and prosperity to Kashmir. Among other things, his policy can be understood as representing the Indian government's tougher stance against Pakistan, Kashmir, and perhaps even China. It is criticized for advancing Hindu majoritarianism at the expense of Indian national and religious pluralism and the rights of the Kashmiris (Guha, 2019; Dorsey, 2019). There is some indication that Kashmir would prefer to be an independent state or under the jurisdiction of Pakistan, not India (Dorsey, 2019). Pakistani Prime Minister Imran Khan voiced his willingness to discuss peaceful negotiations with Modi, who refused to participate in those deliberations. Is the Kashmir issue a "distraction" from a more serious concern, and that the government needs to develop more effective initiatives to address India's slowing economy? The situation in Kashmir is complex and will continue to develop and interact with other issues in the region.

Air Pollution

There are many forms of pollution, but by many measures, the greatest global environmental health risk is air pollution. Air pollution, a harmful and excessive mixture of naturally occurring and **anthropogenic** (human made) chemicals, gases, and particulates in the air, is caused mainly by the burning of fossil fuels. Major sources of ambient airborne particulates include industrial and power plant emissions, burning wood and biomass fuels, wildfires, and construction, as well as sand and dust storms.

While every world region suffers from air pollution, Asia is particularly vulnerable. In 2018, 13 (or 52%) of the 25 countries with the greatest concentration, on average, of ambient airborne particles were in Asia (IQAir AirVisual, 2018). Approximately 89 to 90% of cities in Asia exceed safe exposure to particulates, some by as much as five times (IQAir AirVisual, 2018). The 50 cities with the most heavily polluted air were in four Asian countries: Bangladesh, China, India, and Pakistan. Interestingly, the highest levels of air pollution in the world were in three South Asian countries: Bangladesh, India, and Pakistan. The country with the highest levels of air pollution was Bangladesh, but seven of the 10 most polluted cities in the world were in India, home to the most polluted capital city, Delhi.

Air pollution can irreparably harm the natural environment and human health. It is estimated that 90% of people worldwide (the majority of whom live in Asia) breathe air that is polluted at unsafe levels. Air pollution causes short- and long-term health issues, such as coughing, asthma, decreased lung function, irregular heartbeat, organ damage, and increased premature death among people with heart or lung disease (Environmental Protection Agency, 2018). Approximately seven million people worldwide, most of whom are impoverished, die annually from air pollution; 3.8 million people die from exposure to indoor smoke from cooking fuels, and 4.2 million from ambient, or outdoor, air pollution (World Health Organization, 2020). The "costs" of air pollution are both measurable ($225 billion annual costs globally) and incalculable (e.g., in terms of animal and human life as well as the quality of life). It remains to be seen if countries, in Asia and elsewhere, will endeavor to create urgent and effective policies to address local and transboundary air pollution issues.

References

Chatzky, A., & McBride, J. (2019, May 21). *China's massive belt and road initiative.* Council on Foreign Relations. https://www.cfr.org/backgrounder/chinas-massive-belt-and-road-initiative

CNN Library. (2019, August 22). *Kashmir fast facts.* https://edition.cnn.com/2013/11/08/world/kashmir-fast-facts/index.html?no-st=1565712531

Dahir, A. L. (2018, July 9). Thanks to China, Africa's largest free trade zone has launched in Djibouti. *Quartz Africa.* https://qz.com/africa/1323666/china-and-djibouti-have-launched-africas-biggest-free-trade-zone/

Dorsey, J. M. (2019, August 15). Modi seizes Kashmir. *The Globalist.* https://www.theglobalist.com/kashmir-india-pakistan-narendra-modi/

Environmental Protection Agency. (2018, June 20). Health and environmental effects of particulate matter (PM). Particulate matter (PM) Pollution. https://www.epa.gov/pm-pollution/health-and-environmental-effects-particulate-matter-pm

Foreign Policy. (2019, May 1). *Mining the future: How China is set to dominate the next industrial revolution.* FP Analytics special report. https://foreignpolicy.com/2019/05/01/mining-the-future-china-critical-minerals-metals/

Guha, R. (2019, August 14). India was a miracle democracy. But it's time to downgrade its credentials. *Washington Post.* https://www.washingtonpost.com/opinions/2019/08/14/india-was-miracle-democracy-its-time-downgrade-its-credentials/?utm_campaign=34db0ce18e-EMAIL_CAMPAIGN_2019_08_15_10_02&utm_medium=email&utm_source=Fareed%27s%20Global%20Briefing

Hillman, J. E. (2018, January 25). China's belt and road initiative: Five years later. *Center for Strategic and International Studies.* https://www.csis.org/analysis/chinas-belt-and-road-initiative-five-years-later-0

IQAir AirVisual. (2018). *2018 world air quality report.* https://www.iqair.com/us/blog/press-releases/IQAir-AirVisual-2018-World-Air-Quality-Report-Reveals-Worlds-Most-Polluted-Cities

King, H. M. (2020). REE—Rare earth elements and their uses. Geology.com. https://geology.com/articles/rare-earth-elements/

Legal Information Institute. (n.d.). *Genocide.* Cornell Law School. https://www.law.cornell.edu/wex/genocide#

Martin, P. (2018, December 14). Could China squeeze the U.S. out of its only permanent military base in Africa? *Washington Post*. https://www.washingtonpost.com/national-security/2018/12/14/could-china-squeeze-us-out-its-only-permanent-military-base-africa/?noredirect=on

Office of the UN Special Adviser on the Prevention of Genocide (OSAPG). (n.d.). *Analysis framework*. https://www.un.org/ar/preventgenocide/adviser/pdf/osapg_analysis_framework.pdf

United Nations Human Rights, Office of the High Commissioner (1948). *United Nation's Convention on the Prevention and Punishment of the Crime of Genocide*. https://www.ohchr.org/en/professionalinterest/pages/crimeofgenocide.aspx

World Health Organization. (2020). Air pollution. https://www.who.int/health-topics/air-pollution#tab=tab_1

World Shipping Council. (2020). Top 50 world container ports. http://www.worldshipping.org/about-the-industry/global-trade/top-50-world-container-ports/

Worldometer. (2020, August 16). Asia population. https://www.worldometers.info/world-population/asia-population/#:~:text=The%20current%20population%20of%20Asia,of%20the%20total%20world%20population.

Reading 2.1

India's Women, India's Men

Adam Roberts

ILLIONS WERE MISSING. BIRTH RECORDS, CENSUS DATA, AND child sex ratios and other data analysis revealed who the victims were. In parts of the north of India, in 2015, 120 male babies were being born for every 100 female ones—not at all what nature intended. Heavy societal preference for boys, combined with new technology such as ultrasound scanners, together explained why millions of girl fetuses were being aborted. By one estimate, 12 million girl fetuses had been discarded—because they were girls—in the three decades before 2010. Fatal discrimination continued after birth. An analysis of seven- to fifteen-year-olds, counted in the 2011 census, suggested that another 11 million girls were lost, in addition to those aborted. They had died from neglect, or worse. An expert in the field added a grim detail, explaining how some mothers in Bengal rubbed salt on their breasts to kill newborn daughters, in effect poisoning babies as they tried to feed.

Such statistics and details were appalling, but they did not explain why ill-treatment happened. South Asia was arguably the worst place anywhere to be born female, by the 2010s, at least if you were born poor. Statistics showed that malnutrition, stunting, and other public health–related problems—especially in north India—were especially dire for young women and girls. India had fallen behind almost everywhere on this score. For decades China had done a much better job than India of keeping women alive as they gave birth, for example. For politicians eager to improve well-being, this should have been an obvious area for public spending: devoting an extra billion dollars a year to improving maternal health clinics would have been a far better choice than subsidizing losses at Air India. Getting women better educated and fed, economically stronger, healthier and more powerful: these were obvious paths to raising human capital in India. After all, the well-being of future generations, literally, depended on it.

If India were to enter into its political prime, it needed to achieve dramatic gains by focusing on its women. Women were well represented at the very top of politics, as leaders of some of the largest parties, as a president of the country, and were active in sport, television, art, dance, culture, journalism, academia, and business. The first female voters (though they, like men, had to own land) were enfranchised in Madras, as early as 1921, and universal suffrage came shortly after independence. But by 2014 only 12 percent of national MPs were female, and in regional assemblies the average fell to just 9 percent. Nor did politicians, male or female, make the prospects for Indian women much of a priority.

Schools need to be improved for girls. The first decade or so of this century saw almost all girls get to classes at the primary level for the first time, which counted as welcome progress. Manmohan Singh's government had rolled out free midday meals and enshrined theoretical rights and minimum national standards in schools. But it did too little to get teachers to turn up and give quality instruction. Modi's government did even less. Basic shortages, such as schools that had no toilets, discouraged older girls from sticking with formal education. Corruption, whereby teachers took bribes and let students cheat, meant that many millions of students dropped out or learned little. Girls were especially vulnerable if their parents chose to pay bribes on behalf of sons, who were expected to go to work, rather than for their daughters. A huge number of families, including poor ones, paid for private education, as at least 40 percent of Indian households made some use of private instruction. But because many families favored boys over girls, spending on education for boys was bound to be higher than for girls.

A root problem was that many families simply valued girls less than boys, or women lower than men. Indian society (and many others) over the centuries had a way of measuring this: dowry payments. These became illegal in 1961, but continued anyway in much of Indian society, sometimes disguised as extravagant wedding presents from a bride's family to the parents of the groom. Dowry amounted, in effect, to paying another family to relieve you of the burden of having a daughter. It seems likely that having to pay a dowry was also one reason why some parents much preferred male babies. As in many other countries, sons were favored because they conferred higher social status; brought a higher income, because men were more likely to get jobs beyond the home (plus a dowry); and, by tradition, were supposed to care for parents in old age. By contrast, tradition deemed that a daughter would leave for another household.

Some brides were ill-treated when they arrived in a new family. In 2013 India's Supreme Court lamented "emotional numbness in society," saying that daughters-in-law were sometimes kept as near slaves or attacked over dowry. The judges said "life sparks are extinguished by torture, both physical and mental, because of demand of dowry and insatiable greed."

At the time, nearly seventy thousand trials were pending over dowry violence—brides who had been attacked, even killed, because payments were late or low.

Of course, most Indian women did not suffer in this way, and the problems were not unique to India. It is also true that, for many women, India was an enabling place, especially in more educated, urban, and well-off communities. Yet in some instances even the better-off suffered. One way to get a glimpse into many families was through the eyes of Ajit Singh, who had launched a private detective agency in the 1990s and specialized in the flourishing business of premarital investigations. That gave him an unusual vantage point from which he could trace the changing position of women in society. Investigation of brides (and grooms) was "increasing like anything," he explained. "Now everyone relies on matrimonial portals, websites" to find partners, he said, twitching his moustache a little in disapproval. "Twenty years ago it was only the higher-income group that would hire us. Now people from the weaker section also do," he said. "In the past the poor had their own relatives and sources, now people send each other their resumes and don't tell the truth," he said. "And if you are not telling the truth in relationships, it is much more serious than in business. You are cheating two families."

Extended families of several generations in a single household were growing less common than before, but remained more widespread than in most other countries. A census in 2011 found that 18 percent of homes in India had more than one married couple; barely 1 percent of households in Britain fell into this category. The wider family remained intensely important, and it did much to define what opportunities—social, economic—were possible for women, especially when a bride went to live in her new husband's household. Marriages arranged by parents for their offspring remained the most usual, but even with "love marriages," where the couple already knew each other, the parents of the bride or groom might hire a detective to check out the other family. A simple investigation, for about 20,000 rupees (roughly $300 in 2016), provided basic information about reputation and "general character," plus details from the workplace. Some clients spent as much as 300,000 rupees, said Singh. "Then we will follow the subject. We put more energy into checking the financial status. We offer detailed financial analysis, detailed information into the extended family, monthly income, circles of friends, behavior and habits—for example, whether they are into drinking and partying, what is their weekend style, do they like going to pubs, do they take beer all the night? We talk to maids, drivers, gardeners, nearby persons, neighbors."

Parents of a bride wanted most information about the groom's mother, the future mother-in-law, said Singh. "They ask about the nature of the lady. Is she God-fearing, quarrelsome, friendly with the neighbors? How does she deal with the maid, is she going to temple, does she spend all day in the markets, at kitties [parties], and at the parties is there any drinking? Because the girl who is going to marry [into] that house, she is going to spend a lot of time with that lady. Every day she is going to face the mother-in-law," said Singh. The parents of the groom, however, were most likely to judge the bride, said Singh. The investigator was asked to lay bare the bride's previous "behavior and character, their upbringing. If she is living a lavish life, will there be a difficulty to adjust to the house? What is their temperament? The majority of the girls have a very high expectation of marriage—and it doesn't meet reality. They ask what expectations she has. What friends? Her upbringing, standard of living, the kind of car she has, the brands she wears. If someone is in a Mercedes, shops in malls, buys big brands, will it be a problem when she comes to the in-laws?" Most important was whether she is *gharelu*—literally, "homely," but meaning subservient, timid, hard-working. It all sounded intimidating—families studying each other's women, paying Singh to help them to assess whether the union would raise or diminish social status.

Singh's clients were urban, from Delhi especially, though his agency was spreading nationally. If a woman kept working for a salary after marriage, as became more usual, she would probably be expected to "deposit her salary into the house, to share her income with the husband," said Singh. Double standards were obvious in judging sexual history. "Previous affairs is a big subject," said Singh, because a young woman's past "matters to mothers. We check at the office, we ask about affairs at college, or in the neighborhood, or school even." Lying was common. Around a third of Singh's pre-marriage cases "trend negative," meaning he found that somebody had been dishonest about something serious, perhaps a previous marriage or a falsehood about one's income. It was surprisingly common to be hired by parents of a bride who doubted the sexuality of the groom, he said.

After marriage, the often difficult relationship of brides and their mothers-in-law was a bumper source of extra business. Singh described a woman who had recently asked him to investigate her husband's mother. The client was from Mumbai—"girls from there are very fast. It's a reality. We here, in Delhi, we cannot keep up with them. Life is fast." The woman had moved in with the groom's family in Delhi and things soon went awry. She continued working, but broke convention by sending money to her own parents. Relations soured until she left and each side launched a legal case, accusing the other of deception, abuse, even sorcery. "The daughter-in-law wrote in her FIR [a police charge] that the family were doing tantric worshipping, wrong pujas, against her," he said.

Changing relations between mothers-in-law and daughters-in-law—the *saas-bahu* relationship—were a subject of intense interest because the domestic household was a rare domain in which women dominated. "It is the toughest relationship across the families. In a very rare case the mother-in-law treats the daughter-in-law as her daughter. In the majority of cases the mother-in-law is wrong," suggested Singh, talking of his clients. He saw young women growing more assertive. More were educated, employed, and financially independent than before. "Now they don't tolerate the bullshit," he said. Walking away from an abusive relationship had become possible, something hard to imagine in the past. Books about mothers-in-law offered blunt advice, such as: "Run, she is trying to kill you." Online discussion threads let women share horror stories under titles such as, "I've got a mother-in-law from hell."

A popular soap opera had run with the clunky title *Because the Mother-in-Law Was Once a Daughter-in-Law Too* (Kyunki Saas Bhi Kabhi Bahu Thi). The star, Smriti Irani, an ex-model-turned-actress (who later became education minister, bizarrely), explained to me that, for seven years, viewers—at one point over 20 million nightly—tuned in for its lifelike family drama. It was "the longest-running, biggest-grossing serial in India," she said, describing how her character progressed from being a daughter-in-law to a mother-in-law. It dwelt sympathetically on how a mother-in-law, in a time of changing mores, managed the young women who entered her life. It also tackled previously neglected topics—"for example, the issue of marital rape, it was the first-ever discussion of that on television, and our audience was a family audience. I never projected a girl or a lady as a hapless victim. Everyone recognizes it was a soap, but the soap became a medium for projecting certain ideas," said Irani.

Veena Venugopal, a journalist who turned a sharp eye on Indian society, wrote a study of brides and mothers-in-law.[1] She found educated, prosperous, English-speaking women— with just about the best opportunity of any in India—whose lives were made miserable by their mothers-in-law. "I hadn't expected how bad the stories were going to be," she said, blaming the "unhealthy" joint Indian family "as the source of both the greatest closeness and stress." She described a fabulously wealthy family of nine in Mumbai, whose matriarch wore "diamonds the size of bird's eggs"—a family that feuded for years ostensibly over who controlled the kitchen servants. The daughter-in-law fled when the conflict turned abusive. Venugopal generally blamed the elder women, saying they mistreated the younger ones, and described what she said were elder women's near "obsessive" control of "sex and shame" as a way of keeping a grip on the household. Mothers-in-law "don't trust her to be faithful, so they try to desexualize the daughter-in-law," locking her up, fattening her up, phoning her several times a day. Women competed for attention from the shared man in their lives: the mother's son, the wife's husband. My assistant, Indrani, from Kolkata, explained how in Bengali wedding ceremonies much of this was made explicit. A groom on his wedding day repeated to his mother, three times, "I will bring you a servant." Meanwhile, the burdensome daughter, leaving home to join the new household, would take a handful of rice and tell her own mother, "Your debt is cleared." The message was pretty blunt: a new bride was considered little better than a skivvy, or servant.

But for all the gloomy stories about women in India, there was some progress being made. At least their prospects were being debated intensively in the press, on television, in magazines, on social media, and beyond. For India to tackle the various threats to girls and women, these threats first had to be talked about: a broad cultural change could follow. Some signs pointed to improvements. Divorce rates appeared to be rising (though they remained low by international standards), from almost nonexistent to about 13 dissolutions per 1,000 marriages. Family courts in larger cities, especially, reported a big increase in applications for divorce. That suggested more women were able to leave unhappy or abusive marriages, resulting in increased independence for at least a portion of the female population.

Progress on these scores can be seen in relation to the decline of older, unappealing, practices. One place to hear of old practices that were becoming rarer was in Vrindavan, a pretty town near Agra, a favorite for devotees of Lord Krishna as well as backpackers seeking joints and spiritual highs. The town was famed for its many elderly homeless women who lived out their final years there while begging for alms. At a soup kitchen for the elderly I met Renubala Dasi, a Bengali who had a bent back, a grey smear of mud on her forehead, and oval spectacles. She told a story of years of neglect and toil. It was typical of those told by several elderly women who attended the kitchen. Married at the age of twelve, Dasi had moved to her husband's farming family in Tripura, in northeast India, initially sharing a bed with his widowed mother. She recalled being "very scared of my mother-in-law" and respectfully calling her *ma-goshai,* or "God mother," and "worshipping her as a goddess." She rose at 4 a.m., prepared a hookah for her *shashuri* (the Bengali term for mother-in-law) to smoke, fetched water, and cleaned. "After she had taken her bath, I would wash her clothes, massage her head and body, tie her hair. Whenever she came in[to] sight I would bend and touch her feet to show respect," she said. Submission brought order and Dasi could at least hope that if she produced a son, she would graduate as a mother-in-law herself, and get similar care.

Years later, when it came to arranging a wife for her own son, she said much had changed. She complained that her own daughter-in-law was a "tigress," a woman already thirty years old who had ideas of her own. The younger woman never called her a "God mother": "She calls me nothing, just orders me to sit or stand." The younger woman grew hostile, "denied me food, stopped me speaking to my son," and eventually her son drove her 870 miles to Vrindavan and abandoned her. Resigned to it, she took up singing devotional songs and reciting the 108 names of Krishna. Her son won't light her funeral pyre when she is cremated, she said sadly. Did she think her story reflected a change in the family, and in the place of women in Indian society? She saw only her own sorrow. "We are living in the time of Kali Yuga," the end of civilization, when humans live only for lust, greed, broken vows, and violence, she said. Another widow spoke tearfully of her broken leg, and lamented that "brides arrive in the house prepared, they can't be abused, they do the abuse." A third complained about the influence of soap operas, like Smriti Irani's one, saying: "I blame TV for daughters-in-law being like this. From the age of five they watch TV and learn about money and families."

In fact, though the widows' stories were sad, they reflected a more hopeful turn in society: that many younger women no longer accepted being exploited, shaking off habits that were more common among previous generations. They were less weak than those of an earlier age. Bitter fighting between generations was a welcome sign of power shifting. As women got more paid work, earning income outside of the household, they could dare to assert themselves, leave bad marriages, and defy repressive traditions. Old attitudes—captured in the Hindi saying that "once you go to your in-laws' house, only your dead body should come out"—were fading. The head of a "mother-in-law protection forum" grumbled once to me that "the main problem is that today's women are educated, but not in the proper way. Parents are incapable of teaching the daughter how to stay in her in-laws' house." But the sooner regressive views like hers declined, the better for India.

By 2016 or so, there was mounting evidence that more women were standing up for themselves. Many rejected the old practice of *sindoor*, wearing vermillion at the hair parting to signify devotion to one's husband, for example. Debates also arose over another traditional practice, Karva Chauth, in which women are supposed to fast for a day, each year, to bring their husbands long life and safety. Women were marrying later: at twenty-one or older, on average—up from fifteen years of age in the mid-twentieth century. Later marriages, in turn, gave more women a chance to get educated and to control when the first birth would follow. The more educated expected paid jobs, to work after they wed. Women also had more of a chance of knowing whom they were marrying. Before 1960, fewer than 20 percent of women had any communication or interaction with their future husbands before marriage. By the 1990s that figure had risen to 60 percent of urban women (and about half of rural ones). No doubt, by 2016, it was higher yet.

Change had to come on several more fronts. Only when girls and women were better fed, for example, would fewer underweight babies be born. And only then would India start to be rid of its dreadful record on malnutrition. Surveys showed that bad nourishment persisted even among some wealthy families, suggesting neglect of girls. The grim tendency, especially in north India, to abort female fetuses remained roughly as prevalent in towns as in villages. Modi spoke well, a couple of times, on the subject of horribly skewed child sex ratios in India, but his government did little to change behavior and opinions.

As one consequence of this, northern states including Haryana, which is relatively wealthy and close to Delhi, began to experience a shortage of women (as happened in parts of China). This led to the trafficking of brides from other parts of the country, some tricked or forced against their will. Evidence of this was easy to find. Not far beyond the glass towers of Gurgaon, Delhi's business-satellite suburb, were villages set among wheat fields of Haryana. Dung cakes on the roadside were artfully stacked into house-like structures, drying for use in cooking fires. On one dung stack stood a satellite dish, for receiving cricket games, soap operas, and TV news. Here were mud-built homes and paths thick with people walking from school or leaving fields in chattering groups, a reminder that rural does not always mean lightly populated. In one village, Kotla, in the courtyard of a home where children clambered over walls, Sakina, a mother in her thirties, explained how she had been tricked into marriage while still barely a girl, in the 1990s. She had been brought more than 800 miles to the village by a middleman who trafficked young women as brides. Her husband's family had mistreated her. Sakina explained that "it was when I started having children that I realized I had no time to be upset." She produced nine offspring, eight of them boys—and by producing so many male children, she was elevated in status within the village.

In the dying years of Manmohan Singh's government the mistreatment of women became an issue of national, even international, debate. The spark was the gang rape and murder, on a bus, of a young physiotherapy student, in December 2012. The victim, in Delhi, came to represent an emerging, aspirational group of Indians. Huge protests erupted, helped by intense television and press coverage. Seething crowds appeared, some chanting that they would torture and lynch the attackers. At times, police resorted to tear gas and curfews to restore order. The rape and murder of poorer women never got such attention, but there was a widespread push for more debate over the ill-treatment of women in general. Official rape statistics did not prove that India had a worse problem with sexual violence than other countries, but such statistics were not widely trusted and opinion polls suggested that 90 percent of Indians thought rape was a "very big" concern, and most said it was getting worse.

People in authority mishandled their responses. Some blamed the girls and women who were assaulted for wearing supposedly immodest clothes or for daring to go out after dark. Mulayam Singh Yadav, a leading politician in Uttar Pradesh, said that rapists were treated too harshly—that "boys make mistakes"—and vowed to "revoke the anti-rape laws." A policeman in the same state was seen on television in effect telling villagers to murder a fourteen-year-old girl who had been abducted by older men, saying that if his sister had "eloped" he would have killed her or killed himself in shame. A Bengali politician, the son of Pranab Mukherjee (who became president), scoffed at women protesting against sexual violence, calling them "highly dented-painted." The police chief in Mumbai, where a female photojournalist had been gang-raped, blamed youthful "promiscuous culture."

Thankfully, others promoted women's safety. Ranjana Kumari ran an organization to help women on the edge of a slum in Delhi, for example. "I deal with rape cases on a daily basis." she said. "It is very difficult to believe anything will improve because there is a lack of political will." But at least, as with corruption, democratic India was beginning to confront this enormous, complicated problem. The rise of cities was one reason to be optimistic, because police there were more likely to respond to complaints of sexual assault than those in villages. Kumari dismissed Hindu nationalist commentators who claimed that "Bharat," implying rural India, never saw attacks on women. It was just that such attacks were far less likely to be recorded or publicized than those in town. In cities a new sort of debate was also becoming possible. A decade or two earlier it was almost taboo to utter the Hindi word for rape (*balatkar*), let alone address the problem of how men behaved. But more people in modern India said they refused to be treated as victims.

The photojournalist who was gang-raped in Mumbai said she would keep working, and refused to be shamed by the attack. What needed to change, argued Kumari, was that men and boys should start to have a "fear of law, or at least the semblance of the rule of law." Police have to take the attacks more seriously. It would help, too, if more youngsters got to talk frankly about sex, she said, complaining about "fundamentalists who won't allow sex education in school, and teachers who won't utter the word *sex*."

A judicial commission set up after the Delhi rape and murder received thousands of public suggestions for tackling violence against women. It proposed sensible laws—such as tougher punishment for those who disfigure women by throwing acid at them—which parliament enacted quickly. At least the perpetrators of the Delhi gang rape, men from a nearby slum, were arrested and jailed (though one died in prison) after a swift but fair trial that involved 130 hearings and nearly 200 witnesses. Extra courts—a plan called for 1,800 eventually—helped to speed other prosecutions for rape, to clear a backlog of 23,000 cases. The democracy showed it could function when pressed. The media also got better at discussing sexual violence, dropping euphemistic terms such as *Eve-teasing*, a reference to men's taunting, abuse, or groping of women in public. And although rape statistics in Delhi worsened, that was paradoxically encouraging, suggesting that women there were more willing than before to report attacks and the police were readier to record them.

Growing public anger about the issue at least encouraged those who campaigned to change attitudes. Activists tried to shift opinions. In south Delhi, off a narrow alley, was Maitri, an outfit for battered women. The organizer, Winnie Singh, sporting round tortoise-shell glasses and cropped grey hair, said "our laws are among the strongest in the world," but police and judges failed to implement them. She spoke of being attacked during her first marriage and got only unsympathetic reactions from police. She created her group, one of many, to help battered women lodge legal cases against attackers, though that often proved difficult.

Prospects should improve for women, especially if politicians do more to speed up gains. India spends far too little on public health—1.4 percent of its national wealth, compared with over 3 percent in China. The burden of that is felt hardest by women and girls. Putting more resources there would lift their prospects in general. As of 2014, combined private and public spending on health, per year, averaged $75 per person in India. Even in Delhi, one of the wealthiest corners of India, only one in five women have a midwife or other skilled person present when giving birth, and barely half of the children get a measles jab.

Modi as prime minister, to his credit, did talk about Indians' preferences for sons over daughters as a "psychological illness of the entire country," saying that "we don't have a right to kill our daughters" and "in our neighbourhood, girls are commonly killed in their mothers' wombs and we don't feel the pain."[2] It was welcome to hear him address the difficult subject. But wider efforts are needed, across both political and economic realms. Only if more women are paid for the work they do, for example, will their clout rise. Labor done by women is said to account for only 17 percent of the output of the formal economy, whereas in China it accounts for over 40 percent.[3] Nearly two-thirds of women in China are in the formal workforce (even if many do drudge jobs), vastly more than in India. If manufacturing were to boom in India, even to the level achieved in Bangladesh, with big textile and other factories, then more women would surely start earning salaries. That could have widespread social effects. According to McKinsey Global Institute, India could have an economy 60 percent larger if women were in the paid workforce and more productive—meaning better educated, better fed, and healthier. That is a tremendously hopeful goal for Indians to aim to achieve.

Notes

1. Veena Venugopal, *The Mother-in-Law: The Other Woman in Your Marriage* (Penguin, 2014).
2. Speech given in Haryana state, January 22, 2015, as reported by Reuters, http://uk.reuters.com/article/uk-india-girls-idUKKBN0KV0ZW20150122.
3. Jonathan Woertzel et al., *How Advancing Women's Equality Can Add $12 Trillion to Global Growth* (McKinsey Global Institute, September 2015), p. 35.

Reading 2.2

Afghanistan

Homayun Sidky

Afghanistan is a landlocked mountainous country lying in the heart of the Eurasian continent. Encompassing roughly 647,500 square kilometers, making it slightly smaller than the state of Texas, it borders Pakistan to the south and east, Iran to the west, Turkmenistan to the northwest, Tajikistan and Uzbekistan to the north, and China to the northeast.

During the 1980s Afghanistan attracted considerable international interest as a result of the Soviet invasion in 1979 and the armed resistance by the Afghan people. The true nature of the roles played by external super and regional powers in escalating the scale and intensity of the violence and destruction in Afghanistan has recently come to light and provides insight into the role of the international state system and its web of interdependencies on the nature of modern war (See Reyna & Downs, 1994; Simons, 1999).[1] Several things are now certain (Amnesty International, 1995a, 1995b; Harpviken, 1999; Lansford, 2003). Contrary to the "official version" that the United States became involved in Afghanistan after the Soviets invaded, it is now clear that the intervention in Afghanistan, authorized by President Jimmy Carter in July 3, 1979, began *6 months* before the Soviet troops set foot in the country on December 25, 1979. As Zbigniew Brzezinski (2003), national security advisor to Jimmy Carter, acknowledged in 1998, the CIA aid was directed to support the *mujahideen* (singular mujahid, those who undertake *jihad* or religious struggle in defense of the faith) in order to provoke an inevitable Soviet military response. Brzezinski explained that the aim was to draw the USSR "into the Afghan trap" (Brzezinski, 2003, p. 274) so they would have their own Vietnam.

The plan worked. The Soviets invaded and the United States and its allies showered the *mujahideen* with vast sums of money and a massive array of armaments. This alliance was led by the United States with the help of Saudi Arabia, Pakistan (Grare, 2003), Egypt, the Gulf States, Britain, France, and China. The Soviets, on their part, poured in an equal amount of cash and weaponry to the Kabul regime, which they were supporting. The country, once one of the most peaceful nations in the whole of Asia, thus became a cold war battlefield. The ideological and material conditions for the conflict were created by the interaction of regional and global powers, often with conflicting agendas and strategic designs, that not only provoked the Soviet invasion of Afghanistan, but also cast the conflict solely in terms of a religious or holy war and created an international alliance of countries to facilitate the recruitment, arming, and training of radical militant jihadis from around the world to fight it. In the minds of U.S. politicians, the idea was "the enemy of my enemy is my friend."

Ten years of brutal fighting ensued until the Soviets withdrew in 1989. With the subsequent breakup of the Soviet Union ending the Cold War, the Americans and other Western powers that supported the jihad against the Soviets backed off and disengaged completely (Rubin, 1995). Afghanistan more or less dropped out of the limelight of global politics and Western media attention. Afghanistan was left in ruins and politically fragmented, and its traditional institutional mechanisms for the management of violence eroded (Norchi, 1995).

Left without any functioning political, administrative, law enforcement, or security structures, Afghanistan was abandoned by the international community to the ambitions of Pakistan and other foreign powers (Maley, 2001; Saikal, 2001). This was the context in which a group called the *Taliban* (plural of the Persian word for *madrassa* student) first appeared (Goodson, 2001). Their objective was to impose an extreme intolerance for Islam on the Afghan people. In reality, the Taliban were a Pakistani contrived proxy force (Dorronsoro, 2002; Goodson, 2000; Margolis, 2000). Most Afghans regarded them as a foreign movement whose ideology had no basis in traditional Afghan Islamic or cultural values (Khalilzad & Byman, 1999).

The most controversial policy of the *Taliban*, one that eventually brought about their downfall, was to play host to Osama bin Laden and his operatives (Bodansky, 2001; Miller, 1999; National Commission on Terrorist Attacks Upon the United States, 2010; Weaver, 2000). However, Afghanistan's downward spiral into a hub and sanctuary for international terrorism began in the 1980s, when the CIA, ISI, and *Mukhabarat*, the Saudi Ministry of Intelligence, poured in large sums to finance the *jihad* against the Soviets by bringing Arab volunteers to fight alongside the Afghans after receiving military training in camps run by Pakistan's military intelligence (Griffin, 2001). These mercenaries, nicknamed "Afghan Arabs," came to Afghanistan with the assistance of a facility called *Maktab al Khidmat ili-mujahideen al-Arab*, run by the wealthy Arab businessman Osama bin Laden.

In 1988, utilizing the financial resources and technical expertise put in place for the war against the Soviets, bin Laden formed *al-Qaeda* (The Base), an organization with an international scope. The following year the Soviet army departed from Afghanistan (see Jacquard, 2002; National Commission on Terrorist Attacks Upon the United States, 2010; Reeve, 1999).

For bin Laden, the defeat and collapse of the atheist superpower and triumph of the Afghan jihad was a defining moment in Islamic history, a triumph that could be repeated against other superpowers (Orbach, 2001).[2]

From 1993 onward, bin Laden's camps in Afghanistan, nicknamed "terrorist universities" by U.S. officials, became the training grounds for a new generation of *jihadi* recruits. Attacks against U.S. targets carried out by trainees of these camps include the World Trade Center bombing in 1993; the attacks at Dhahran, Saudi Arabia, in 1996 that killed 19 American soldiers; the bombing of the U.S. embassies in Kenya and Tanzania in 1998 that left 258 dead and 5,000 injured; the attack on the *USS Cole* in Aden, Yemen, in 2000, killing 17 U.S. servicemen. These attacks demonstrated al-Qaeda's capacities for globally coordinated operations (Griffin, 2001; see also Katzman, 2001a, 2001b). By 1998, bin Laden had shifted his focus on the United States as the main enemy of Islam, and in a *fatwa* issued that year he called on his followers to kill Americans, military or civilian, anywhere in the world.

The Afghan-Arab jihadis had thus found a new global mission, to defend the *ummah* from incursions by non-believers everywhere. Hailed up to that time as heroic holy warriors and "freedom fighters" in the Western media, the jihadis would henceforth be referred to as "terrorists." The Cold War battleground in Afghanistan thus produced a generation of Islamist militants, emboldened by their encounter with the Soviet army and ready to expand their jihad beyond the Afghan theater to the international scene against new enemies: the United States, Israel, pro-Western Arab governments, and India in Kashmir. The weapons that the United States and its allies shipped into Afghanistan at a time when jihad directed at the Red Army was deemed a commendable battle cry was now redirected against their donors (Griffin, 2001). Some analysts call this "blowback," a term that means the unintended consequences of covert U.S. policies abroad result in retaliation against unsuspecting U.S. citizens (Johnson, 2000, 2002; Weaver, 1996).

By the start of the 21st century, there was an entirely different American perception of Afghanistan. It was now viewed as a grim "Kalashnikov culture," located near some other "stan," the home of heavily armed militant Muslims, warlords, opium czars, and terrorists, a place where women were oppressed and beaten in public, and where Islam "had gone crazy" (Vogelsang, 2002, p. ix). Many in the West did not understand what was transpiring in Afghanistan and many more simply did not care. The September 11, 2001, attacks on New York City and Washington, DC, changed all of that. Afghanistan became a household word. It was also in the days immediately after the collapse of the Twin Towers that some Americans first heard, to their horror, of al-Qaeda, Osama bin Laden, and the "atavistic" bearded radicals, called *Taliban*, and their global *jihad* or holy war against the United States.

The September 11th tragedy not only brought Afghanistan back into the center stage of global politics, but it also brought to the fore the fundamentally problematic nature of the relationship between the United States and the Islamic world (Halliday, 2002; Marsden, 2002). Shortly after 9/11, the United States invaded Afghanistan. The Taliban were defeated, most of their leadership and a large number of their followers are still at large, and the movement remains viable with a base of operations in Pakistan. Along with the Taliban leadership went Osama bin Laden and his Al Qaeda forces. It would take a decade before U.S. troops hunted down and killed bin Laden, who was hiding in plain sight in the town of Abbotabad, in Pakistan. To prevent a Taliban comeback, these events also committed the United States to one of the longest wars in its history.

After the expulsion of the Taliban from Kabul, the capital of Afghanistan, the United States backed Hamid Karzai, an ethnic Pashtun from Kandahar, as the head of a 30-member government with a timetable for transition to a democratic government. In June 2002 Karzai was elected as head of an interim government by an emergency *Loya Jirga* (tribal council). In April 2003 the initial draft of a new constitution endorsing a system of government was completed, and the *Loya Jirga* approved the constitution on January 4, 2004. National elections in Afghanistan scheduled for June 2004 were held in October 2004 due to security concerns. Costing approximately $200 million in international contributions, the outcome of the election was never in doubt. Karzai emerged as the victor. However, in reality the United States established an illegitimate government put in place by a foreign power through "regime change." This U.S.-dependent puppet regime has never had legitimacy in the provinces.

The country is now firmly divided along ethnic and sectarian lines, with many minorities, especially the Hazara people, being victimized more than ever before. This issue is aggravated because the current U.S.-backed president, Mr. Ashraf Ghani, has chosen to employ ethnicity as his favorite instrument of control and authoritarianism. The central authority is overtly engaged in ethnic politics through the domination of the Pashtuns in all areas of government. Non-Pashtuns see the United States as culpable for the abuses and for repression because of its support for a corrupt regime. The result has been the magnification of ethnic tensions in what is a multi-ethnic society where non-Pashtuns have been victims of Pashtun-controlled central government for over 2 centuries. This has also contributed to the failure to create a functional, reliable, and effective national military because the central government has no legitimacy and is Pashtun dominated.

The U.S.-sponsored regime in Afghanistan is entirely dependent on foreign aid. Access to such funds has contributed to massive levels of government corruption and abuse of power. None of this helps to rectify the legitimacy issues of the central authority or the outside forces that are seen as supporting its officials. The Taliban continue to be potential challengers for state power as long as their foreign sponsors continue to push their own political and strategic agendas and interfere in Afghanistan's internal affairs (Conetta, 2002; Cordesman,

2003; Danish Immigration Service, 2003; Langton, 2003; Raman, 2003; Rohde, 2003; UN Secretary-General, 2003; United States Institute of Peace, 2003).

After over 17 years of active military involvement and billions of dollars spent, mostly for military purposes, the Afghan military remains unable to meet the challenges and threats posed by regime enemies. The most persuasive evidence that the current strategies are not working is the length of the conflict with no resolution in sight and the ongoing efforts by our politicians and military planners to find some sort of workable alternative and possibly an exit strategy.

Notes

1. Although anthropologists have written about war (the anthropology of war) from a variety of perspectives, this international dimension of modern war has not been sufficiently addressed.

2. Such claims by the Islamist to the credit for defeating the Soviet Union overlooks the significant role of the United States and its allies and their money and arms assistance to the *mujahideen*, without which the rebellion would most likely have been defeated in the mid-1980s. Also, not everyone agrees that the Soviet Union collapsed as a result of the war in Afghanistan (see Cordovez & Harrison, 1995).

References

Amnesty International. (1995a). *Women in Afghanistan: A human rights catastrophe*. Author.

Amnesty International. (1995b). *International responsibility for human rights disaster*. Author.

Bodansky, Y. (2001). *Bin Laden: The man who declared war on America*. Copenhagen, Denmark: Forum Publishers.

Brzezinski, Z. (2003). "Some stirred up Muslims": Reflections on Soviet intervention in Afghanistan. In M. Gettleman & S. Schaar (Eds.), *The Middle East and Islamic World Reader* (pp. 273–276). New York, NY: Grove Press.

Conetta, C. (2002). *Strange victory: A critical appraisal of Operation Enduring Freedom and the Afghanistan War*. Project on Defense Alternatives Research Monograph 6 (30 January). http://184.73.243.18:8080/jspui/bitstream/azu/3266/1/azu_acku_pamphlet_ds371_3_c66_s77_2002_w.pdf

Cordesman, A. (2003). *The lessons of Afghanistan: War, fighting, intelligence, and force transformation*. Center for Strategic and International Studies.

Cordovez, D., & Harrison, S.S. (1995). *Out of Afghanistan: The inside story of the Soviet withdrawal*. New York, NY: Oxford University Press.

Danish Immigration Service. (2003). *The political, security and human rights situation in Afghanistan: Report on fact-finding mission to Kabul and Mazar-i-Sharif (Afghanistan) and Islamabad (Pakistan)*.

22 September–5 October 2002. https://www.refworld.org/docid/3ef7f0c84.html [accessed 23 January 2020]

Dorronsoro, G. (2002). Pakistan and the Taliban: State policy, religious networks, and political connections. In C. Jaffrelot (Ed.), *Pakistan: Nationalism without a nation?* (pp. 161–178). London, UK: Zed Books.

Goodson, L. (2000). Foreign policy gone awry: The Kalashnikovization and Talibanization of Pakistan. In C. Baxter & C. H. Kennedy (Eds.), *Pakistan 1999* (pp. 107–128). New York, NY: Oxford University Press.

Goodson, L. (2001). *Afghanistan's endless war: State failure, regional politics, and the rise of the Taliban.* Seattle, WA: University of Washington Press.

Grare, F. (2003). *Pakistan and the Afghan conflict, 1979–1985: With an afterword covering events from 1985–2001.* New York, NY: Oxford University Press.

Griffin, M. (2001). *Reaping the whirlwind: The Taliban movement in Afghanistan.* London; Sterling, VA: Pluto Press.

Halliday, F. (2002). *Two hours that shook the world, September 11, 2001: Causes and consequences.* London, UK: Saqi Books.

Harpviken, K. B. (1999). War and change in Afghanistan: Reflections on research priorities. In M. Juntunen & B. N. Schylter (Eds.), *Return to silk routes: Current Scandinavian research on Central Asia* (pp. 167–186). New York, NY: Routledge.

Jacquard, R. (2002). *In the name of Osama bin Laden: Global terrorism and the bin Laden brotherhood* (G. Holoch, Trans.). Durham, NC: Duke University Press.

Johnson, C. (2000). *Blowback: The cost and consequences of American empire.* New York, NY: Henry Holt.

Johnson, C. (2002, December). September 11th blowback. *Radical Historian Newsletter,* 86–87.

Katzman, K. (2001a). *Terrorism: Near Eastern groups and state sponsors, 2001.* CRS report for Congress. https://nsarchive2.gwu.edu/NSAEBB/NSAEBB55/crs20010910.pdf

Katzman, K. (2001b). *Afghanistan: Current issues and U.S. policy concerns.* CRS report for Congress. https://digital.library.unt.edu/ark:/67531/metacrs1781/m1/1/high_res_d/RL30588_2001Nov15.pdf

Khalilzad, Z., & Byman, D. (1999). Afghanistan: The consolidation of a rogue state. *Washington Quarterly, 23*(1), 64–78.

Langton, C. (2003, June 13). *Instability threatens reconstruction.* Institute for War and Peace Reporting, no. 13914. http://www.iwpr.net/index.pl?archive/arr/arr_200306_64_2_eng.txt

Lansford, T. (2003). *A bitter harvest: US foreign policy and Afghanistan.* Burlington, VT: Ashgate.

Maley, W. (2001). Moving forward in Afghanistan. In S. Harris, W. Maley, R. Price, C. Reus-Smith, & A. Saikal (Eds.), *The day the world changed? Terrorism and world order* (pp. 18–24). Department of International Relations.

Margolis, E. (2000). *War at the top of the world: The struggle for Afghanistan, Kashmir, and Tibet*. New York, NY: Routledge.

Marsden, P. (2002). *The Taliban: War and religion in Afghanistan*. London, UK: Zed Books.

Miller, J. (1999). Greetings, America. My name is Osama bin Laden. Now That I have Your Attention. *Esquire, 131*, 96–103.

National Commission on Terrorist Attacks Upon the United States. (2010). *The 9–11 Commission Report: Final Report*. Cosimo.

Norchi, C. H. (1995). *Afghanistan after the Soviets: Time, culture, and chaos*. Modern Asia Research Center.

Orbach, B. (2001). Usama bin Laden and *al-Qaeda*: Origins and doctrines. *Middle East Review of International Affairs, 5*(4), 54–68.

Raman, B. (2003, October 23). The fall and rise of the Taliban. *Asia Times*. http://atimes.com/atimes/Central_Asia/EJ23Ag02.html

Reeve, S. (1999). *The new jackals: Ramzi Yousef, Osama bin Laden, and the future of terrorism*. Boston, MA: Northeastern University Press.

Reyna, S. P., & Downs, R. E. (Eds.). (1994). *Studying war: Anthropological perspectives*. Langhorn, PA: Gordon and Breach.

Rohde, D. (2003, September 1). Taliban raids widen in parts of Afghanistan. *The New York Times*. https://www.nytimes.com/2003/09/01/world/taliban-raids-widen-in-parts-of-afghanistan.html

Rubin, B.R. (1995). *The search for peace in Afghanistan: From buffer state to failed state*. New Haven, CT: Yale University Press.

Saikal, A. (2001). The Afghan tragedy and the US response. In S. Harris, W. Maley, R. Price, C. Reus-Smith, & A. Saikal (Eds.), *The day the world changed? Terrorism and world order* (pp. 9–17). Department of International Relations.

Simons, A. (1999). War: Back to the future. *Annual Review of Anthropology, 28*, 73–108.

UN Secretary-General. (2003). *Report of the secretary-general on the situation in Afghanistan and its implications for international peace and security*. https://unama.unmissions.org/secretary-general-reports

United States Institute of Peace. (2003, April). *Unfinished business in Afghanistan: Warlordism, reconstruction, and ethnic Harmony*. Special Report, 105. https://www.usip.org/publications/2003/04/unfinished-business-afghanistan-warlordism-reconstruction-and-ethnic-harmony

Vogelsang, W. (2002). *The Afghans*. Malden, MA: Blackwell Publishers.

Weaver, M. A. (1996). Blowback. *The Atlantic*. https://www.theatlantic.com/magazine/archive/1996/05/blowback/376583/#Weaver

Weaver, M. A. (2000, January 24). The real bin Laden. *New Yorker*. https://www.newyorker.com/magazine/2000/01/24/the-real-bin-laden

Reading 2.3

Mining the Future
How China Is Set to Dominate the Next
Industrial Revolution

FP Analytics—Special Report

*A fight between the United States and China is brewing over 5G and
the question of who can be trusted to control the world's wireless
infrastructure. But scant attention is being paid to an issue of arguably
greater importance to the future of the world's economy and security:
China's control of the raw materials necessary to the digital economy.*

N O NEW PHONE, TABLET, CAR, OR satellite transferring your data at lightning speed can be
made without certain minerals and metals that are buried in a surprisingly small number
of countries, and for which few commonly found substitutes are available. Operating in niche
markets with limited transparency and often in politically unstable countries, Chinese firms
have locked up supplies of these minerals and metals with a combination of state-directed investment and state-backed capital, making long-term strategic plays, sometimes at a loss. Through

Illustration by Gwen Keraval.

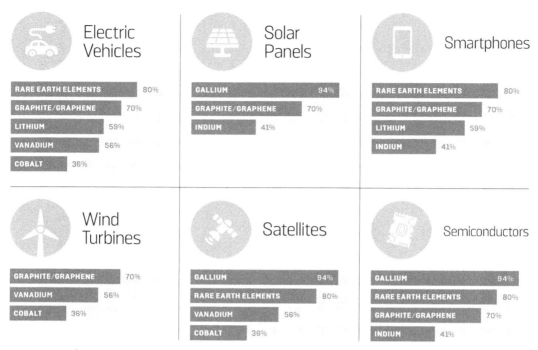

A Vast Sum of Parts China's control or influence over critical minerals and metals that power modern technology is unrivaled.

Sources: USGS; FPA Analysis of Company Filings, Deal Flows, Equity Stakes and Off-Take Agreements

in-depth analysis of company reports and disclosures, mapping of deal flows, quantification of direct and indirect equity stakes, and other primary research, FP Analytics has produced the first consolidated review of this unprecedented concentration of market power. Without rhetoric or hyperbole, this fact-based analysis reveals how rapidly and effectively China has executed its national ambitions, with far-reaching implications for the rest of the world.

China's 13th Five-Year Plan declared 2016 to 2020 a "decisive battle period" for the non-ferrous metal industry and for building a well-off society.[1] Its hallmark initiative, "Made in China 2025," aims to build strategic industries in national defense, science, and technology. To meet these objectives, in October 2016, the Ministry of Industry and Information Technology announced an action plan[2] for its metals industry to achieve world-power status: By deploying state-owned enterprises and private firms to resource-rich hot spots around the globe, China would develop and secure other countries' mineral reserves—including minerals in which China already holds a dominant position.

The timing could not have been better. The fall in metal commodities prices from 2011 to 2015 left many mining companies desperate for capital. Even the largest global players, such as Anglo American, had to slash their workforces and shed assets.[3,4] By directly acquiring mines, accumulating equity stakes in natural-resource companies, making long-term agreements to buy mines' current or future production (known as "off-take agreements"), and investing in new projects under development, Chinese firms traded much-needed capital for outright control or influence over large shares of the global production of these resources. Despite China's slowing growth and a major pullback in its foreign direct investment in other sectors, the government has maintained robust financial support for resource acquisition; mergers and acquisitions in metals and chemicals hit a record high in 2018.[5]

PART I
'Going Out and Bringing In'

Though it boasts a rich endowment of natural resources at home, China lacks significant reserves of three resources vital to its tech ambitions: cobalt, platinum-group metals, and lithium. It has successfully employed two strategies to secure control of them. One is driven by China's state-owned enterprises (SOEs), which use development finance and infrastructure investment to embed themselves in higher-risk countries, establishing close ties with government leaders. The second is investment by state-linked private firms in market-based economies. Both strategies have shown agility and an ability to effectively adapt to local circumstances to achieve the same end.

SOE Strategy, Cobalt, and the Case of the Democratic Republic of the Congo

With few governments having articulated, let alone implemented, an explicit resource strategy, China is more than a decade ahead in the game. At a gathering last June in Lubumbashi, the mining capital of the Democratic Republic of Congo (DRC), representatives from 35 Chinese mining companies announced the creation of the Union of Mining Companies with Chinese Capital to coordinate communication with the DRC's government.[6] The announcement was less an inauguration than a formalization of the deep, long-term relationships between Chinese industry and DRC government officials that have been cultivated for decades: China now owns or has influence over half of the DRC's cobalt production,[7] and has a massive stake in its mining industry. Six months ahead of the presidential elections, the event also sent a strong message to candidates about China's deep investment in copper and cobalt mining—which constitutes 80 percent of the DRC's export revenue[8] and thousands of jobs—and its capacity to influence the future of the DRC's economy.

China's notably high tolerance for political and security risk and its ability to embed firms in the development of local industry have not only enabled Chinese SOEs to gain footholds in complex natural-resource markets, but given them a competitive edge over their rivals in the industry. Its patient acquisition of the DRC's cobalt resources serves as a case in point.

The DRC is home to nearly two-thirds of the world's cobalt production and half of its known reserves.[9] Those resources are the prime target of investors for the booming battery industry. Over a decade of steady engagement, China has staked out a dominant position by developing strong political ties and investing in production assets and related infrastructure. Using development financing, in 2007, the Export-Import Bank of China issued[10] $6 billion for infrastructure (a figure later reduced to $3 billion) and $3 billion for copper and

A worker watches a conveyor belt loaded with chunks of raw cobalt at a plant in Lubumbashi, the mining capital of the Democratic Republic of the Congo, on Feb. 16, 2018. SAMIR TOUNSI/AFP/ GETTY IMAGES

cobalt mine development.[11] Projects were run by Sinohydro and China Railway Group in exchange for a 68 percent mineral stake in the Sicomines copper and cobalt mine, thought to be one of Africa's largest.[12] China deepened the DRC's reliance on Chinese capital by committing to finance the revitalization of the DRC's state-run company Gécamines,[13] strengthen the country's core industrial sector, and create needed jobs through additional sector investments.[14]

By targeting debt-stressed mining companies already established in the DRC, China's SOEs and private firms have secured equity shares and influence over a majority of its mines, including majority stakes in the Tenke Fungurume mine, which holds one of the world's largest, highest-grade deposits of copper and cobalt. China Molybdenum bought the majority stake (56 percent) from U.S. company Freeport-MacMoRan in 2016, and recently bought an additional 24 percent stake from Chinese private-equity firm BHR Partners.[15,16,17] Over time, China has secured ownership over 10 out of the DRC's 18 major operational mines, six major development projects, and a three-year off-take deal from the DRC's (and the world's) largest cobalt mine,[18] effectively establishing influence over 52 percent of the country's production.[19]

Recognizing the continued demand from global industry, former President Kabila and DRC officials implemented a 50 percent tax on superprofits in a revised mining code,[20] creating even more uncertainty about the country's future cobalt production. Before leaving office, Kabila declared cobalt a "strategic" metal and tripled the royalty tax, to boost local governments' profit share from the sector.[21] Similar taxes are being considered in neighboring Zambia.

Despite the DRC's recent election and uncertainty about how the new president will engage with the mining industry, China and its local firms continue to reinforce their impact on the local economy and engage collectively with the DRC's political establishment. The recent formalization of the Union of Mining Companies with Chinese Capital has been set up to do just that.

Replicating the State-Owned Enterprise Model

China's SOE-driven strategy remains dominant throughout Africa, where adverse market sentiment and financial hardship in the mining industry have opened the door for SOE investment across the region. Notably, SOEs, in partnership with the China-Africa Development Fund, a Chinese state-funded institution, have expanded in South Africa's Bushveld Complex,[22] a mineral-rich geological formation that contains the world's largest reserves of platinum-group metals[23]—critical for making catalytic converters, which are essential for reducing automobile emissions—and the world's highest-grade and third-largest deposit of vanadium, a resource integral to a broad range of high-tech industries, from renewable-energy storage to aerospace and defense.

By leveraging state resources, China's SOEs and private firms have made at least eight major equity and off-take plays in platinum-group metals in the Bushveld Complex.[24] Such investments in South Africa's highly concentrated and strategic resource deposits have helped make metals the country's leading source of export growth,[25] with nearly 50 percent of its metal exports going to China[26]—tying South Africa's economic welfare directly to Chinese investment.

Private Firms and the Extension of State Strategy Abroad

China is also proving agile at adapting to conditions in market-oriented, democratic countries, using privately owned companies that are backed by state capital. By incrementally acquiring equity stakes in major local resource companies and financing junior developers, Chinese firms are strengthening their market presence while overcoming local concerns about foreign control over strategic domestic resources, such as niobium in Brazil and tantalum in Australia. Nowhere is this privately driven resource strategy more evident than in the three countries where nearly 90 percent of global lithium production and more than three-quarters of the world's known lithium reserves are located: Chile, Argentina, and Australia.[27] In just six years, China has come to dominate the global market: More than 59 percent of the world's lithium resources are now under its control or influence.[28]

With the backing of state-owned banks, China's industrial chemical giants—Tianqi Lithium and Ganfeng Lithium—have become the world's third-largest producer of lithium[29] and third-largest producer of lithium chemical compounds,[30] respectively. The chairmen of both companies have risen within the ranks of Chinese politics over the past few years, just as China was beginning to prioritize securing supplies of rare metals. In 2013, Tianqi's chairman, Jiang Weiping, became a member of the Standing Committee of the Political Consultative Conference of Sichuan province,[31] and he was made a delegate to the National People's Congress in 2018.[32] Ganfeng's chairman, Li Liangbin, became a member of the Standing Committee of the 12th Political Consultative Conference of Jiangxi province in 2018.[33] These two companies, along with other Chinese firms, have expanded their investments and integrated operations in three distinct markets by acquiring a major stake in the leading producer in Chile, financing new development in Argentina, and acquiring mines and building up processing capacity in Australia.

Growing Equity in Latin America's Lithium Leaders

In early 2018, Tianqi Lithium made a bold play to acquire a 24 percent stake in Chilean rival Sociedad Química y Minera (SQM), the world's second-largest lithium producer. Chile is home to 57 percent of the world's known lithium reserves,[34] the world's largest known concentration, and SQM controls roughly half the country's production. In the industry's biggest mergers-and-acquisitions deal to date, Tianqi made a $4.1-billion bid on SQM's shares, $3.5 billion of which was financed by China's CITIC Bank International,[35] whose parent company, CITIC Group, is among China's largest state-owned financial and industrial conglomerates.[36]

The Chilean government has traditionally held a relatively tight rein on its lithium resources, which have long been considered strategic for the nation's nuclear industry. The size of the deal with Tianqi heightened concerns in Chile over a foreign entity controlling those resources, and the potential for a cartel to form—spurring public opposition and antitrust and constitutional court challenges by SQM's majority shareholder. After months of legal battles and debate, the Constitutional Court of Chile dismissed the antitrust claims,[37] allowing Tianqi to secure the deal in December. Though the final agreement[38] included restrictions on Tianqi's board and committee participation and its access to SQM's sensitive data, Tianqi's equity position still confers considerable influence over SQM.

But the SQM deal is just one piece of a deepening economic relationship[39] with Chile, including Chinese investments in the local lithium industrial base, exports of electric buses to Chile, and an upgraded trade agreement between the two countries that just came into force in March 2019.[40] In April 2018, China's ambassador to Chile, Xu Bu, stated to local news outlets that opposition to the sale "could leave negative influences on the development of economic and commercial relations between both countries,"[41] and has since reportedly made other economic threats.[42] Tianqi is now seeking permission to develop Salar de La Isla, Chile's second-largest lithium brine deposit,[43] in partnership with U.S.-based lithium

COBALT

Democratic Republic of the Congo

PRODUCTION: 61%

RESERVES: 49%

CHINA'S INFLUENCE:
Influence over 52% of cobalt production with equity stakes and supply agreements

NIOBIUM

Brazil

PRODUCTION: 88%

RESERVES: 80%

CHINA'S INFLUENCE:
Stakes in 100% production

PLATINUM GROUP METALS (PGMs)

South Africa

PRODUCTION: 54%

RESERVES: 91%

CHINA'S INFLUENCE:
Stakes in ⅔ of all major PGM sites

LITHIUM

Argentina

PRODUCTION: 10%

RESERVES: 14%

CHINA'S INFLUENCE:
Stakes in 41% of major planned projects accounting for 37% of reserves

Australia

PRODUCTION: 58%

RESERVES: 19%

CHINA'S INFLUENCE:
Stakes in 61% of production

Bolivia

PRODUCTION: None

RESERVES:
Believed to be among the world's largest

CHINA'S INFLUENCE:
Stakes in 100% of development via an equity agreement

Chile

PRODUCTION: 21%

RESERVES: 57%

CHINA'S INFLUENCE:
Stakes in 67% of Chile's output

PRODUCTION AND RESERVES FOR 2017. SOURCES: USGS; FPA ANALYSIS OF COMPANY FILINGS, DEAL FLOWS, EQUITY STAKES AND OFF-TAKE AGREEMENTS

Chinese Resource Strategy
China is securing minerals and metals for which it is net import reliant.

company Albemarle, the other major player in Chile's lithium industry. Tianqi has the majority stake in the joint venture.[44]

Leveraging Capital Across Developing and Developed Markets

In a cash-strapped industry, Chinese firms are financing mine expansion and new development in exchange for a guaranteed supply of lithium in both mature and emerging markets. In Argentina, where President Mauricio Macri is eliminating mineral export taxes, reducing corporate tax rates, and allowing profit repatriation, China is establishing a dominant position in the nascent sector with "streaming deals," which provide development capital in exchange for future lithium yields to help projects get off the ground. Chinese firms, led by Ganfeng, have stakes in 41 percent of the country's major planned projects that account for 37 percent of Argentina's reserves.[45] This raw-material strategy is already coming to fruition: Lithium export volumes from Argentina to China rose nearly fourfold from 2015 to 2017,[46] and China has secured access to the country's lithium for the longer term.

This same strategy, combined with asset acquisition, has also been successful in Australia, whose proximity to China, significant lithium reserves, and broad political support for mining investment have attracted Chinese investment. Tianqi and Ganfeng have established stakes in 91 percent of the lithium mining projects underway and 75 percent of the country's reserves, including some of the world's largest.[47] By taking over Talison Lithium, Tianqi captured a majority stake in the Greenbushes mine, which accounts for roughly 40 percent of global lithium production.[48] Together, Chinese firms have secured deals with nine of the 11 major operations and projects in the pipeline in Australia, two-thirds of which are exclusive.[49]

Growing the Global Footprint

Having already consolidated control over global lithium supplies, Tianqi and Ganfeng are just getting started. Both filed for initial public offerings last fall with the intent to raise capital for further expansion. Ganfeng raised $421 million in its October 2018 initial public offering,[50] which included four state-linked cornerstone investors.[51] Last November, Tianqi received the necessary approvals from the China Securities Regulatory Commission to prepare for its Hong Kong listing,[52] the proceeds from which will be deployed in global markets.

PART 2
China Reinforcing Its Resource Dominance

China is also making moves to take an even stronger position in resources it already controls on the global market. Natural resources are abundant in China; it is the No. 1 producer and processor of at least ten critical minerals and metals[53,54] that are essential to high-tech industries and upon which China's commercial and strategic competitors depend. To reinforce its strength, Chinese firms are acquiring mines and output from the next-largest producers and reserves, giving China both an economic edge in the next high-tech industrial revolution and increasing geopolitical power.

Perhaps the best-known example both of China's natural-resource dominance and its willingness to exploit it is rare-earth elements, a group of 17 elements that (despite their name) are commonly found, but rarely in concentrations that can be economically extracted. They are important materials for the defense, aerospace, electronics, and renewable energy industries. Over the past two decades China has produced more than 80 percent of the world's production of rare-earth elements and processed chemicals.[55] In 2010 it cut off exports to Japan[56] amid rising tensions over the East China Sea, and the following year it imposed export quotas[57] that threw governments and manufacturers into a panic.[58] But with the exception of Japan, the attention to this critical vulnerability was short-lived, and little action was taken by other countries reliant on imports to diversify their resources or develop minerals action plans of their own.

China declared rare-earth elements a strategic resource in 1990 and prohibited foreign investment in the sector.[59] Six state-owned enterprises control the industry, and the government cut production quotas in 2018 by 36 percent.[60] With global demand for rare-earth elements projected at a compound average growth rate of more than 17 percent to 2025,[61] a supply crunch is likely approaching—and China is already securing other nations' supplies.

Chinese firms have been increasing stakes in mines and securing off-take deals from the world's largest deposits of rare-earth elements. While Russia strictly limits foreign participation in rare-earth element development, Chinese firms have accumulated off-take agreements and stakes in rare-earth element mines in Australia and Brazil. Though Australia's Foreign Investment Review Board denied a 2009 takeover of Australian company Lynas' mine at Mount Weld,[62] the second-largest rare-earth element oxide producer outside China, Chinese firms have locked in output from the site.[63] Northern Minerals, owned by Chinese firms,[64] is also developing Australia's other major rare-earth elements site, Browns Range; 100 percent of the mine's dysprosium, an element used in magnets and superalloys, will go to China's Lianyungang Zeyu New Materials Sales Co. Ltd.[65]

And in the United States in 2017, China's Shenghe Resources and two U.S. private equity firms acquired the sole U.S. and North American rare-earth element producer and processor, Molycorp, and its idled mining operations at Mountain Pass, California.[66] The operation went bankrupt in 2015 due in large part to low prices for Chinese supplies of rare-earth elements, and its sale briefly spurred debate over whether the deal posed risks to national security,[67] but opponents could not make the legal case to block it. Shenghe holds rights to the mine's output; meanwhile the United States' rare-earth element imports continue to increase, at a cost of $160 million in 2018 alone.[68] Though President Donald Trump has since called for a defense review and assessment of critical minerals, the Committee on Foreign Investment in the United States has not taken further action on the site. Meanwhile, Shenghe and its subsidiaries are continuing to expand internationally, with a major joint-venture development project in rare-earth elements now underway in Green land.[69,70] China's decades-long consolidation of strategic resources has only compounded its commercial and geopolitical capabilities, and it shows no sign of slowing down.

Vanadium and Graphite

China is also seeking to expand its dominant market position in vanadium and graphite, securing additional supplies and building integrated supply chains. Vanadium is a transition metal that is used in flow batteries, superconducting magnets, and high-strength alloys for jet engines and high-speed aircraft. Chinese firms already produce 56 percent of the world's vanadium domestically, and China is home to 48 percent of the world's reserves.[71] Now, they are targeting South Africa, ranked third in vanadium production and reserves behind China and Russia.[72]

In 2015, Hong Kong-based International Resources Ltd., a company whose ownership is opaque, executed a takeover of a major vanadium mine from Russia's Evraz High veld Steel and Vanadium, which was facing bankruptcy.[73] In 2016, China's Yellow Dragon Holdings Ltd. co-invested with Bushveld Minerals, the primary vanadium developer in South Africa's massive Bushveld Complex, to acquire Strategic Minerals, which owned the Vametco vanadium mine and plant.[74] Yellow Dragon subsequently increased its investment in Bushveld Minerals and has become the fifth-largest shareholder.[75] The holdings deepen China's influence over South Africa's vanadium resources and its role in the country's emerging high-tech sector. Bushveld Minerals is moving to develop an integrated platform to produce vanadium redox flow batteries for distributed energy across South Africa.[76] The vanadium resources will also flow toward China, feeding its battery industry and the National Development and Reform Commission's planned rollout of 100-megawatt stationary energy storage stations to manage its wind and solar energy.[77]

China's position is even stronger in graphite, a crystalline form of the element carbon whose high conductivity makes it a major component in electrodes, batteries, and solar panels, as well as industrial products such as steel and composites. For the last 20 years, China has been the leading global supplier of graphite, representing nearly 70 percent of the world's production in 2018 and 24 percent of its reserves.[78] While synthetic graphite, which is produced from petroleum coke, is an alternative, unfavorable economics constrain its use.

A worker walks across the Jin Yang graphite factory in the town of Mashan, China, on May 28, 2016. MICHAEL ROBINSON CHAVEZ/THE WASHINGTON POST VIA GETTY IMAGES

Rapidly growing demand for batteries and other end uses, coupled with environmental restrictions in China, are driving prices higher and stimulating investment. New projects are concentrated in Mozambique, where the world's largest graphite mine and fourth-largest known reserves are located.[79] Already, Chinese firms have secured off-take agreements with the three major developers in Mozambique for the majority of their graphite production,[80,81] and they are financing new development.[82]

Now that it controls most of the world's graphite, China has expanded down the supply chain, becoming the world's leading producer of anodes, positively charged electrodes that are essential for making lithium-ion batteries. That industry is also highly concentrated: China's Shenzhen BTR New Energy Materials accounts for roughly 70 percent of global anode production.[83] The next-largest player is Japan's Hitachi Chemical, at 20 percent;[84] Japan is 90 percent reliant on China for its graphite.[85] China is channeling increasing volumes of graphite toward its booming domestic battery and new electric-vehicle industries, stockpiling domestic production and reducing graphite exports, which could result in a supply crunch for other end users. In 2016, China consumed 35 percent of the world's graphite production.[86]

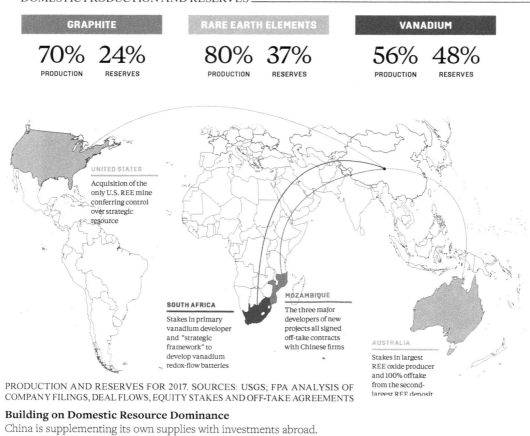

GRAPHITE

70% **PRODUCTION** 24% **RESERVES**

RARE EARTH ELEMENTS

80% **PRODUCTION** 37% **RESERVES**

VANADIUM

56% **PRODUCTION** 48% **RESERVES**

UNITED STATES
Acquisition of the only U.S. REE mine conferring control over strategic resource

SOUTH AFRICA
Stakes in primary vanadium developer and "strategic framework" to develop vanadium redox-flow batteries

MOZAMBIQUE
The three major developers of new projects all signed off-take contracts with Chinese firms

AUSTRALIA
Stakes in largest REE oxide producer and 100% offtake from the second-largest REE deposit

PRODUCTION AND RESERVES FOR 2017. SOURCES: USGS; FPA ANALYSIS OF COMPANY FILINGS, DEAL FLOWS, EQUITY STAKES AND OFF-TAKE AGREEMENTS

Building on Domestic Resource Dominance
China is supplementing its own supplies with investments abroad.

PART 3
Controlling the Fuel of the Future

This resource consolidation could determine whether China is able to overcome the last major hurdle to achieving its ambitions: a competitive semiconductor industry. The life-blood of high-tech industries, semiconductors are made of the very minerals and metals over which China is securing control. Semiconductors can be pure elements or compounds and altered with impurities to improve their conductivity. Several materials are now being used to improve speed and performance, including rare-earth elements, graphite, indium, gallium, tantalum, and cadmium. China is the dominant producer of five out of the six, controls more than 75 percent of the world's supply of three,[87] and is consolidating control over them all.

However, China still lacks the technological capability to produce semiconductors on par with the industry's leading companies and remains highly dependent on imports, at a cost of roughly $260 billion per year.[88] The government is keenly focused on ending its dependency by acquiring the technological expertise to surpass its rivals. It poured nearly $20 billion into highly targeted research and development to that end from 2014 to 2017,[89] and it is only intensifying its focus.

Should China succeed technologically, its capacity to scale production and flood markets (as it has already done with solar panels and wind turbines) has serious implications not only for leading semiconductor producers, but also for national security, if Chinese-manufactured chips are embedded in the devices upon which our data-driven lives, our economies, and our defense systems increasingly depend. While government and industry officials have started to restrict semiconductor sales and scrutinize Chinese acquisition of technology firms—e.g., the United States' temporary ban on selling semiconductors to ZTE, or the recent flare-up over Huawei—such moves are strengthening China's resolve to develop its domestic industry. More attention should be paid to its efforts to consolidate critical raw materials and the computing power they confer.

This is not a foregone conclusion. It will, however, require us to fundamentally rethink how we understand strategic industries and the long-term investments needed to ensure economic prosperity and national security in the digital age. Some countries are waking up to these strategic vulnerabilities and starting to act on them. In April, U.S. government officials announced plans to meet with lithium industry leaders and automakers with the intention of developing a national electric-vehicle supply chain strategy. It is a start.

Notes

1   Ministry of Industry and Information Technology of the People's Republic of China, "Nonferrous Metal Industry Development Plan 2016–2020," October 2016, http://www.miit.gov.cn/n1146290/n4388791/c5288773/content.html.

2   Ministry of Industry and Information Technology of the People's Republic of China, "Nonferrous Metal Industry Development Plan 2016–2020," October 2016, http://www.miit.gov.cn/n1146290/n4388791/c5288773/content.html.

3   "Annual Report 2015: Driving Change, Defining our Future," Anglo American, https://www.angloamerican.com/~/media/Files/A/Anglo-American-PLC-V2/documents/aa-ar-15.pdf.

4   Peter Koven, "Anglo American's massive restructuring involving 85,000 layoffs shows miners bracing for prolonged downturn," *Financial Post*, Dec. 8, 2015, https://business.financialpost.com/commodities/mining/anglo-american-to-cut-85000-workers-sell-60-of-its-assets-and-suspend-dividend.

5   "PwC M&A 2018 Mid-Year Review and Outlook," PricewaterhouseCoopers, https://www.pwccn.com/en/deals/publications/ma-2018-mid-year-review-and-outlook.pdf.

6   William Clowes, "China Marks Cobalt, Copper Ascendancy in Congo With New Group," *Bloomberg*, June 18, 2018, https://www.bloomberg.com/news/articles/2018-06-18/china-marks-cobalt-copper-ascendancy-in-congo-with-new-group.

7   FP Analytics analysis.

8   "The World Bank in DRC," The World Bank, May 16, 2018, https://www.worldbank.org/en/country/drc/overview.

9   "BP Statistical Review of World Energy," BP, June 2018, https://www.bp.com/content/dam/bp/business-sites/en/global/corporate/pdfs/energy-economics/statistical-review/bp-stats-review-2018-full-report.pdf.

10   "Accord Protocol," Ministry of Infrastructure, Public Works and Reconstruction, Democratic Republic of Congo, Sep. 17, 2007, http://congomines.org/system/attachments/assets/000/000/274/original/B8-Sicomines-2007-ProtocoleDAccordConsortiumEntreprisesChinoises-RDC.pdf?1430928299.

11   Martyn Davies, "How China is Influencing Africa's Development," OECD Development Centre, April 2010, https://www.oecd.org/dev/pgd/45068325.pdf.

12   David G. Landry, "Sicomines: A Resource-for-Infrastructure Case Study," China Africa Research Initiative, Johns Hopkins University School of Advanced International Studies, March 1, 2017, https://static1.squarespace.com/static/526eec2ce4b0178a935d2104/t/58bddf5e9f-745699f218aa48/1488838500718/NRGI+Blog+-+Sicomines+A+Resource+for+Infrastructure+Case+Study+(David+G.+Landry).pdf.

13   "Announcement on Investment in PE527 Copper-Cobalt Project in Congo-Kinshasa," Zhejiang Huayou Cobalt, March 15, 2018, http://www.huayou.com/downloadRepository/61e1b228-ac24-4c2d-8a64-494595c3debe.pdf.

14   "Announcement: Proposed Acquisition of 51% Shareholding in La Compagnie Minière de Musonoie Global SAS," Zijin Mining Group, http://www.zijinmining.com/Portals/1/LTN201411032180.pdf.

15   "2017 Annual Report," China Molybdenum, http://www.chinamoly.com/06invest/DOC/2018/E_03993_04207.pdf.

16   Siyamend Al Barazi et al., "Cobalt from the DR Congo—Potential, Risks and Significance for the Global Cobalt Market," July 2017, https://www.researchgate.net/publication/326060301_COBALT_FROM_THE_DR_CONGO_-_POTENTIAL_RISKS_AND_SIGNIFICANCE_FOR_THE_GLOBAL_COBALT_MARKET_1_Commodity_Top_News_53.

17   Cecilia Jamasmie, "China Moly ups stake in giant Tenke copper mine to 80%," *Mining*, Jan. 18, 2019, http://www.mining.com/china-moly-ups-stake-giant-tenke-copper-mine-80/.

18   "GEM Announcement Regarding Strategic Purchase Agreement for Cobalt and Raw Materials for Batteries," Shenzhen Stock Exchange, March 15, 2018, http://www.szse.cn/disclosure/listed/bulletinDetail/index.html?415fcfb8-75e4-4ee8-8283-237d8a31c727.

19 FP Analytics analysis.

20 "A new mining code for the DRC," *DLA Piper*, August 10, 2018, https://www.dlapiper.com/en/morocco/insights/publications/2018/08/democratic-republic-of-congo-mining-code/.

21 "Congo declares battery metal cobalt 'strategic' in move that triples royalties," *Financial Times*, Dec. 3, 2018. https://www.ft.com/content/382c3d24-f726-11e8-8b7c-6fa24bd5409c.

22 Zhen Han, "China's Current Involvement in Mining in Africa," *Mining Journal*, Jan. 19, 2016, https://s3.amazonaws.com/documents.lexology.com/efec9be3-a177-43e6-97e4-24e64ac6ef41.pdf.

23 "Mineral Commodities Summaries: Platinum-Group Metals," U.S. Geological Survey, 2019, https://minerals.usgs.gov/minerals/pubs/commodity/platinum/mcs-2019-plati.pdf.

24 FP Analytics analysis.

25 "Statistical Release P0441: Gross Domestic Product, Fourth quarter 2017," Statistics South Africa, June 5, 2018, http://www.dmr.gov.za/Portals/0/files/P04414thQuarter2017(1).pdf?ver=2018-03-09-063718-170.

26 "South Africa Minerals Exports By Country 2017," World Integrated Trade Solution (WITS), The World Bank, https://wits.worldbank.org/CountryProfile/en/Country/ZAF/Year/LTST/TradeFlow/Export/Partner/by-country/Product/25-26_Minerals.

27 "BP Statistical Review of World Energy," BP, June 2018, https://www.bp.com/content/dam/bp/business-sites/en/global/corporate/pdfs/energy-economics/statistical-review/bp-stats-review-2018-full-report.pdf.

28 FP Analytics analysis.

29 Tianqi Lithium, http://en.tianqilithium.com.

30 Ganfeng Lithium, http://www.ganfenglithium.com/about_en.html.

31 "List of members of the Standing Committee of the 11th Political Consultative Conference of Sichuan Province," The People's Government of Sichuan Province, Jan. 9, 2013, http://www.sc.gov.cn/10462/10464/10797/2013/1/9/10243666.shtml.

32 "Sichuan Province People's Congress Announcement (No. 1)," People.cn, Feb. 1, 2018, http://sc.people.com.cn/n2/2018/0201/c345514-31206075.html.

33 "The 2018 list of representatives of the 'two sessions' of Jiangxi Province was announced!" Jan. 18, 2018, https://baijiahao.baidu.com/s?id=1589931694452543678&wfr=spider&for=pc.

34 Mineral Commodities Summaries," U.S. Geological Survey, 2019, https://minerals.usgs.gov/minerals/pubs/mcs/2019/mcs2019.pdf.

35 "Tianqi Lithium Industry Co., Ltd.'s Announcement on Its Reply to the Shenzhen Stock Exchange's Restructuring Inquiry, June 20, 2018," http://www.szse.cn/disclosure/listed/bulletinDetail/index.html?0a2b7923-9c60-4893-84b3-2423db4c6549.

36 CITIC Group Corporation of Beijing was founded by Rong Yiren, vice president of China from 1993 to 1998 and known as "the Red Capitalist."

37 "Tianqi and Nutrien Comment on Chilean Constitutional Court Ruling," *BNamericas*, October 26, 2018, https://subscriber.bnamericas.com/en/news/miningandmetals/tianqi-and-nutrien-comment-on-chilean-constitutional-court-ruling?position=1&aut=true&idioma=en.

38 Fabian Cambero, "China's Tianqi agrees truce in battle over Chilean lithium miner SQM," Reuters, April 11, 2019, https://www.reuters.com/article/us-sqm-tianqi-lithium/chinas-tianqi-agrees-truce-in-battle-over-chilean-lithium-miner-sqm-idUSKCN1RN2B0.

39 Jeppe Saarinen, "China-Chile FTA Upgraded, New Opportunities for Investors," *China Briefing*, March 4, 2019, https://www.china-briefing.com/news/china-chile-fta-upgraded-market-opportunities-investors/.

40 "China-Chile Free Trade Agreement Upgrade Protocol enters into force today," Ministry of Commerce of the People's Republic of China, March 1, 2019, http://www.mofcom.gov.cn/article/ae/ai/201903/20190302839160.shtml.

41 "China warns Chile against blocking $5bn SQM lithium deal," *Financial Times*, April 26, 2018, https://www.ft.com/content/238bda20-48b0-11e8-8ee8-cae73aab7ccb.

42 "The China lobby: How the Asian country deploys its influence in the Chilean Congress," *La Tercera*, Nov. 7, 2018, https://www.latercera.com/la-tercera-pm/noticia/un-lobby-chino-como-el-pais-asiatico-despliega-su-influencia-en-el-congreso-chileno/391266/.

43 "Lithium Report 2018," Swiss Resource Capital, http://www.advantagelithium.com/_resources/pdf/en_Doppelseite_Lithium_2018.pdf.

44 Tianqi is seeking permission to develop Salar de La Isla through its joint venture partnership, Talison, with U.S.-based lithium company Albemarle, the other major player in Chile; Tianqi has the majority stake in Talison and the joint venture has a 50 percent stake in the play. The partners are also working with Canada-based Wealth Minerals, which holds the other 50 percent stake.

45 FP Analytics analysis.

46 United Nations Comtrade Database, accessed Feb. 6, 2019, https://comtrade.un.org.

47 FP Analytics analysis.

48 "Greenbushes project—Western Australia," Lithium Australia, https://lithium-au.com/greenbushes/.

49 FP Analytics analysis.

50 Kristian John Dayrit, "Report: Ganfeng Lithium prices Hong Kong IPO at US$421M," S&P Global Market Intelligence, https://www.spglobal.com/marketintelligence/en/news-insights/trending/ijk96vubsklahzczseolvq2.

51 Ganfeng IPO Prospectus, p. 266–267, http://www3.hkexnews.hk/listedco/listconews/sehk/2018/0927/ltn20180927025.pdf.

52 "Tianqi Lithium Gets Securities Regulator Approval To Issue Offshore Shares, List in Hong Kong," Reuters, Nov. 8, 2018, https://www.reuters.com/finance/stocks/002466ta.SZ/key-developments/article/3934258.

53 "Mineral Commodities Summaries," U.S. Geological Survey, 2019, https://minerals.usgs.gov/minerals/pubs/mcs/.

54 The definition of "critical" or "strategic" and the exact list of minerals, metals, or materials varies by jurisdiction, but a literature review of major studies assessing "criticality" identifies the resources most commonly categorized and cited in official documents. China is the leading global producer of the majority of those listed, including natural graphite, rare-earth elements, vanadium, indium, tungsten, gallium, antimony, tellurium, cadmium, and molybdenum. Also see: https://www.sciencedirect.com/science/article/pii/S0301420718301296?via%3Dihub.

55 U.S. Geological Survey annual commodity data.

56 Keith Bradsher, "Amid Tension, China Blocks Vital Exports to Japan," *The New York Times*, Sep. 22, 2010, https://www.nytimes.com/2010/09/23/business/global/23rare.html.

57 Nabeel A. Mancheri, "China's export restrictions on rare earths," East Asia Forum, Oct. 6, 2011, https://www.eastasiaforum.org/2011/10/06/china-s-export-restrictions-on-rare-earths/.

58 "China's cut to rare earth output unnerves global manufacturers," Reuters/*The Japan Times*, https://www.japantimes.co.jp/news/2018/10/25/business/china-cutting-rare-earth-output-unnerving-global-manufacturers/#.XLDqJetKjGI.

59 Pui-Kwan Tse, "China's Rare-Earth Industry: Open-File Report 2011–1042," U.S. Geological Survey, https://pubs.usgs.gov/of/2011/1042/of2011-1042.pdf.

60 "Barbara Lewis and Ernest Scheyder, "China cutting rare earth output, unnerving global manufacturers," Reuters, Oct. 24, 2018, https://www.reuters.com/article/us-china-rareearths/china-cutting-rare-earth-output-unnerving-global-manufacturers-idUSKCN1MY2GZ.

61 "United States Securities and Exchange Commission Form 10–K: Rare Element Resources Ltd.," fiscal year ended Dec. 31, 2017, http://www.rareelementresources.com/docs/default-source/financial-reports/p05218_rare-element-resources_2018_10k_v2.pdf?sfvrsn=0.

62 "Australia blocked China investment on supply concerns," *The Sydney Morning Herald*, Feb. 15, 2011, https://www.smh.com.au/business/australia-blocked-china-investment-on-supply-concerns-20110215-1au8x.html.

63 "2018 Annual Report," Lynas Corporation, https://www.lynascorp.com/Pages/Reporting-centre-Annual-report.aspx.

64 Conglin Investment Group, accessed March 2019, http://www.conglingroup.com.au/profile.html.

65 Christopher Ecclestone, "Northern Minerals Strategy: Long," Hallgarten & Company, Feb. 7, 2018, http://northernminerals.com.au/wp-content/uploads/2018/02/NTU_Hallgarten-Feb2018.pdf.

66 "Rare Earths: Mountain Pass sold to Chinese-led consortium," *Roskill*, June 21, 2017, https://roskill.com/news/rare-earths-mountain-pass-sold-chinese-led-consortium/.

67 "Rare-earth rancor: Feds must stop Chinese purchase of US mine," *The Hill*, June 26, 2017, https://thehill.com/blogs/pundits-blog/economy-budget/339528-Rare-earth-rancor%3A-Feds-must-stop-Chinese-purchase-of-US-mine.

68 "Mineral Commodities Summaries: Rare Earths," U.S. Geological Survey, 2019, https://minerals.usgs.gov/minerals/pubs/commodity/rare_earths/mcs-2019-raree.pdf.

69 "New Chinese JV for rare earth minerals from Greenland," *World Nuclear News*, Jan. 23, 2019, http://www.world-nuclear-news.org/Articles/New-Chinese-JV-for-rare-earth-minerals-from.

70 "2017 Annual Report: Materials for an Energy Efficient Future," Greenland Minerals and Energy, http://www.ggg.gl/assets/Uploads/Annual-Reports/43ab98ed04/2017-Annual-Report.pdf.

71 "Mineral Commodities Summaries 2019," U.S. Geological Survey, https://minerals.usgs.gov/minerals/pubs/mcs/2019/mcs2019.pdf.

72 Ibid.

73 Terence Creamer, "Hong Kong resources group named as winning Highveld bidder," *Mining Weekly*, http://www.miningweekly.com/article/hong-kong-resources-group-named-as-winning-highveld-bidder-2015-09-16/rep_id:3650.

74 "Bushveld Gets USD5.2 Million for Strategic Minerals Acquisition," *Morningstar*, June 3, 2016, http://www.morningstar.co.uk/uk/news/AN_1464938425301552800/bushveld-gets-usd52-million-for-strategic-minerals-acquisition-(alliss).aspx; In 2017, Bushveld Minerals moved to acquire Yellow Dragon Holding's shares of Bushveld Vametco in exchange for 9.24% of the larger integrated Bushveld Minerals resource platform, with businesses in vanadium, tin, coal and power. "Bushveld Minerals acquisition of Bushveld Vametco Limited," Bushveld Minerals, December 2017, http://www.bushveldminerals.com/wp-content/uploads/2017/12/Bushveld-Minerals-acquisition-of-Bushveld-Vametco-Limited_Final.pdf.

75 Bushveld Minerals Capital Structure Shareholder Information, March 29, 2019, http://www.bushveldminerals.com/capital-structure-shareholder-information/.

76 "Bushveld Minerals: Right commodity, right asset, right time," Alternate Resource Capital, March 1, 2018, http://www.bushveldminerals.com/wp-content/uploads/2018/03/BMN_010318.pdf.

77 "Bushveld Minerals acquisition of Bushveld Vametco Limited," Bushveld Minerals, December 2017, http://www.bushveldminerals.com/wp-content/uploads/2017/12/Bushveld-Minerals-acquisition-of-Bushveld-Vametco-Limited_Final.pdf.

78 "Mineral Commodities Summaries: Graphite (Natural)," U.S. Geological Survey, 2019, https://minerals.usgs.gov/minerals/pubs/commodity/graphite/mcs-2019-graph.pdf.

79 Mozambique has the fourth highest reserves at 17 million tons, tied with Tanzania which also as 17 million tons of estimated reserves. "Mineral Commodities Summaries: Graphite (Natural),"

U.S. Geological Survey, 2019, https://minerals.usgs.gov/minerals/pubs/commodity/graphite/mcs-2019-graph.pdf.

80 "Battery Minerals secures fourth offtake deal for Mozambique graphite," *Small Caps*, Jan. 22, 2018, https://smallcaps.com.au/battery-minerals-fourth-offtake-deal-mozambique-graphite/.

81 "Triton cements second major graphite supply deal with China; shares gain," *Stockhead*, May 10, 2018, https://stockhead.com.au/special-report/triton-cements-second-major-graphite-supply-deal-with-china/.

82 "Mozambique: Triton signs MoU for Ancuabe development," *The Mozambique Resources Post*, March 15, 2019, https://mozambiqueminingpost.com/2019/03/15/mozambique-triton-signs-mou-for-ancuabe-development/.

83 "Batteries: POSCO begins aggressive lithium-ion battery anode materials expansion," Roskill, Nov. 15, 2018, https://roskill.com/news/batteries-posco-begins-aggressive-lithium-ion-battery-anode-materials-expansion/.

84 Ibid.

85 United Nations Comtrade Database, https://comtrade.un.org/data/.

86 "Mineral Commodities Summaries: Graphite (Natural)," U.S. Geological Survey, 2017, https://minerals.usgs.gov/minerals/pubs/commodity/graphite/mcs-2017-graph.pdf.

87 "Mineral Commodities Summaries 2019" U.S. Geological Survey, https://minerals.usgs.gov/minerals/pubs/mcs/2019/mcs2019.pdf.

88 Shunsuke Tabeta, "Chinese companies rush to make own chips as trade war bites," *Nikkei Asian Review*, Nov. 7, 2018, https://asia.nikkei.com/Business/China-tech/Chinese-companies-rush-to-make-own-chips-as-trade-war-bites.

89 E. Jan Vardaman, "Semiconductor Industry in China," TechSearch International, 2017, https://forums.ni.com/t5/NI-Test-Leadership-Council-Forum/TLF-2017-Presentation-The-Semiconductor-Industry-in-China-Supply/gpm-p/3785289?profile.language=en.

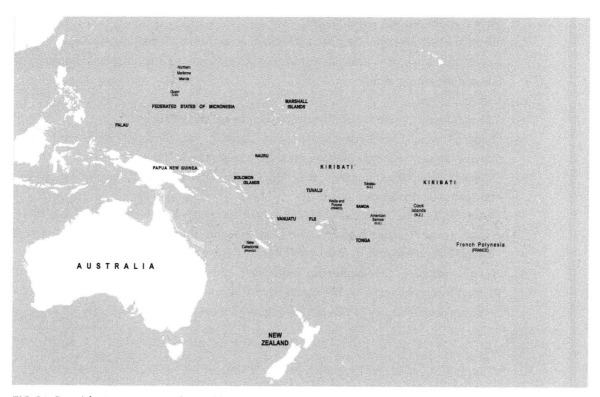

Chapter III

Oceania

List of countries included in the world region of Oceania:

- Australia
- Fiji
- Kiribati
- Marshall Islands
- Federated States of Micronesia
- Nauru
- New Zealand
- Palau
- Papua New Guinea
- Samoa
- Solomon Islands
- Tonga
- Tuvalu
- Vanuatu

Additional island countries and/or territories:

- American Samoa (United States)
- French Polynesia (France)
- Guam (United States)
- New Caledonia (France)
- Tokelau (New Zealand)
- Wallis and Futuna (France)

Other islands in Oceania:

- Cook Islands and Niue: States in free association with New Zealand; not in UN. Most countries do not recognize them as sovereign states. Citizens carry NZ passports.
- Northern Mariana Islands (like Puerto Rico, a commonwealth in political union with the United States; a self-governing U.S. jurisdiction with its own written constitution; only two jurisdictions with U.S. commonwealth status, Puerto Rico and Northern Mariana Islands)

Introduction

Stretching from the coast of Malaysia to the Americas, the region of Oceania is the world's largest in terms of territory. Oceania covers about 100 million square kilometers, or 38.6 million square miles, the equivalent of one fifth of the planet (Countries of Australia and Oceania, 2020).

Yet, this vast world region, largest in terms of territory, is the smallest in landmass (about 5.6% of Earth's total landmass). Its varied landscapes include lagoons, tropical rainforests, mountains, grasslands, and atolls, as well as coralline and volcanic islands. Oceania includes most of the South Pacific Ocean islands, approximately 25,000, some of which are uninhabited. While Australia is generally considered a continent, Oceania (including Australia) can be understood as one of the seven continents, along with Africa, Antarctica, Asia, Europe, North America, and South America. With a population of about 43 million, Oceania is the second smallest continent in population and population density, after Antarctica.

The four major sub-regions of Oceania are Australasia (Australia and New Zealand), Melanesia (Fiji, New Caledonia, Papua New Guinea, Solomon Islands, Vanuatu), Micronesia (Guam, Kiribati, Mariana Islands, and the Federal States of Micronesia), and Polynesia (French Polynesia, Samoa, and Tonga). In terms of area, the largest Oceanic country is Australia (over 7.692 square kilometers, or 2.967 square miles) and the smallest is also the world's smallest independent republic, Nauru (21 square kilometers, or 8 square miles). Most of Oceania is located in the southern hemisphere. But the islands of Oceania's Kiribati straddle the equator and International Dateline, putting this small island nation in four different hemispheres. So depending on the time of day, it is two different days at the same time in Kiribati.

Oceania is home to wealthy and developed countries as well as several of the most impoverished and least developed in the world. Australia and New Zealand are among the world's most developed states, with large, modern, and industrialized economies. Australia, the wealthiest country in Oceania, is perennially among the top three countries of the United Nations' Human Development Index. Australia and New Zealand have diverse, modern, and industrialized economies, yet most of the Pacific Island nations have relatively few natural resources and small economies based on agriculture, including subsistence fishing and farming, seafood and ocean products, coconut, bananas, papaya, taro, and sugarcane. Multinational corporations own and operate fish canneries and freshwater bottling facilities, while others extract timber, minerals, and fossil fuels in the Pacific Islands. Some of the countries of Oceania make revenue by selling fishing rights to other countries, like the United States and Japan. Travel and tourism is another major economic sector of Oceania, home to some of the most beautiful islands and pristine beaches on Earth (World Travel & Tourism Council, 2019).

While most Pacific Islands are relatively small, defenseless, and remote, they have long been exploited by outsiders due to their strategic location, wide open spaces, deep seas, and sparse populations. In the late 1500s, Spain and Portugal began colonizing South Pacific islands, mainly to secure strategic islands and protect trade routes to the Spice Islands, the present-day Maluku Islands of Indonesia. Early explorers were inspired by fables of South Sea Islands that held fabulous gold and riches. Australia was discovered by the Dutch in 1606 but later colonized by the British. After 1600, waves of Europeans began colonizing Oceania and decimating the relatively small local populations due to forced labor and exposure to diseases introduced by the Europeans to which the Indigenous Peoples had no resistance. The Pacific Islands have served foreign military purposes. For example, between World Wars I and II, they were colonized by the Japanese. From approximately 1946 until 1962, the United States conducted scores of nuclear tests, including the detonation of dozens of bombs, in the Marshall Islands in a remote area of Oceania called the Pacific Proving Grounds. The United States has been forced to pay millions of dollars in restitution to compensate the victims among the resident population who were unwittingly exposed to radiation contamination, which created an epidemic of cancers and birth defects (Barker, 2013).

Garbage Patches at Sea

Ocean gyres are part of an immense marine system that circulates ocean water and currents clockwise around the planet (National Ocean Service, n.d.). Like gears in a giant mechanism, these ancient oceanic verticils revolve, sustained by prevailing sea, wind, and seasonal patterns, as well as the earth's rotation. Found in the Atlantic, Pacific, and Indian Oceans, the five major gyres include the North Atlantic Gyre, the South Atlantic Gyre, the North Pacific Gyre, the Indian Ocean Gyre, and the South Pacific Gyre.

Each of these ocean gyres has a corresponding offshore **garbage patch,** often called a garbage accumulation zone or plastic gyre. The first oceanic garbage patch was documented in 1997. The most recent, the South Pacific Plastic Waste Gyre in Oceania, was discovered in 2013 (Bedolfe, 2013). The term *patch* is somewhat misleading, since it implies a small area. However, each garbage vortex is colossal even by oceanic standards. For example, the South Pacific Plastic Waste Gyre, located in Oceania between Australia and South America, covers about three million square kilometers, or 1.9 million square miles, of ocean. This patch, nearly the size of Argentina, is considerably smaller than the largest garbage gyre, the Great Pacific Garbage Patch (located in the North Pacific Gyre, halfway between the coasts of California and Hawaii). In 2019, this hellish vortex of debris, approximately 1.6 million square kilometers, or over 617,763 square miles, was bigger than Mongolia (Eriksen et al., 2013; Moore & Phillips, 2012).

Gyres contain some natural debris but are comprised mostly of some of the 8 million tons of plastic garbage that migrates annually, mainly from coastal areas (The problem with plastic, 2019). Garbage patches contain primarily hard or ridged plastic materials but also fishing gear (like net and rope fragments), single-use plastic waste, and cosmetic microbeads made of polyethylene or polypropylene (Gallo et al., 2018; Ocean Cleanup, 2019). While some plastic waste breaks down somewhat due to the sun, waves, and marine life exposure, many plastics are not biodegradable and may be in the environment for centuries breaking down into smaller and smaller pieces (Lebreton et al., 2018). Although 92% of the trash in the Great Pacific Garbage patch is larger than 5 mm, garbage gyres contain trillions of **microplastics**, which are solid non biodegradable and insoluble plastic particles. The size of microplastics range from smaller than 5 millimeters, or about 3/16th of an inch, to a few nanometers, so small they cannot be seen by the naked eye (Ocean Cleanup, 2019). **Bioaccumulation** refers to microplastics that collect in the bodies (including the stomach and flesh) of animals, including humans, in the entire food web. Microplastics pose significant health risks to humans, including damage to reproductive organs and the central nervous system (National Ocean Service, 2020; Consumer Reports, 2019). These are among the "costs" of wasteful single-use plastics and inefficient garbage collection infrastructures. The oceans now contain over 150 million tons of plastic pollution, which is accumulating far more rapidly than it is disappearing. Marine pollution, including millions of tons of toxic chemical additives, is expected to double by 2025 (Gallo et al., 2018; Ocean Conservancy, 2020).

Ring of Fire

The **Ring of Fire**, or Circum-Pacific belt, is a long chain of the world's most numerous and destructive volcanoes as well as other tectonically and seismically active geologic structures. The Ring of Fire is approximately 40,000 kilometers, or 24,900 miles, in length, extending from Oceania to Latin America. Starting in New Zealand, it arcs along the Pacific Ocean basin and ends at the tip of South America. Most (13) of the 31 countries in the Ring of Fire are in Oceania. Moreover, Oceania states are among the most vulnerable to the environmental threats found in this formidable geologic area. The Ring of Fire contains the world's greatest concentration (75%, or 450 total) of active and dormant volcanoes. Over the past 100 years or so, it has produced about 90% of the 16 most powerful volcanic eruptions, 81% of the world's largest earthquakes, and 80% of the world's tsunamis. A **tsunami** is a series of often extreme and fast-moving sea waves that can be caused by an earthquake, landslide, volcanic eruption, explosion, or meteorite. A tsunami may go unnoticed at sea, but these waves often become deadly and destructive as they approach shallow coastal waters and make landfall (Conners, 2016; National Geographic, 2020; Australian Government Bureau of Meteorology, 2020).

Natural Disaster Risks

Much of Oceania is particularly vulnerable to natural disasters, In fact, Oceania is home to the top five countries considered most at-risk for natural disasters, including the first, Vanuatu, and the second, Tonga (Institute for International Law of Peace and Armed Conflict, 2018). **Natural disasters** include but are not limited to rising sea levels, earthquakes, landslides, tsunamis, volcanic eruptions, meteorites, droughts, and floods. For instance, one strong **typhoon,** or tropical storm, can destroy the vegetation, groundwater, and infrastructure of an entire island. Coastal erosion, storm surge flooding, and king tides, or unusually high tides and waves, are more common examples of Oceania's natural disaster risks. Natural disaster risks can be caused, singly or in combination, by geophysical forces, often beyond human control, or climate change.

The Anthropocene and Climate Change

The **Anthropocene** is a geologic term that describes the current epoch, from the Industrial Age to the present, when human beings have had a tremendous impact on global climates and ecosystems. The most pressing issue of the Anthropocene is **climate change**. Climate can be understood variously, but for our purposes it is the 30-year average of weather in an area. There is no consensus definition of climate change, a term that refers to any substantial change in the Earth's climate that lasts for decades or longer. The Intergovernmental Panel on Climate Change (IPCC) provides a frequently-cited definition of climate change:

> A change in the state of the climate that can be identified (e.g., by using statistical tests) by changes in the mean and/or variability of its properties and that persists for an extended period, typically decades or longer. Climate change may be due to natural internal processes or external forcings, or to persistent anthropogenic changes in the composition of the atmosphere or in land use (2012, p. 577).

Climate change is largely **anthropogenic**, a term that means human made or caused by human activities, primarily the burning of fossil fuels in industrialized countries. The release of heat-trapping carbon and greenhouse gas emissions (GHGs) into the atmosphere causes a broad range of catastrophic climate change effects, including but not limited to global warming, ice mass loss, rising sea levels, shifting agricultural and disease patterns, and extreme weather intensification and events, such as more prolonged and destructive droughts, hurricanes or typhoons, and wildfires. For example, between 2012 and 2018, 65% out of 131 major weather events were attributed to climate change (Herring et al., 2018). Moreover, hotter and drier weather has increased the frequency and severity of wildfires (most of which are caused by human activities) worldwide. They release tons of carbon dioxide into the atmosphere, exacerbating climate change, making wildfires not only the result but also a major catalyst of climate change.

Managed Retreat

There are multiple adaptations and strategies for dealing with natural disaster risks. For instance, there are three major ways to address rising sea levels: 1) fortify or create natural-based defenses (such as establishing coral reefs and coastal mangrove forests); 2) augment the land to control and mitigate erosion and floods (like building retaining walls and adding beach fill); and 3) relocate people to higher ground and away from areas prone to flooding (World Economic Forum, 2019). **Managed retreat** is a natural disaster risk strategy that involves relocating individuals and even whole communities, as well as the moveable structures and other natural assets, from an area (Hino et al., 2017). To illustrate, when the island nation of Kiribati is uninhabitable due to impending rising sea levels, its people, the I-Kiribati, will relocate to land its government purchased in 2014 in Fiji, nearly 2,000 kilometers, or over 1,200 miles, away. The Indigenous Peoples of Kiribati, as well as many other Oceanic nations, will likely be the last to live in their ancestral islands as rising sea levels are expected to displace between 72 and 187 million people globally (Lindsey, 2019; Hino et al., 2017).

The environment is more than the physical or natural environment. It includes sociocultural dimensions, such as the fluidity and plurality of human meanings and attachments to all aspects and forms of life (Pascht & Durr, 2017). The Peoples of Oceania have a long history in this region. For millennia their knowledge and values have been shaped by the sea. Over time they have developed sophisticated knowledge about navigation, the sea, and marine life as well as conserving and safeguarding ocean resources. Ocean-oriented knowledge and cultural traditions have been integral to Oceanic seafaring, land-based, and linguistically diverse identities. What is at risk of being lost through climate change and subsequent managed retreat displacement and resettling is the existence of whole communities, cultures, histories, and economies in Oceania. The Peoples of Oceania are societally vulnerable to climate change and natural disasters, which endanger the continuation of Pacific Islanders' knowledge, worldviews, and ways of life as it threatens to diminish our understandings of what it means to be human. There are myriad tangible and intangible costs as well as manifold political, sociocultural, and economic entanglements inextricably bound with managed retreat displacement. Dealing effectively with natural disaster, climate change, and associated risks will require **praxis**, the combination of reflection and action directed at what needs to be transformed, in the making and remaking of resilient environments.

References

Australian Government Bureau of Meteorology. (2020). *Tsunami Facts and Information*. http://www.bom.gov.au/tsunami/info/index.shtml

Barker, H. M. (2013). *Bravo for the Marshallese: Regaining control in a post-nuclear, post-colonial world*. Wadsworth.

Bedolfe, S. (2013, 29 January). South Pacific plastic gyre discovered. *One World One Ocean*. https://www.oneworldoneocean.com/blog/entry/south_pacific_plastic_gyre_discovered#:~:text=Researchers%20announced%20last%20week%20that,Garbage%20Patch%2C%20discovered%20in%201997.

Conners, D., Byrd, D., & Gonzaga, S. (2019, December 9). *What is the ring of fire?* EarthSky. https://earthsky.org/earth/what-is-the-ring-of-fire

Consumer Reports. (2019, October 7). You're literally eating microplastics. How you can cut down exposure to them. *The Washington Post*. https://www.washingtonpost.com/health/youre-literally-eating-microplastics-how-you-can-cut-down-exposure-to-them/2019/10/04/22ebdfb6-e17a-11e9-8dc8-498eabc129a0_story.html

Countries of Australia and Oceania (2020). *Facts about Australia and Oceania*. The Nations Online Project. https://www.nationsonline.org/oneworld/oceania.htm

Eriksen, M., Maximenko, N., Theil, M., Cummins, A., Lattin, G., Wilson, S., Hafner, J., Zellers, A., & Rifman, S. (2013, March 15). Plastic pollution in the South Pacific subtropical gyre. *Marine Pollution Bulletin 68*(1–2), 71–76. https://doi.org/10.1016/j.marpolbul.2012.12.021

Gallo, F., Fossi, C., Weber, R., Santillo, D., Sousa, J., Ingram, I., Nadal, A., & Romano, D. (2018). Marine litter plastics and microplastics and their toxic chemical components: The need for urgent preventative measures. *Environmental Sciences Europe 30*(13). https://doi.org/10.1186/s12302-018-0139-z

Hernandez-Montilla, M., & Gomez, C. (2019, April 29). *Continent news: Oceania 2019*. International Union for Conservation of Nature (IUCN). https://iucnrle.org/blog/continent-news-oceania-2019/

Herring, S. C., Christidis, N., Hoell, A., Kossin, J. P., Schreck, C. J., III, & Stott, P. A. (Eds). (2018). Explaining extreme events of 2016 from a climate perspective. *Bulletin of the American Meteorological Society, 99*(1). https://doi.org/10.1175/BAMS-ExplainingExtremeEvents2016.1

Hino, M., Field, C. B., & Mach, K. J. (2017). Managed retreat as a response to natural hazard risk. *Nature Climate Change, 7*, 364–370. https://doi.org/10.1038/NCLIMATE3252

Institute for International Law of Peace and Armed Conflict (IFHV). (2019). *WorldRiskReport 2018* https://weltrisikobericht.de/wp-content/uploads/2019/03/190318_WRR_2018_EN_RZonline_1.pdf

Intergovernmental Panel on Climate Change (IPCC). (2012). Glossary of terms. In C. B. Field, V. Barros, T. F. Stocker, D. Qin, D. J. Dokken, K. L. Ebi, M. D. Mastrandrea, K. J. Mach, G.-K. Plattner, S. K. Allen, M. Tignor, & P. M. Midgley (Eds.), *Managing the risks of extreme events and disasters to advance climate change adaptation* (pp. 555–564). Cambridge University Press.

Lebreton, L., Slat, B., Ferrari, F., Sainte-Rose, B., Aitken, J., Marthouse, R., Hajbane, S., Cunsolo, S., Schwarz, A., Levivier, A., Noble, K., Debeljak, P., Maral, H., Schoeneich-Argent, R., Branbini, R., & Reisser, J. (2018, March 22). Evidence that the Great Pacific Garbage Patch is rapidly accumulating plastic. *Scientific Reports 8*, 4666. https://www.nature.com/articles/s41598-018-22939-w

Lindsey, R. (2019, November 19). *Climate change: Global sea level*. National OAA (NOAA) Climate. gov. https://www.climate.gov/news-features/understanding-climate/climate-change-global-sea-level

Moore, C. J., & Phillips, C. (2012). *Plastic ocean: How a sea captain's chance discovery launched a determined quest to save the oceans*. Avery.

National Geographic. (2020). *Tsunamis*. https://www.nationalgeographic.com/environment/natural-disasters/tsunamis/

National Ocean Service. (n.d.). *Garbage patches: How gyres take our trash out to sea*. https://oceanservice.noaa.gov/podcast/mar18/nop14-ocean-garbage-patches.html

National Ocean Service. (2020). What are microplastics? https://oceanservice.noaa.gov/facts/microplastics.html

National Oceanic and Atmospheric Administration (NOAA). (2019). *Global climate report for January 2019*. https://www.ncdc.noaa.gov/sotc/global/201901

Ocean Cleanup. (2019). *The Great Pacific Garbage patch*. https://theoceancleanup.com/great-pacific-garbage-patch/

Ocean Conservancy. (2020). *Fighting for trash-free seas*. https://oceanconservancy.org/trash-free-seas/plastics-in-the-ocean/

Pacific Coastal and Marine Science Center. (2019). *Low-lying areas of tropical Pacific Islands*. United States Geologic Survey. https://www.usgs.gov/centers/pcmsc/science/low-lying-areas-tropical-pacific-islands?qt-science_center_objects=0#qt-science_center_objects

Pascht, A., & Durr, E. (2017). Engaging with environmental transformation in Oceania. In E. Durr & A. Pascht (Eds.), *Environmental transformations and cultural responses: Ontologies, discourses, and practices in Oceania* (pp. 1–18). Palgrave Macmillan.

United Nations. (2019). *World economic situation and prospects 2019*. https://unctad.org/en/PublicationsLibrary/wesp2019_en.pdf

World Economic Forum. (2019). *The global risks report 2019* (14th ed). Geneva, Switzerland. http://www3.weforum.org/docs/WEF_Global_Risks_Report_2019.pdf

World Travel & Tourism Council. (2019). *Travel & tourism economic impact 2019*. https://www.wttc.org/-/media/files/reports/economic-impact-research/regions-2019/world2019.pdf

Marine Conservation in Oceania
Past, Present, and Future

Alan M. Friedlander

Pristine Seas, National Geographic Society, Washington, DC, USA
Fisheries Ecology Research Lab, University of Hawai'i, Honolulu, HI, USA

ABSTRACT

The people of Oceania have long relied on the ocean for sustenance, commerce, and cultural identity, which promulgated a sophisticated understanding of the marine environment and its conservation. Global declines in ocean health now require innovative solutions that can benefit from customary knowledge and practices, which in the past led to sustainable marine resource use. The resurgence of local stewardship, which incorporates customary practices and governance, has shown promise in many locations throughout the Pacific, although a complete return to past practices is not fully implementable owing to the loss of traditional knowledge, centralized governmental structures, economic development, and globalization. Hybrid systems that incorporate elements of customary and contemporary management can overcome some of these limitations to implementation of successful local management, and lead to greater food security, social cohesion, and the creation of an adaptive system that can potentially mitigate the effects of climate change and other stressors.

Introduction

Owing to the failures of conventional ocean management, there is a growing interest in exploring new and innovative approaches to conserving marine ecosystems and the benefits they provide to current and future generations. Nowhere is this more critical than in the islands of Oceania, where the ocean has provided important cultural connections and life sustaining services for

Alan M. Friedlander, "Marine Conservation in Oceania: Past, Present, and Future," *Marine Pollution Bulletin*, vol. 135, pp. 139–149. Copyright © 2018 by Elsevier B.V. Reprinted with permission.

millennia. The knowledge and values of indigenous peoples are increasingly being recognized as essential to the sustainable management of the coupled human-natural world (Berkes, 2012). Integrating traditional ecological knowledge and customary management practices into contemporary marine management has shown promise in many places, and these practices provide adaptive approaches to confront changing socio economic and environmental conditions (Johannes, 2002a; Cinner and Aswani, 2007). Because of their long history of ocean use, much can be learned from the indigenous practices of the people of Oceania, and how these practices can contribute to innovative thinking about ecosystem-based management in the modern-day world.

In this article, I explore the knowledge and values that allowed the people of Oceania to develop sustainable use of their marine resources, followed by the demise of these systems after western colonization and the breakdown of traditional societies. The current renaissance of customary stewardship has resulted in not only more effective management, but also a cultural reawakening in many of these island nations. The integration of customary and contemporary management regimes holds great promise for reducing reliance on foreign goods and services, while also improving social cohesion. Finally, I explore how the future management of the region's marine resources may be affected by climate change and other global, as well as local stressors, and how these management regimes may be able to adapt to these changes.

This review is based on my 35+ years of experience working throughout the Pacific region, with an emphasis on artisanal fisheries and traditional and local ecological knowledge. While much has been written about various aspects of marine conservation in Oceania, this work strives to take a more holistic view of how current practices have been influenced by the culture and history of the region and how these can help inform sustainability of people and place well into the future. I conducted a comprehensive review of the literature and attempted to synthesize these findings based on my previous experiences, as well as a multitude of discussions with practitioners, researchers, and governmental and non-governmental actors. Although it is not possible to fully describe the wealth of knowledge and information found within this vast region, attempts were made to be as wide-ranging and unbiased as possible. The intent of this review is to provide a broad overview of past, present, and potential future stewardship and conservation approaches across Oceania, which can also help identify solutions to ocean degradation elsewhere around the world.

Early Colonization

The focus of this article is on what is described as remote Oceania, which included the islands of Polynesia, Melanesia (excluding New Guinea), and Micronesia (Fig. 3.1.1, Table 3.1.1,

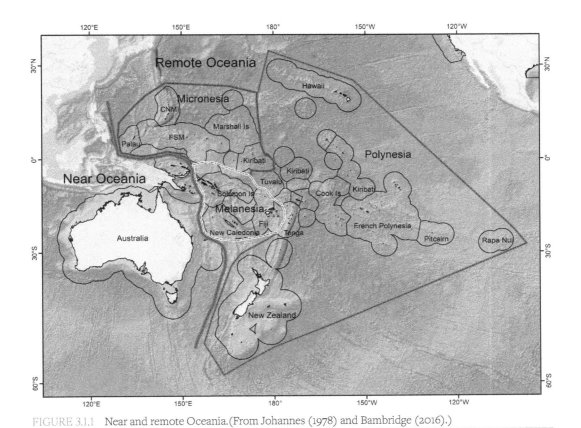

FIGURE 3.1.1 Near and remote Oceania.(From Johannes (1978) and Bambridge (2016).)

Johannes, 1978; Bambridge, 2016). Melanesian ancestors arrived first to the region, settling in the high islands of the Western Pacific where they found abundant resources and complex topographies (Bellwood, 1980). In contrast, the resource-poor low islands of Polynesia and Micronesia provided the impetus for extensive sea travels and expansion into the outer edges of the Pacific (Sheppard et al., 2011). The first colonists to this region likely came from Southeast Asia between 4000 and 2000 BCE, with the earliest archaeological evidence found on the island of Saipan in the Northern Marianas Islands, dating back to ~1500 BCE (Carson and Kurashina, 2012). As colonization continued to the east across ever increasing distances between islands, these people developed progressively more sophisticated navigational skills and a growing knowledge of the oceanic environment. Long before Europeans were sailing out of sight of land, Pacific Island navigators were voyaging thousands of kilometers across the entire Pacific (Finney, 1977). The knowledge acquired as these islanders crossed this vast region led to the creation of social systems that fostered sustainable use of the marine environment.

TABLE 3.1.1 Country, Territory, States Within Remote Oceania. EEZ—Exclusive Economic Zone. Land = km², Pop Density = People km⁻².

Country, Territory, State	Governance Type	Pop.	EEZ	Land	Pop. Density
Polynesia					
Am. Samoa (USA)	Territory of USA	54,194	405,844	197	275.1
Cook Islands	Self-governing in free assoc. w/ NZ (1965)	19,379	1,969,507	180	107.7
French Poly. (Fra.)	Overseas collectivity of France	280,208	4,766,884	3521	79.6
Hawai'i (USA)	State of USA (1959)	1,428,557	2,480,124	16,636	85.9
Kingdom of Tonga	Constitutional monarchy	103,036	666,079	696	148.0
Niue (NZ)	Self-governing state in free assoc. w/ NZ (1974)	1624	318,144	258	6.3
Pitcairn Is. (UK)	British overseas territory w/ local government	55	842,345	5	11.0
Rapa Nui (Chile)	Special territory of Chile	6600	729,763	164	40.2
Samoa	Independent (1962)	192,342	130,474	2934	65.6
Tokelau (NZ)	Dependent territory of NZ	1499	320,617	12	124.9
Tuvalu	Independent from UK (1978)	10,640	753,126	26	409.2
Wallis & Futuna (France)	French overseas collectivity	11,899	262,751	124	96.0
Micronesia					
CNMI (USA)	Commonwealth of USA	53,467	763,555	475	112.6
FSM	Self-governing in free association w/ USA since 1979	104,937	3,010,628	702	149.5
Guam (USA)	Unincorporated territory of USA	162,742	208,211	549	296.4
Republic of Nauru	Independent since 1968 from UN trust of NZ, Australia, and UK	10,084	309,261	21	480.2
Republic of Kiribati	Independent from UK since 1979	110,136	3,439,873	726	151.7
Republic of Palau	Presidential republic in free association with US since 1982	21,503	614,805	500	43.0
Republic of the Marshall Islands	Independent (1979), Compact of Free Association with USA (1986)	53,066	2,001,386	720	73.7
Melanesia					
New Caledonia (France)	Special collectivity of France	286,767	1,175,906	19,103	15.0
Republic of Fiji	Independent from UK (1970)	879,760	1,283,244	18,376	47.9
Solomon Islands	Independent from UK (1978)	599,419	1,605,256	29,785	20.1
Vanuatu	Independent from UK & France (1980)	270,402	623,417	12,189	22.2

While there is evidence that the regions that make up Oceania had different processes of cultural diversification owing in part to environmental settings and the differential size of the islands (Sand, 2002), many communities throughout the tropical Pacific share a similar knowledge of basic resource conservation principles that are the result of centuries of continuing experimentation and innovation (Wilhelm et al., 2014). Localized adaptive management was based on customary knowledge and practices and was responsive to changes in local environmental and social conditions (Ruddle, 1996; Johannes, 1998a). Long before western societies recognized the limits of ocean resources, the people of Oceania developed methods to safeguard against the collapse of these invaluable resources (Johannes, 1978). Their long history of conservation was motivated by scarcity, limited resources, and climate variability. Some species were referred to as "famine foods", suggesting that food needs were not always met (Titcomb, 1972). Some Pacific Island cultures learned that their resources were limited and introduced appropriate conservation measures, while others exceeded those limits, which ultimately led them to overshoot their carrying capacity (Johannes, 2002a; Tainter, 2006).

Not all these practices were developed for conservation purposes; many had cultural roots and were designed to maintain political structure and order (Ruddle, 1996; Colding and Folke, 2001). In contrast to the densely populated islands of Polynesia and Micronesia, human population densities in parts of Melanesia prior to European colonial intrusions were likely too low to have generated sufficient fishing pressure to drive the evolution of a conservation ethic (Foale et al., 2011; 2016). Therefore, customary marine tenure and fishing taboos in this region were primarily designed to manage relationships between social groups, rather than to sustain food security (Foale et al., 2016). Although tenure and taboo systems were not inherently designed to ensure sustainable management outcomes in these areas, stable resource availability for local use was sometimes a by-product (Jupiter, 2017).

In parts of Oceania, especially lightly populated coastal areas of Melanesia, marine resources existed in quantities sufficient for the needs of the local populations to be met (Johannes, 1989). In some of these areas, there is little evidence of a marine conservation ethic, because people never experienced overexploitation of these resources (Johannes and MacFarlane, 1991) or relied more heavily on terrestrial resources for sustenance (Chapman, 1985). Traditional political structure also played a role in conservation in Oceania. In Polynesia and Micronesia, political authority was through heredity and these lineages were considered of divine origin, while in Melanesia, leadership was often acquired through achievements such as wealth accumulation, oratory skill, courage in warfare, or benevolence toward their followers (Chapman, 1987). Because of greater social stratification, higher occupational specialization, and larger political units, Polynesian and Micronesian societies often had a greater emphasis on conservation knowledge and practices compared with Melanesia.

The people of Oceania relied on the sea for much of their protein, as well as other essential nutrients and minerals that were lacking in the poor-quality soils of many atolls and small islands (Johannes, 1978). In addition, other important resources such as building materials, fishing gear, jewelry, medicines, and household tools were obtained from the sea. Marine resource management was often in the hands of the local resource users who were knowledgeable of the natural rhythms and processes that controlled resource abundance (Johannes, 1978; Poepoe et al., 2007). Fishermen were often held in high regard within the community and master fishermen held extensive knowledge that was passed down from generation to generation (Titcomb, 1972; Johannes, 1982).

Many fishing restrictions were associated with spiritual and cultural beliefs. Certain species that were considered sacred were often rare or susceptible to overfishing, and as a result were prohibited from consumption by certain groups (e.g., women, commoners, clans, age groups) (Abbott, 1984). For example, turtles were typically reserved for chiefs in many locations throughout Oceania (Allen, 2007). In Hawai'i, only ruling chiefs could consume Pacific threadfin (*Polydactylus sexfilis*), which is a protandric hermaphrodite (changing sex from male to female), and therefore particularly vulnerable to overharvest (Friedlander and Ziemann, 2003).

Species of importance often have multiple names, depending on various life history characteristics (e.g., size, sex, color). In Rapa Nui, the rudderfish *Kyphosus sandwicensis*, locally known as *nānue*, in one of the most important nearshore fisheries species and has seven secondary names based on size and five secondary names based on color pattern (Randall and Cea, 2011). Names were also associated with various life history phases, which often connoted an understanding of the ecology of the species. In Palau, the juvenile stage of the sweetlip *Plectorhinchus obscurus* (*bikl*) lives at mangrove edges near river mouths, where it is called *melimralm*, which means to drink fresh water (Helfman and Randall, 1972). These distinctions often had important conservation and management implications. Hawaiians recognized four life history phases for the hermaphroditic Pacific threadfin (juveniles—*moi li'i*, males—*mana moi*, hermaphrodites—*pala moi*, and female—*moi*), and conservation principles included restrictions on harvest of *pala moi* or *moi*, depending on inter-annual fluctuations in population structure (Poepoe et al., 2007).

Societies were strongly stratified through chieftainships and community leadership that were based on matrilineal or patrilineal systems, which were inherited and/or merit-based and often associated with ritual and spiritual protocols (Lal and Fortune, 2000). The first fish of a catch was often offered to the gods, and the next fish to the chief, before consumption by an individual (Bambridge, 2016). In Hawai'i, gathering of shellfish and seaweed was primarily conducted by women, and their harvest was then surrendered to the representative of the high chief who would divide it among the community (Titcomb, 1978). Despite this hierarchy, the egalitarian nature of many Pacific Island cultures meant that food was shared among most sectors of society (Allen, 2007). Sharing also helped maintain kinship and other social linkages, which reinforced reciprocal sharing during seasonal shortages or other times of need (Campbell, 2015).

Many of the marine management rules and regulations we have today (e.g., closed areas, closed seasons, size restrictions, restricted entry) were employed thousands of years ago by Pacific Islanders (Johannes, 1998a). The traditional systems in many of these islands emphasized social and cultural controls on marine resource use, with a code of conduct that was strictly enforced (Johannes, 1982; Ruddle, 1988). Draconian penalties were often administered for violating these restrictions owing to the importance of maintaining a secure food supply and social order.

Pacific Islanders developed an encyclopedic knowledge of their resources, especially as they related to seasonal movements, feeding behavior, and spawning seasons and locations (Johannes, 1981, 1982). Approaches to harvest management were often based on identifying the specific times and places that fishing could occur so as not to disrupt basic processes and habitats of important food resources (Johannes and Yeeting, 2001; Poepoe et al., 2007). Many natural processes affect the distribution of these marine resources, but some of the most important are related to seasons and moon phases. This knowledge helped to inform lunar calendars, which were mental models based on a holistic understanding of marine and terrestrial environments and emphasized certain repetitive ecological processes (e.g., spawning, aggregations, feeding habits) that function at different time scales (e.g., seasonal, monthly, and daily), which were adapted to fishermen's own observations for specific locations (Friedlander et al., 2002; Poepoe et al., 2007).

The most important marine conservation measure in Oceania was local marine tenure, where the right to fish in a location was controlled by a clan, chief, or family (Johannes, 1978; Ruddle et al., 1992). Spatial closures within these tenure systems were employed throughout Oceania for various purposes, and these closures were often imposed to ensure large catches for special events, or as a cache for when resources in the commonly accessed fishing grounds ran low (Johannes, 1978; Cinner et al., 2006). Temporal closures were widely used to reduce intensive harvest of spawning fishes or other predictable aggregations (e.g., migration routes, Johannes, 1978, 1981). The collective practices described above were developed through much trial and error and fostered sustainability under highly variable and scare resource conditions.

Post-Western Contact

European Colonization

The age of European exploration of the Pacific began with the voyage of Magellan in 1519–21, which led to the rise of global trade and the creation of European colonial empires throughout the region. Except for the interiors of the largest Melanesian islands and some small and remote islands, missionaries soon penetrated much of the region, and by the late nineteenth century entrepreneurial traders from Europe and the US were present throughout Oceania. Soon after western contact, depopulation of the native peoples occurred in many areas due to disease and servitude.

The whaling industry, primarily centered in Hawai'i but also prevalent in Guam, Fiji, Pohnpei, Tahiti, and the Gilbert Islands, led to great economic and social transformation (Lal and Fortune, 2000). Pacific Islanders began to supply labor for provisioning European ships, and as crew, while also becoming involved in the extraction and processing of marine products (Lal and Fortune, 2000). Europeans and Americans involved in the China trade established export fisheries for bêche-de-mer (dried sea cucumber) in the early 1800s throughout Oceania (Preston, 1993). Bêche-de-mer traders introduced firearms and trade goods such as iron tools and fishhooks, which led to increased efficiencies, but also increased conflict, leading to major demographic and political changes in the region (Ward, 1972).

The establishment of cash economies and the presence of foreigners led to the development of commercial fisheries around many islands to feed and resupply merchant ships and the ever-growing non-native populations. Commercialization of fishing created distance markets and led to a dismantling of the conservation ethic in many locations. In Hawai'i, the early 1900s saw the centralization of economic activities and fisheries with large increases in commercial fish landings. The Hawaiian Tuna Packing Company began operations in 1917 and by the 1930s employed 500 men and produced nearly ten million cans of tuna per year, making it the third largest export commodity in Hawai'i at that time, behind sugar and pineapple (Schug, 2001).

Traditional local authority mostly disintegrated due to colonization, commercialization, and economic development (Johannes, 1978; Ruddle and Hickey, 2008). In Kiribati many traditional marine management practices were abandoned during the colonial era, and customary marine management is now uncommon in the country (Vierros et al., 2010). Colonial governments were generally ignorant of traditional management structures and introduced various types of ineffective centralized natural resource management policies that often greatly weakened local authority (Johannes, 1998b).

Post-Colonial Rule

World War II brought about profound changes in the Pacific—once remote and isolated villages were rapidly exposed to an entirely new world view. Following World War II, many countries gained independence, while others developed various forms of association with their former colonial powers (Table 3.1.1). The shift to market-based economies led to increased commercialization of fisheries, particularly industrial tuna fishing (Barclay, 2014). While the economic value and total tonnage of the industrial tuna catch dwarfs all other fisheries in Oceania, coastal fisheries are far more important for livelihoods and food security, as well as cultural identity (Gillett, 2009). These near-shore fisheries also became increasing commercialized with assistance from international and national interests.

The post-war period witnessed the growth of regionalism. Regional conservation action in Oceania illustrates how mechanisms for international cooperation, standard setting and implementing institutions such as convention secretariats are mutually supportive, with interested governments, non-governmental organizations and international organizations working together through a combination of formal agreements, action plans, intergovernmental meetings and scientific symposia to build interest in and capacity for nature conservation in the region (Dahl, 2017). The South Pacific Commission (SPC, now known as the Pacific Community) was formed in 1947 as the principal scientific and technical organization in the region. In 1971, the newly independent states formed the South Pacific Forum, renamed the Pacific Islands Forum (PIF), to address political and social issues. The Forum Fisheries Agency, created in 1979, negotiates licensing agreements with foreign fishing companies on behalf of the PIF members. In 1982, the South Pacific Regional Environment Program, was established by SPC, PIF, and the United Nations, to promote sustainable development throughout the region. The Council of Regional Organizations in the Pacific under the PIF ensures cooperation among the regional organizations, both governmental and non-governmental.

Beginning in the 1970, secondary education programs began to develop more relevant curricula for Pacific Island schools that included an indigenous perspective (Thaman, 1993). The University of the South Pacific has provided higher education to students from throughout the region since 1967 and now has 14 campuses across 12 countries. Other universities that serve the region include the University of Guam, the University of Hawai'i system, the National University of Samoa, the University of French Polynesia, and the University of New Caledonia.

Present

Impacts of Globalization

Modernization and a cash economy have driven many coastal communities to overexploit their resources, often at the expense of the very resources on which they rely. Declines in marine resources have resulted from myriad factors including: intensive fishing pressure, landbased pollution, destruction of habitat, and invasive species. The distal drivers of these declines stem from growing human populations, cash economies and globalization, access to technological innovations (e.g., motorized boats and freezers for storing catch), introduction of overly efficient fishing techniques (e.g., inexpensive monofilament gill nets, scuba, GPS), and loss of traditional conservation practices (Johannes, 1978; Cinner and Kittinger, 2015). In the Solomon Islands, the use of more efficient gear was positively related to both human population density and market proximity, which collectively contributed to declines in marine resources (Brewer et al., 2013).

Most Pacific Island countries and territories do not have coastal fisheries policies, and the low levels of government support and the large spatial scale of these coastal resources present significant management challenges (Gillett and Cartwright, 2010; Govan, 2015). Poor government effectiveness is, in part, a result of under-resourced agencies, particularly in rural areas where the fisheries mostly occur (Govan et al., 2013). The lack of effective coastal management has led to a call for the development of innovative solutions to address these problems.

Renaissance of Customary Management

Recognition that westernization produced a concomitant decline in marine resources and cultural identity has led to a revival of customary management practices throughout Oceania. This resurgence is being driven by increasing scarcity of resources, re-establishment of local authority and tenure, improved education, and more effective assistance and advice from governmental and non-governmental organizations (Johannes, 2002b). In many locations customary management systems have achieved positive social outcomes by improving local social order and identity, which promotes historical continuity and links ancestry and place (McClenachan and Kittinger, 2013; Cinner and Huchery, 2014). This localized management also reduces the cost of enforcement, as well as social and political conflicts (Hviding, 1998).

The success of community tenure of marine resources is often related to the proximity of the community to their area of responsibility, and to the level of cultural and social cohesion extant within the community (Aswani, 2005; Cinner et al., 2012). Local authority is most relevant in remote areas where centralized government is not cost-effective nor effectual. Even where state institutions exist at the local level, they co-exist with customary institutions, resulting in "legal pluralism", or the existence of multiple legal systems within one geographic area (Corrin Care and Zorn, 2001; Bambridge, 2016).

Throughout much of Oceania, compliance with local resource management rules relies to a large extent on respect for traditional authority and decision-making processes (Aswani, 2005; Hoffmann, 2002). Current barriers to compliance include conflict between customary management rules and national legal frameworks, as well as incentives to overfish from growing global markets (Clarke and Jupiter, 2010). National legislation in many Pacific island countries recognizes and protects indigenous land tenure; however, recognition of customary marine tenure has been more uneven, reflecting a historical conflict between Pacific marine tenure systems and the "open access" traditions of colonizing European states (Govan et al., 2009; Clarke and Jupiter, 2010). In Fiji, enforcement of community management rules is constrained by the national legal system, whereas local communities have no formal authority to enforce management rules, and certain community-imposed sanctions may breach national criminal laws (Veitayaki, 2000).

Locally Managed Marine Areas

Communities throughout Oceania are currently engaged in bottom-up management of their coastal and marine resources with technical support and resources from groups such as the Locally-Managed Marine Area network (LLMA; Jupiter et al., 2014). LMMAs are often supported and guided by co-management partners (e.g., NGOs, government agencies, or research institutes) who promote a diverse range of objectives, including biodiversity conservation, fisheries management, livelihood diversification, and climate change adaptation (Weeks and Jupiter, 2013). However, for most communities the main driver for local management is the desire to maintain or improve livelihoods and is often related to perceived threats to food security, commerce, or culture (Govan et al., 2009). More than 900 communities, comprising ~8% of coastal communities in the Pacific region, are documented as having implemented Community-Based Fisheries Management (CBFM; Govan, 2015). However, more than half of these CBFMs are in Fiji and Samoa, leaving > 90% of the coastal villages in the region without support to implement local management (Table 3.1.2). There are likely hundreds to thousands of communities throughout the Pacific implementing their own coastal and marine actions that are not officially documented and therefore lack support from government institutions (Jupiter et al., 2014; Govan, 2015). Despite their proliferation and popularity, there are relatively few empirical examples describing how these areas were established or how they are performing from either an ecological or socio-economic perspective (Jupiter et al., 2014; Wamukota et al., 2012).

In Hawai'i, communities can enter co-management with the State to protect Native Hawaiian subsistence, cultural, and religious fishing practices (Ayers and Kittinger, 2014). Despite interest from > 19 communities only two communities in over 20 years have been successfully designated, and none have approved management plans (Levine and Richmond, 2014). This co-management approach has been hindered by a lack of capacity in communities and institutional rigidity at resource management agencies, as well as an ambiguous, complicated administrative rulemaking processes. Despite the numerous obstacles to formal governmental authorization, numerous communities in Hawai'i are strengthening local influence and accountability for their marine resources, oftentimes independent of government support (Friedlander et al., 2013, 2014).

TABLE 3.1.2 Marine managed areas in remote Oceania. Data from World Database on Protected Areas (UNEP-WCMC and IUCN, 2018; Govan, 2015; O'Leary et al., 2018). Local management areas include: indigenous owners, communities, individual landowners, joint and collaborative.

Region/Country-Territory	No. CBFM[a] (% of total)	Government (km²)	Local Management (km²)
Melanesia			
Fiji	448 (53%)	–	12,696
New Caledonia	1 (ND)	3747	8884
Solomon Is.	184 (5%)	155	1414
Vanuatu	13 (1%)	–	123
Micronesia			
FSM	10 (13%)	472[b]	3
Guam	0	15	4
Kiribati	5 (3%)	539[c]	–
Marshall Is.	13 (13%)	–	7470
N. Mariana Is.	0	14	8
Nauru	0	–	–
Palau	5 (31%)	–	1104
Polynesia			
Am. Samoa	13 (18%)	–	23
Cook Is.	6 (16%)	–	2
Niue	1 (7%)	–	54
Pitcairn Is.	0	–	–
French Polynesia	27 (56%)	207	–
Rapa Nui	0	–	–
Tokelau	3 (100%)	10	–
Samoa	102 (31%)	8	107
Tonga	10 (6%)	37[d]	158
Tuvalu	9 (100%)	40	24
Wallis and Futuna	0	–	–

[a] Govan (2015).
[b] 99% in Oroluk Sanctuary—subsistence fishing by residents only.
[c] 60% on Kiritimati Atoll.
[d] Excluding Ha'apai Archipelago, which is a multi-use conservation area (9879 km²).

Hybrid Management

Integrating traditional ecological knowledge and customary practices into contemporary marine management has shown promise in many locations (Cinner, 2005; Kittinger et al., 2014). Hybridization of customary beliefs and institutions with modern management concepts such as marine protected areas (MPAs) and ecosystem-based management (EBM) can help address broader concerns such as coastal degradation, climate change, weak governance, corruption, limited resources, and increasing poverty (Aswani and Ruddle, 2013). This integration is particularly relevant in coastal communities that have or have had traditional rights-based fishery management systems and/or are more socio-culturally homogeneous (Aswani, 2005).

Customary and contemporary "western-style" systems of governance often have different objectives, values, and time horizons that can lead to conflict. While there are distinct differences between customary and contemporary regimes, there are commonalities that can lead to effective management. The Pacific Islanders' holistic world view of the inseparability of people and nature corresponds largely with the principles of EBM, recognizing the strong interdependencies of ecological, social, economic, and institutional perspectives. Local tenure allows inclusive members to institute spatial and temporal restrictions that also lie at the core of EBM. Customary tenure systems have hybridized with modern rights-based fisheries management measures such as individual transferable quotas (ITQs), as in the *Trochus* fisheries in the Cook Islands and Vanuatu (Aswani, 2005; Hickey and Johannes, 2002). The perceived success of hybrid MPAs in Samoa and Vanuatu has inspired neighboring communities to adopt similar strategies (Johannes, 2002b).

Marine Protected Areas

Closing certain areas to harvest for periods of time has been practiced for centuries by Pacific Islanders to help sustain healthy populations of marine resources (Johannes, 1978, 1982; Cinner et al., 2006). Incorporating elements of these established practices into a contemporary framework has shown biological and social success, and can increase the legitimacy of decisions regarding MPAs, as well as aid in compliance (Aswani et al., 2012). Incorporating fishermen's local knowledge into designing marine protected areas in the Solomon Islands produced conservation areas that represented natural and social seascapes recognized by indigenous communities (Aswani and Lauer, 2006). Protection of spawning sites is a central tenant of MPA design, and identification and conservation of these aggregations has been greatly aided by traditional and contemporary fishers' knowledge (Johannes, 1998a, 1998b; De Mitcheson et al., 2008).

In Palau, conservation has evolved from the traditional "bul" to more contemporary MPAs with effective enforcement, by most standards, owing to strong community support

(Gruby and Basurto, 2013; Friedlander et al., 2017). In Fiji, where enforcement capacity rests largely with communities, most MPAs are located near communities to improve surveillance (Jupiter and Egli, 2011). In many cases, opportunistically placing MPAs where there is community support may be more beneficial than implementing, or failing to implement, a more optimal design in the future (Ban et al., 2011).

Permanent "western-style" area closures have been implemented throughout the region, particularly in more developed localities where customary practices are less prevalent. In areas where customary tenure is strong, permanent "no-take" reserves are likely to be disregarded, owing to concerns for human welfare or different objectives as seen by the community (Aswani et al., 2012). However, in some more urban areas and areas where customary or local management is weak due to increased market influence, population size, immigration and development, imposition of larger no-take areas may be a more effective strategy.

The establishment of permanent or indefinite closures appears to be a departure from customary practices, and this shift may be due, in part, to both declining resources and changing social structure (Bartlett et al., 2009). Periodic closures based on customary norms are likely most effective where local socio-cultural institutions are strong, and communities have the capacity to enforce regulations (Johannes, 2002b; Muehlig-Hofmann, 2007). Some have argued that permanent no-take closures are largely incompatible with customary tenure because the scale of population replenishment for most marine species is considerably larger than that of most community-based management area boundaries (Foale and Manele, 2004). However, localized recruitment of many species has been shown to be important for many nearshore species, and networks of no-take areas can enhance regional population replenishment (Grorud-Colvert et al., 2014). One example is Palau where the government was instrumental in establishing the Micronesia Challenge—a conservation initiative to protect > 30% of the marine ecosystems of the region by 2020 through the establishment of a Protected Areas Networks, which been shown to be successful from at least an ecological perspective (Baker et al., 2011; Friedlander et al., 2017). Elsewhere in Micronesia, MPA effectiveness varies widely and depends on the proximity to human populations, the level of reef degradation, and wave exposure, which can be a proxy for accessibility (Houk et al., 2015). In Fiji, efforts are underway to scale up its LMMA network by encouraging communities to work together with adjacent communities (Mills et al., 2011).

The World Database on Protected Areas (WDPA, UNEP-WCMC and IUCN, 2018) maintains information on marine and terrestrial protected areas. Most countries in Oceania do not maintain up to date lists of MPAs and therefore reported areas should be treated with caution. As reported in the WDPA, most of the marine protected areas in Oceania have some form of local co-management (Table 3.1.2). Solely government managed MPAs are less common and are often associated with remote locations, important conservation areas (e.g., spawning sites), or to benefit tourism. Despite government control, local influence is still important in the management of many of these MPAs.

Some conservation measures have violated the rights of indigenous peoples, resulting in poverty and societal problems (Colchester, 2004). The term "ocean grabbing" has been used to describe actions, policies or initiatives that deprive small-scale fishers of resources, dispossess vulnerable populations of coastal lands, and/or undermine historical access to areas of the sea (Bennett et al., 2015). These concerns highlight the need for proponents and implementers of ocean-related initiatives involving re-allocation of space or resources to incorporate input from and be mindful of potential consequences to local communities.

Large-Scale MPAs

Increasing attention is being paid to the natural and cultural heritage value of remote ocean spaces and this recognition has led to the designation of Large-Scale MPAs (LSMPAs, $\geq$ 100,000 km^2), particularly in Oceania (Toonen et al., 2013; Wilhelm et al., 2014). These LSMPAs offer benefits that are not obtainable at smaller scales, primarily the ability to protect whole ecosystems and interdependent habitats so that biologically connected ecosystems can be included within the same management area (Toonen et al., 2013). Large no-take LSMPAs have been established in several areas (e.g., Hawai'i and US Pacific, Palau, Pitcairn, Kiribati), while a few jurisdictions have declared or promised to create their entire EEZs as multi-use LSMPAs (O'Leary et al., 2018; Fig. 3.1.2, Table 3.1.3).

Many of the existing LSMPAs are remote areas in the Pacific that share common natural history, threats, culture, as well as scientific and management needs. The distinctive challenges faced by LSMPAs, especially the governance and protection of vast tracks of open ocean, led to the formation of a unique conservation organization in 2010, "Big Ocean: A Network of the World's Large-Scale Marine Managed Areas" (http://bigoceanmanagers.org), which is a peer-to-peer learning and sharing network of LSMPA managers (Wilhelm et al., 2014). Several LSMPAs in the Pacific have collaborated in bilateral agreements, and learning exchanges, as well as research, monitoring, and enforcement activities (Friedlander et al., 2016). Papahānaumokuākea Marine National Monument (PMNM) is one of the world's largest MPAs (> 1.5 million km^2) and its UNESCO World Heritage inscription identified its outstanding universal value for both natural and cultural heritage, and as the world's first cultural seascape for its continuing connections to indigenous people (Kikiloi et al., 2017). Management of PMNM emphasizes integration of science, policy, cultural knowledge, traditions, and practices to create successful management strategies appropriate for both natural and cultural resources.

The creation of LSMPAs is not without controversy. The rapid growth of LSMPAs runs the risk of being biased toward places that are remote or unpromising for extractive activities

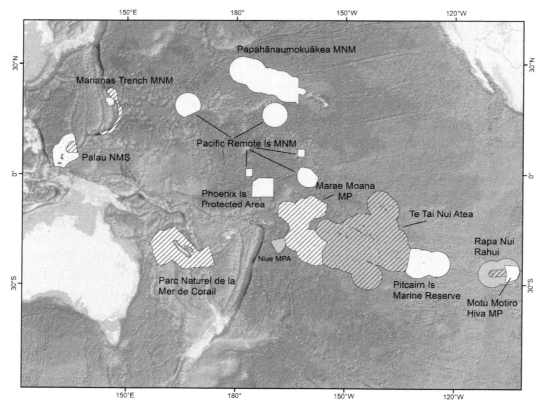

FIGURE 3.1.2   Distribution of designated and promised LSMPAs in Oceania as of June 2017. LSMPAs that are designated are in olive and those promised are in pink. Multiple-use MPAs are designated by hatched lines. Strongly or fully protected are shown without hatches. MNM—Marine National Monument, NMS—National Marine Sanctuary, MP—Marine Park. Should Easter Island Marine Park be designated, Motu Motiro Hiva MP would be encompassed by this designation. (adapted from O'Leary et al., 2018). (For interpretation of the references to color in this figure legend, the reader is referred to the web version of this article.)

and hence residual to commercial uses (Devillers et al., 2015). In addition, the implementation and the management of LSMPAs have not been well explored in practice or theory (Leenhardt et al., 2013). Some of the criticisms of LSMPAs are valid and need addressing, however, none pertain exclusively to LSMPAs and many involve challenges ubiquitous to all management (O'Leary et al., 2018).

Future

It is estimated that coastal fisheries of most countries and territories in the region will not meet their food security needs by 2030 due to population growth, overfishing, reduced productivity because of climate change, and inadequate national distribution networks

TABLE 3.1.3 Large-Scale Marine Protected Areas (LSMPAs) in Oceania. Year is the year proposed. Data from O'Leary et al. (2018).

LSMPA Name	Country	Year	Designated	Area (km²)	Management Type
Parc Naturel de la Mer de Corail, New Caledonia	France	2014	Yes	1,291,643	Multi-use
Phoenix Is. Protected Area	Kiribati	2008	Yes	408,250	Strong protection
Marianas Trench Marine National Monument	USA	2009	Yes	246,608[a]	Multi-use
Palau National Marine Sanctuary	Palau	2015	Yes	503,521[b]	Strong protection
Marae Moana Marine Park	Cook Is	2017	No	1,900,000	Multi-use
Niue Marine Park	Niue	2017	No	127,000	Strong protection
Pitcairn Is. Marine Reserve	UK	2016	Yes	834,334	Strong protection
Te Tai Nui Atea, French Polynesia	France	2017	No	5,000,000	Multi-use
Rapa Nui Rahui MPA	Chile	2015	No	720,016[c]	Strong protection
Motu Motiro Hiva Marine Park	Chile	2010	Yes	150,340[c]	Strong protection
Papahanaumokuakea Marine National Monument	USA	2006	Yes	1,508,859[d]	Strong protection
Pacific Remote Islands Marine National Monument	USA	2009	Yes	1,269,094[e]	Strong protection

[a] Commercial fishing is permitted in waters of the Trench and Volcanic Units but not in the Islands Unit of the Monument (~17%).
[b] Palau National Marine Sanctuary fully protects 80% of the EEZ with the remainder reserved for domestic fishing only.
[c] Once designated the Rapa Nui Rahui MPA will encompass the Motu Motiro Hiva Marine Park. A local fishing zone of 89,834 km² (22% of EEZ) around Easter Island will permit the Rapa Nui to continue using the marine resources.
[d] Expanded from 362,061 in 2016.
[e] Expanded from 214,969 in 2014.

(Hanich et al., 2018). The stagnation of coastal fishery production and the lack of management investment means food and employment must be spread among a growing number of people. The utility of nearshore fisheries laws in the face of climate change requires resilient coastal fisheries policies (Gourlie et al., 2018). New legislation with the appropriate balance between state-driven management efforts and bottom-up community stewardship must allow for management flexibility to ensure that scientific understanding of climate effects supports management decisions, and minimizes adverse effects of climate change on the lives, livelihoods, and rights of communities. Improving coastal fisheries management in the short term should be better addressed through improved management frameworks, use of human resources, and allocation of increased and decentralized budgets. An example of this is the Pacific Oceanscape Initiative, which has been endorsed by 23 Pacific Island nations, regional intergovernmental agencies, and the conservation community to advocate for conservation and sustainable development of ~40 million km² of Pacific Ocean (Govan, 2017).

Climate Change

Global climate change is imperiling ecosystems worldwide, but especially in Pacific Islands, which is one of the most vulnerable regions to climate change impacts (Bell et al., 2013; Cheung et al., 2016). Climate change is already affecting the region through increasing temperatures, sea-level rise, saltwater intrusion of freshwater resources, coastal erosion, an increase in extreme weather events, altered rainfall patterns, coral bleaching, and ocean acidification (Hanich et al., 2018). Potential pelagic fish catch is projected to decrease by > 50% across many areas, with the largest impacts in the western Pacific (Cheung et al., 2016). However, these impacts will be in even more pronounced in coastal regions, with significant declines expected in the abundance of nearshore fisheries species, including export products such as *Trochus* and bêche de mer, due to degradation of coral reefs and other essential habitats, such as mangroves and seagrass beds (Bromhead et al., 2015).

Pacific Islanders and their knowledge-practice-belief systems have a long history of resilience to environmental variability and unpredictability, including periodic and severe disturbances (e.g., droughts, floods, storms, and tsunamis) (McMillen et al., 2014). Improved climate predictions can assist governments and coastal communities in reducing the impacts of climatic variability, but policy and management responses will need to be adaptive to the same time scales as climatic variability (Dunstan et al., 2018). While reductions in CO_2 are the only way to reverse climate change, reducing non-climate stresses that contribute to ecosystem degradation can moderate the vulnerability of species and ecosystems to direct climate change impacts. Modeling results suggest that strong local mitigation measures (e.g., regional fishing allocation schemes, effective MPA networks, decentralized coastal management) can substantially reduce fisheries declines, particularly in areas that are projected to have the largest decreases in catch (Asch et al., 2018). Community-based and participatory approaches can complement and ground-truth climate models and guide culturally appropriate resource management, research, and adaptation measures (McMillen et al., 2014).

Other Global Threats

Illegal, unreported, and unregulated (IUU) fishing is an ever-growing existential threat to the Pacific region. IUU fishing harms legitimate fishing activities and livelihoods, jeopardizes food and economic security, benefits transnational crime, distorts markets, contributes to human trafficking, and undermines ongoing efforts to implement sustainable fisheries policies (Petrossian, 2015). International efforts to counter IUU fishing have grown over the past decades. Advances in satellite technology and vessel tracking had made huge advances in surveillance. The public accessibility of automatic ship identification system (AIS) data has made it possible to observe vessel activity anywhere in the world and has revolutionized how we monitor fisheries (Kroodsma et al., 2018). Curtailing IUU fishing can produce rapid improvements in fishery profits and catches and creates an opportunity for countries to reform their fisheries while avoiding many of the short-run costs of reducing domestic fishing efforts and catches (Cabral et al., 2018). The recent implementation of the Port State Measures Agreement establishes a minimum set of standard measures for States to apply when foreign vessels seek entry into their ports and verifies that such vessels have not engaged in IUU fishing and other inspection and enforcement violations (FAO, 2016).

As more Pacific Island countries and territories have increased management of their EEZs, fishing effort has shifted to the adjacent high seas where rules of fishing are less rigorous, and revenues are not shared with island nations. Recent research shows that closing the high seas to fishing would increase fisheries yield in countries' exclusive economic zones by 30% and fisheries profits by > 100% (White and Costello, 2014). This would also increase the social equitability of fishing, by shifting benefits to local fishers and away from large foreign fleets (Sumaila et al., 2015).

Deep-sea mineral companies are particularly interested in the exploration and exploitation of the rich mineral deposits of the Pacific region. The Clarion-Clipperton Fracture Zone (CCZ) in the abyssal eastern Pacific has the largest known concentrations of high-value polymetallic nodules, and the International Seabed Authority (ISA), created under the Law of the Sea Convention, has granted numerous contracts to explore for minerals on the deep seabed in this region (Wedding et al., 2015). Because of the scale of the impacts and the sensitivity of the deep sea, the ISA developed a precautionary approach in the CCZ by developing the deep seabed's first environmental management plan, and one that included MPAs based on the recommendations of a scientific working group (Wedding et al., 2015). The Cook Islands and Kiribati have implemented national deep-sea mineral policies, and many other countries in the region have draft policies or existing legislation that includes management of national deep-sea mineral resources (Govan, 2017).

Whole-Island and Whole-Ocean Approaches

The connectivity between terrestrial and marine ecosystems in nearly all aspects of life in Oceania requires a major shift from current thinking toward a more integrated approach. Marine spatial planning (MSP) is a strategic, coordinated, and comprehensive effort that provides a framework for engaging stakeholders at all levels to maximize resilience of ecosystems and communities (Crowder et al., 2006). MSP can help mitigate some threats by planning for sustainable coastal development, appropriate waste and marine pollution management, and best practices for watershed and marine resource management (Grantham et al., 2011).

Trends toward adaptive management are essential in this time of rapid environmental change. While larger MPAs are thought to be better buffers from the effects of climate change, the small size of many MPAs in developing nations means that adaptive management can be done by communities and decisions can be made and implemented rapidly (Aswani et al., 2007; Ban et al., 2011). In the Republic of the Marshall Islands, atoll communities have formed Natural Resource Management Committees, with responsibilities for assessing environmental impacts and making recommendations for management implementation (Baker et al., 2011). The Cook Islands recent declaration to declare their entire EEZ as an LSMPA may represent a model for achieving integrated ocean management and conservation through inclusive processes of consultation and spatial planning.

Understanding how to build effective, culturally grounded measurement systems is a fundamental step toward supporting adaptive management and resilience in the face of environmental, social, and economic change (Sterling et al., 2017a). By incorporating multiple worldviews and knowledge systems, biocultural approaches can help better understand the links in social-ecological systems and increase the chances of long-term success of conservation interventions (Gavin et al., 2015; Sterling et al., 2017b). These hybrid systems have limitations as not all views and values have equal importance, and rapid cultural and environmental changes will require a prioritization of goals and objectives that are largely place-based.

The increasing threats of climate change impacts, coupled with declining coastal fisheries and food security challenges requires bottom-up, as well as top-down governance that will benefit from traditional ecological knowledge that is adapted to a modern and changing planet. The people of Oceania are at the frontline of climate change and while these changes will fundamentally change the world of the future in ways we cannot fully predict, the resilience shown by the people of Oceania in the past gives us some hope.

References

Abbott, L.A., 1984. *Limu. An Ethnobotanical Study of Hawaiian Seaweeds*. PacificTropical Garden, Honolulu.

Allen, M.S., 2007. Three millennia of human and sea turtle interactions in remote Oceania. *Coral Reefs* 26 (4), 959–970.

Asch, R.G., Cheung, W.W., Reygondeau, G., 2018. Future marine ecosystem drivers, biodiversity, and fisheries maximum catch potential in Pacific Island countries and territories under climate change. *Mar. Policy* 88, 285–294.

Aswani, S., 2005. Customary sea tenure in Oceania as a case of rights-based fishery management: does it work? *Rev. Fish Biol. Fish.* 15 (3), 285–307.

Aswani, S., Lauer, M., 2006. Incorporating fishermen's local knowledge and behavior into geographical information systems (GIS) for designing marine protected areas in Oceania. *Hum. Organ.* 65 (1), 81–102.

Aswani, S., Albert, S., Sabetian, A., Furusawa, T., 2007. Customary management as precautionary and adaptive principles for protecting coral reefs in Oceania. *Coral Reefs* 26 (4), 1009.

Aswani, S., Christie, P., Muthiga, N.A., Mahon, R., Primavera, J.H., Cramer, L.A., Barbier, E.B., Granek, E.F., Kennedy, C.J., Wolanski, E., Hacker, S., 2012. The way forward with ecosystem-based management in tropical contexts: reconciling with existing management systems. *Mar. Policy* 36 (1), 1–10.

Aswani, S., Ruddle, K., 2013. Design of realistic hybrid marine resource management programs in Oceania. *Pac. Sci.* 67 (3), 461–476.

Ayers, A.L., Kittinger, J.N., 2014. Emergence of co-management governance for Hawai'i coral reef fisheries. *Glob. Environ. Chang.* 28, 251–262.

Baker, N., Beger, M., McClennen, C., Ishoda, A., Edwards, F., 2011. Reimaanlok: a national framework for conservation area planning in the Marshall Islands. *J. Mar. Biol.* 2011, 273034.

Bambridge, T., 2016. *The Rahui: Legal Pluralism in Polynesian Traditional Management of Resources and Territories*. Anu Press.

Ban, N.C., Adams, V.M., Almany, G.R., Ban, S., Cinner, J.E., McCook, L.J., Mills, M., Pressey, R.L., White, A., 2011. Designing, implementing and managing marine protected areas: emerging trends and opportunities for coral reef nations. *J. Exp. Mar. Biol. Ecol.* 408 (1–2), 21–31.

Barclay, K., 2014. *History of industrial tuna fishing in the Pacific Islands. In: Historical Perspectives of Fisheries Exploitation in the Indo-Pacific*. Springer, Dordrecht, pp. 153–171.

Bartlett, C.Y., Pakoa, K., Manua, C., 2009. Marine reserve phenomenon in the Pacific islands. *Mar. Policy* 33 (4), 673–678.

Bell, J.D., Ganachaud, A., Gehrke, P.C., Griffiths, S.P., Hobday, A.J., Hoegh-Guldberg, O., Johnson, J.E., Le Borgne, R., Lehodey, P., Lough, J.M., Matear, R.J., 2013. Mixed responses of tropical Pacific fisheries and aquaculture to climate change. *Nat. Clim. Chang.* 3 (6), 591.

Bellwood, P.S., 1980. The peopling of the Pacific. *Sci. Am.* 243 (5), 174–185.

Bennett, N.J., Govan, H., Satterfield, T., 2015. Ocean grabbing. *Mar. Policy* 57, 61–68.

Berkes, F., 2012. *Sacred Ecology*. Routledge, New York.

Brewer, T.D., Cinner, J.E., Green, A., Pressey, R.L., 2013. Effects of human population density and proximity to markets on coral reef fishes vulnerable to extinction by fishing. *Conserv. Biol.* 27 (3), 443–452.

Bromhead, D., Scholey, V., Nicol, S., Margulies, D., Wexler, J., Stein, M., Hoyle, S., Lennert-Cody, C., Williamson, J., Havenhand, J., Ilyina, T., 2015. The potential impact of ocean acidification upon eggs and larvae of yellowfin tuna (*Thunnus albacares*). *Deep-Sea Res. II Top. Stud. Oceanogr.* 113, 268–279.

Cabral, R.B., Mayorga, J., Clemence, M., Lynham, J., Koeshendrajana, S., Muawanah, U., Nugroho, D., Anna, Z., Ghofar, A., Zulbainaeni, N., Gaines, S.D., Costelle, C., 2018. Rapid and lasting gains from solving illegal fishing. *Nat. Ecol. Evol.* 2, 650–658.

Campbell, J.R., 2015. Development, global change and traditional food security in Pacific Island countries. Reg. Environ. *Chang.* 15 (7), 1313–1324.

Carson, M.T., Kurashina, H., 2012. Re-envisioning long-distance Oceanic migration: early dates in the Mariana Islands. *World Archaeol.* 44 (3), 409–435.

Chapman, M.D., 1985. Environmental influences on the development of traditional conservation in the South Pacific region. Environ. *Conserv.* 12 (3), 217–230.

Chapman, M.D., 1987. Traditional political structure and conservation in Oceania. *Ambio* 16 (4), 201–205.

Cheung, W.W., Reygondeau, G., Frölicher, T.L., 2016. Large benefits to marine fisheries of meeting the 1.5 C global warming target. *Science* 354 (6319), 1591–1594.

Cinner, J., 2005. Socioeconomic factors influencing customary marine tenure in the Indo-Pacific. *Ecol. Soc.* 10 (1).

Cinner, J.E., Aswani, S., 2007. Integrating customary management into marine conservation. *Biol. Conserv.* 140 (3–4), 201–216.

Cinner, J., Huchery, C., 2014. A comparison of social outcomes associated with different fisheries co-management institutions. *Conserv. Lett.* 7 (3), 224–232.

Cinner, J.E., Kittinger, J.N., 2015. Linkages between social systems and coral reefs. In: Mora, Camilo (Ed.), *Ecology of Fishes on Coral Reefs*. Cambridge University Press, Cambridge, UK, pp. 215–220.

Cinner, J., Marnane, M.J., McClanahan, T.R., Almany, G.R., 2006. Periodic closures as adaptive coral reef management in the Indo-Pacific. *Ecol. Soc.* 11 (1).

Cinner, J.E., McClanahan, T.R., MacNeil, M.A., Graham, N.A., Daw, T.M., Mukminin, A., Feary, D.A., Rabearisoa, A.L., Wamukota, A., Jiddawi, N., Campbell, S.J., 2012. Comanagement of coral reef social-ecological systems. *Proc. Natl. Acad. Sci.* 109 (14), 5219–5222.

Clarke, P., Jupiter, S.D., 2010. Law, custom and community-based natural resource management in Kubulau District (Fiji). Environ. *Conserv.* 37 (1), 98–106.

Colchester, M., 2004. Conservation policy and indigenous peoples. *Environ. Sci. Pol.* 7 (3), 145–153.

Colding, J., Folke, C., 2001. Social taboos: "invisible" systems of local resource management and biological conservation. *Ecol. Appl.* 11 (2), 584–600.

Corrin Care, J., Zorn, J.G., 2001. Legislating pluralism: statutory 'developments' in Melanesian customary law. *J. Leg. Pluralism Unofficial Law* 33 (46), 49–101.

Crowder, L.B., Osherenko, G., Young, O.R., Airamé, S., Norse, E.A., Baron, N., Day, J.C., Douvere, F., Ehler, C.N., Halpern, B.S., Langdon, S.J., 2006. Resolving mismatches in US ocean governance. *Science* 313 (5787), 617.

Dahl, A.L., 2017. Island conservation issues in international conventions and agreements. *Environ. Conserv.* 44 (3), 1–19.

De Mitcheson, Y.S., Cornish, A., Domeier, M., Colin, P.L., Russell, M., Lindeman, K.C., 2008. A global baseline for spawning aggregations of reef fishes. *Conserv. Biol.* 22 (5), 1233–1244.

Devillers, R., Pressey, R.L., Grech, A., Kittinger, J.N., Edgar, G.J., Ward, T., Watson, R., 2015. Reinventing residual reserves in the sea: are we favouring ease of establishment over need for protection? Aquat. Conserv. Mar. Freshwat. *Ecosyst.* 25 (4), 480–504.

Dunstan, P.K., Moore, B.R., Bell, J.D., Holbrook, N.J., Oliver, E.C., Risbey, J., Foster, S.D., Hanich, Q., Hobday, A.J., Bennett, N.J., 2018. How can climate predictions improve sustainability of coastal fisheries in Pacific Small-Island Developing States? *Mar. Policy* 88, 295–302.

FAO, 2016. Agreement on Port State Measures to Prevent, Deter, and Eliminate Illegal, Unreported and Unregulated Fishing. Food and Agriculture Organization of the United Nations, Roma, Italy.

Finney, B.R., 1977. Voyaging canoes and the settlement of Polynesia. *Science* 196, 1277–1285.

Foale, S., Manele, B., 2004. Social and political barriers to the use of marine protected areas for conservation and fishery management in Melanesia. *Asia Pacific Viewpoint* 45 (3), 373–386.

Foale, S., Cohen, P., Januchowski-Hartley, S., Wenger, A., Macintyre, M., 2011. Tenure and taboos: origins and implications for fisheries in the Pacific. *Fish.* 12 (4), 357–369.

Foale, S., Dyer, M., Kinch, J., 2016. The value of tropical biodiversity in rural Melanesia. *Valuation Studies* 4 (1), 11–39.

Friedlander, A.M., Ziemann, D.A., 2003. Impact of hatchery releases on the recreational fishery for Pacific threadfin (*Polydactylus sexfilis*) in Hawaii. *Fish. Bull.* 101 (1), 32–43.

Friedlander, A., Poepoe, K., Poepoe, K., Helm, K., Bartram, P., Maragos, J., Abbott, I., 2002. Application of Hawaiian traditions to community-based fishery management. In: Proceedings of the Ninth International Coral Reef Symposium, Bali, 23–27 October 2000, vol. 2. pp. 813–815.

Friedlander, A.M., Shackeroff, J.M., Kittinger, J.N., 2013. Customary marine resource knowledge and use in contemporary Hawai'i. *Pac. Sci.* 67 (3), 441–460.

Friedlander, A.M., Stamoulis, K.A., Kittinger, J.N., Drazen, J.C., Tissot, B.N., 2014. Understanding the scale of marine protection in Hawai'i: from community-based management to the remote Northwestern Hawaiian Islands. *Adv. Mar. Biol.* 69, 153–203 (Academic Press).

Friedlander, A.M., Wagner, D., Gaymer, C.F., Wilhelm, T.A., Lewis, N.A., Brooke, S., Kikiloi, K., Varmer, O., 2016. Co-operation between large-scale MPAs: successful experiences from the Pacific Ocean. *Aquat. Conserv. Mar. Freshwat. Ecosyst.* 26 (S2), 126–141.

Friedlander, A.M., Golbuu, Y., Ballesteros, E., Caselle, J.E., Gouezo, M., Olsudong, D., Sala, E., 2017. Size, age, and habitat determine effectiveness of Palau's Marine Protected Areas. *PLoS One* 12 (3), e0174787.

Gavin, M.C., McCarter, J., Mead, A., Berkes, F., Stepp, J.R., Peterson, D., Tang, R., 2015. Defining biocultural approaches to conservation. *Trends Ecol. Evol.* 30 (3), 140–145.

Gillett, R., 2009. *Fisheries in the Economies of the Pacific Island Countries and Territories.* Asian Development Bank.

Gillett, R., Cartwright, I., 2010. *The Future of Pacific Island Fisheries.* Secretariat of the Pacific Community, Noumea and the Forum Fisheries Agency, Honiara.

Gourlie, D., Davis, R., Govan, H., Marshman, J., Hanich, Q., 2018. Performing "A New Song": suggested considerations for drafting effective coastal fisheries legislation under climate change. *Mar. Policy* 88, 342–349.

Govan, H., 2015. *Preliminary Review of Public Expenditure of the Fisheries Agencies of Pacific Island Countries and Territories: Policy, Operational Budget and Staffing Support for Coastal Fisheries.* Report for Secretariat of the Pacific Community. FAME Division, Noumea. http://dx.doi.org/10.13140/RG.2.1.4949.9363. http://bit.ly/FishPEIR.

Govan, H., 2017. Ocean governance—our sea of islands. In: Katafono, R. (Ed.), *A Sustainable Future for Small States: Pacific 2050.* Commonwealth Secretariat, London (ISBN 978-1-84929-163-7).

Govan, H., et al., 2009. *Status and Potential of Locally-managed Marine Areas in the South Pacific: Meeting Nature Conservation and Sustainable Livelihood Targets Through Wide-spread Implementation of LMMAs.* SPREP/WWF/WorldFish-Reefbase/CRISP.

Govan, H., Kinch, J., Brjosniovschi, A., 2013. *Strategic Review of Inshore Fisheries Policies and Strategies in Melanesia-Fiji, New Caledonia, Papua New Guinea, Solomon Islands and Vanuatu-Part II:* Country Reports to the Secretariat of the Pacific Community for the Melanesian Spearhead Group, Noumea, New Caledonia. http://bit.ly/1dhIxv4.

Grantham, H.S., McLeod, E., Brooks, A., Jupiter, S.D., Hardcastle, J., Richardson, A.J., Poloczanska, E.S., Hills, T., Mieszkowska, N., Klein, C.J., Watson, J.E.M., 2011. Ecosystem-based adaptation in marine ecosystems of tropical Oceania in response to climate change. *Pac. Conserv. Biol.* 17 (3), 241–258.

Grorud-Colvert, K., Claudet, J., Tissot, B.N., Caselle, J.E., Carr, M.H., Day, J.C., Friedlander, A.M., Lester, S.E., De Loma, T.L., Malone, D., Walsh, W.J., 2014. Marine protected area networks: assessing whether the whole is greater than the sum of its parts. *PLoS One* 9 (8), e102298.

Gruby, R.L., Basurto, X., 2013. Multi-level governance for large marine commons: politics and polycentricity in Palau's protected area network. *Environ. Sci. Pol.* 33, 260–272.

Hanich, Q., Wabnitz, C.C., Ota, Y., Amos, M., Donato-Hunt, C., Hunt, A., 2018. Small-scale fisheries under climate change in the Pacific Islands region. *Mar. Policy* 279–284.

Helfman, G.S., Randall, J.E., 1972. Palauan fish names. *Pac. Sci.* 27 (2), 136–153.

Hickey, F.R., Johannes, R.E., 2002. Recent evolution of village-based marine resource management in Vanuatu. In: *SPC Traditional Marine Resource Management and Knowledge Information Bulletin.* 14. pp. 8–21.

Hoffmann, T.C., 2002. Coral reef health and effects of socio-economic factors in Fiji and Cook Islands. *Mar. Pollut. Bull.* 44 (11), 1281–1293.

Houk, P., Camacho, R., Johnson, S., McLean, M., Maxin, S., Anson, J., et al., 2015. The Micronesia Challenge: assessing the relative contribution of stressors on coral reefs to facilitate science-to-management feed-back. *PLoS One* 18, e0130823.

Hviding, E., 1998. Contextual flexibility: present status and future of customary marine tenure in Solomon Islands. *Ocean Coast. Manag.* 40, 253–269.

Johannes, R.E., 1978. Traditional marine conservation methods in Oceania and their demise. *Annu. Rev. Ecol. Syst.* 9 (1), 349–364.

Johannes, R.E., 1981. *Words of the Lagoon: Fishing and Marine Lore in the Palau District of Micronesia.* Univ of California Press.

Johannes, R.E., 1982. Traditional conservation methods and protected marine areas in Oceania. *Ambio* 11-5 (11), 258–261.

Johannes, R.E., 1989. Managing small-scale fisheries in Oceania: unusual constraints and opportunities. In: Campbell, H., Menz, K., Waugh, G. (Eds.), *Economics of Fisheries Management in the Pacific Islands Region.* Australian Centre for International Agricultural Research, Canberra, A.C.T., pp. 85–93.

Johannes, R.E., 1998a. The case for data-less marine resource management: examples from tropical nearshore finfisheries. *Trends Ecol. Evol.* 13 (6), 243–246.

Johannes, R.E., 1998b. Government-supported, village-based management of marine resources in Vanuatu. *Ocean Coast. Manag.* 40 (2–3), 165–186.

Johannes, R.E., 2002a. Did indigenous conservation ethics exist. In: *SPC Traditional Marine Resource Management and Knowledge Information Bulletin*, vol. 14. pp. 3–7.

Johannes, R.E., 2002b. The renaissance of community-based marine resource management in Oceania. *Annu. Rev. Ecol. Syst.* 33 (1), 317–340.

Johannes, R.E., MacFarlane, J.W., 1991. *Traditional Fishing in the Torres Strait Islands.* CSIRO Division of Fisheries, Marine Laboratories, Hobart, Tasmania.

Johannes, R.E., Yeeting, B., 2001. I-Kiribati knowledge and management of Tarawa's lagoon resources. *Atoll Res. Bull.* 489, 1–24.

Jupiter, S., 2017. Culture, kastom and conservation in Melanesia: what happens when worldviews collide? *Pac. Conserv. Biol.* 23 (2), 139–145.

Jupiter, S.D., Egli, D.P., 2011. Ecosystem-based management in Fiji: successes and challenges after five years of implementation. *J. Mar. Biol.* 2011.

Jupiter, S.D., Cohen, P.J., Weeks, R., Tawake, A., Govan, H., 2014. Locally-managed marine areas: multiple objectives and diverse strategies. *Pac. Conserv. Biol.* 20 (2), 165–179.

Kikiloi, K., Friedlander, A.M., Wilhelm, A., Lewis, N.A., Quiocho, K., 'Āila Jr., W., Kaho'ohalahala, S., 2017. Papahānaumokuākea: integrating culture in the design and management of one of the world's largest marine protected areas. *Coast. Manag.* 45 (6), 436–451.

Kittinger, J.N., Cinner, J.E., Aswani, S., White, A.T., 2014. Back to the future: integrating customary practices and institutions into comanagement of small-scale fisheries. In: Kittinger (Ed.), *Marine Historical Ecology in Conservation: Applying the Past to Manage for the Future*, pp. 135–160.

Kroodsma, D.A., Mayorga, J., Hochberg, T., Miller, N.A., Boerder, K., Ferretti, F., Wilson, A., Bergman, B., White, T.D., Block, B.A., Woods, P., 2018. Tracking the global footprint of fisheries. *Science* 359 (6378), 904–908.

Lal, B.V., Fortune, K. (Eds.), 2000. *The Pacific Islands: An Encyclopedia*. vol. 1 University of Hawaii Press.

Leenhardt, P., Cazalet, B., Salvat, B., Claudet, J., Feral, F., 2013. The rise of large-scale marine protected areas: conservation or geopolitics? *Ocean Coast. Manag.* 85, 112–118.

Levine, A., Richmond, L., 2014. Examining enabling conditions for community-based fisheries comanagement: comparing efforts in Hawai'i and American Samoa. *Ecol. Soc.* 19 (1).

McClenachan, L., Kittinger, J.N., 2013. Multicentury trends and the sustainability of coral reef fisheries in Hawai'i and Florida. *Fish Fish.* 14 (3), 239–255.

McMillen, H.L., Ticktin, T., Friedlander, A., Jupiter, S.D., Thaman, R., Campbell, J., Veitayaki, J., Giambelluca, T., Nihmei, S., Rupeni, E., Apis-Overhoff, L., 2014. Small islands, valuable insights: systems of customary resource use and resilience to climate change in the Pacific. *Ecol. Soc.* 19 (4).

Mills, M., Jupiter, S.D., Pressey, R.L., Ban, N.C., Comley, J., 2011. Incorporating effectiveness of community-based management in a national marine gap analysis for Fiji. *Conserv. Biol.* 25 (6), 1155–1164.

Muehlig-Hofmann, A., 2007. Traditional authority and community leadership: key factors in community-based marine resource management and conservation. In: *SPC Traditional Marine Resource Management and Knowledge Information Bulletin*, vol. 21. pp. 31–44.

O'Leary, B.C., Ban, N.C., Fernandez, M., Friedlander, A.M., García-Borboroglu, P., Golbuu, Y., Guidetti, P., Harris, J.M., Hawkins, J.P., Langlois, T., McCauley, D.J., 2018. Addressing criticisms of large-scale marine protected areas. *Bioscience* 68 (5), 359–370.

Petrossian, G.A., 2015. Preventing illegal, unreported and unregulated (IUU) fishing: a situational approach. *Biol. Conserv.* 189, 39–48.

Poepoe, K., Bartram, P., Friedlander, A., 2007. The use of traditional Hawaiian knowledge in the contemporary management of marine resources. In: Haggan, N., Neis, B., Baird, I. (Eds.), *Fishers' Knowledge in Fisheries Science and Management*. UNESCO, Paris, pp. 117–141.

Preston, G.L., 1993. Beche-de-mer. In: *Nearshore Marine Resources of the South Pacific: Information for Fisheries Development and Management*. Forum Fisheries Agency, Honiara, Solomon Islands, pp. 371–401.

Randall, J.E., Cea, A., 2011. *Shore Fishes of Easter Island*. University of Hawai'i Press.

Ruddle, K., 1988. Social principles underlying traditional inshore fishery management systems in the Pacific Basin. Mar. *Resour. Econ.* 5 (4), 351–363.

Ruddle, K., 1996. Traditional management of reef fishing. In: NVC, Pollunin, Roberts, C.M.P. (Eds.), *Reef Fisheries*. Springer, Netherlands, pp. 315–335.

Ruddle, K., Hickey, F.R., 2008. Accounting for the mismanagement of tropical nearshore fisheries. *Environ. Dev. Sustain.* 10 (5), 565–589.

Ruddle, K., Hviding, E., Johannes, R.E., 1992. Marine resources management in the context of customary tenure. *Mar. Resour. Econ.* 7 (4), 249–273.

Sand, C., 2002. Melanesian tribes vs. Polynesian chiefdoms: recent archaeological assessment of a classic model of sociopolitical types in Oceania. *Asian Perspect.* 41 (2), 284–296.

Schug, D., 2001. Hawaii's commercial fishing industry: 1820–1945. *Hawaii. J. Hist.* 35, 15–34.

Sheppard, P.J., Bedford, S., Bellwood, P., Burley, D.V., Chiu, S., Irwin, G., Kirch, P.V., Lilley, I., Matisoo-Smith, L., Pawley, A., Ross, M., 2011. Lapita colonization across the Near/Remote Oceania boundary. *Curr. Anthropol.* 52 (6), 799–840.

Sterling, E., Ticktin, T., Morgan, T.K.K., Cullman, G., Alvira, D., Andrade, P., Bergamini, N., Betley, E., Burrows, K., Caillon, S., Claudet, J., 2017a. Culturally grounded indicators of resilience in social-ecological systems. *Environ. Soc.* 8 (1), 63–95.

Sterling, E.J., Filardi, C., Toomey, A., Sigouin, A., Betley, E., Gazit, N., Newell, J., Albert, S., Alvira, D., Bergamini, N., et al., 2017b. Biocultural approaches to well-being and sustainability indicators across scales. *Nat. Ecol. Evol.* 1 (12), 1798.

Sumaila, U.R., Lam, V.W., Miller, D.D., Teh, L., Watson, R.A., Zeller, D., Cheung, W.W., Côté, I.M., Rogers, A.D., Roberts, C., Sala, E., 2015. Winners and losers in a world where the high seas is closed to fishing. *Sci. Rep.* 5, 8481.

Tainter, J.A., 2006. Archaeology of overshoot and collapse. *Annu. Rev. Anthropol.* 35, 59–74.

Thaman, K.H., 1993. Culture and the curriculum in the South Pacific. *Comp. Educ.* 29 (3), 249–260.

Titcomb, M., 1972. *Native use of fish in Hawai'i*. University of Hawai'i Press, Honolulu, Hawai'i.

Titcomb, M., 1978. Native use of marine invertebrates in old Hawaii. *Pac. Sci.* 32, 325–375.

Toonen, R.J., Wilhelm, T.A., Maxwell, S.M., Wagner, D., Bowen, B.W., Sheppard, C.R., Taei, S.M., Teroroko, T., Moffitt, R., Gaymer, C.F., Morgan, L., Lewis, N., Sheppard, A.L.S., Parks, J., Friedlander,

A.M., Big Ocean Think Tank, 2013. One size does not fit all: the emerging frontier in large-scale marine conservation. *Mar. Pollut. Bull.* 77 (1–2), 7–10.

UNEP-WCMC and IUCN, 2018. *Marine Protected Planet.* UNEP-WCMC and IUCN, Cambridge, UK Available at: www.protectedplanet.net (On-line, March, 2018).

Veitayaki, J., 2000. Fisheries resource-use culture in Fiji and its implications. In: Hooper, A. (Ed.), *Culture and Sustainable Development in the Pacific*, pp. 116–130.

Vierros, M., Tawake, A., Hickey, F., Tiraa, A., Noa, R., 2010. *Traditional Marine Management Areas of the Pacific in the Context of National and International Law and Policy.* United Nations University, Traditional Knowledge Initiative, Darwin, Australia.

Wamukota, A.W., Cinner, J.E., McClanahan, T.R., 2012. Co-management of coral reef fisheries: a critical evaluation of the literature. *Mar. Policy* 36 (2), 481–488.

Ward, R.G., 1972. The Pacific bêche-de-mer trade with special reference to Fiji. In: Ward, R.G. (Ed.), *Man in the Pacific Islands: Essays on Geographical Change in the Pacific Islands*, pp. 91–123.

Wedding, L.M., Reiter, S.M., Smith, C.R., Gjerde, K.M., Kittinger, J.N., Friedlander, A.M., Gaines, S.D., Clark, M.R., Thurnherr, A.M., Hardy, S.M., Crowder, L.B., 2015. Managing mining of the deep seabed. *Science* 349 (6244), 144–145.

Weeks, R., Jupiter, S.D., 2013. Adaptive comanagement of a marine protected area network in Fiji. *Conserv. Biol.* 27 (6), 1234–1244.

White, C., Costello, C., 2014. Close the high seas to fishing? *PLoS Biol.* 12 (3), e1001826.

Wilhelm, T.A., Sheppard, C.R., Sheppard, A.L., Gaymer, C.F., Parks, J., Wagner, D., Lewis, N., 2014. Large marine protected areas–advantages and challenges of going big. *Aquat. Conserv. Mar. Freshwat. Ecosyst.* 24 (S2), 24–30.

Reading 3.2

The New in the "New Normal" for the Post-Covid Pacific Islands

Richard Herr

F INDING A "NEW NORMAL" HAS BECOME a ubiquitous catchphrase expressing the hope that the instability and uncertainties of the Covid-19 pandemic will end soon. The concept describes either a temporary transitional state on the way back to an old pre-Covid normal or the altered reality of a transformed post-Covid order.

For the Pacific Community's 21 Pacific Island countries and territories (PICTs), their post-Covid options will be determined more by the choices made elsewhere than by their own preferences. Ironically, their new normal is likely to be business as usual for the PICTs. External influences have limited the extent to which they can control own their fate for centuries.

The course of the current pandemic illustrates this. The states of the region responded to the threat of infection in much the same way as responsible, larger states elsewhere and, in most cases, more swiftly. Most shut their borders, closed schools, imposed shelter-at-home regimes and quarantined the infected. And, at time of writing, these measures appear to have worked.

From the declaration of a pandemic, only six of the 21 PICTs (Commonwealth of the Northern Marianas (CNMI), Papua New Guinea (PNG), Fiji, French Polynesia, Guam, and New Caledonia) have had reportable cases with very few deaths. By May 27, just two–the CNMI and Guam–have had a case within the incubation period of 14 days. The other four have not had a reportable case within at least one, and most more than two, incubation periods.

Without minimizing the heroic efforts made by the PICTs, arguably much of this success would have been imposed on the region had the Islands not reacted. Travel across the region was cut off at source. Almost immediately flights into the region were cut to nothing and cruise ships stopped sailing. Quarantine on travelers at transit or entry points into the region discouraged using what access was available.

Richard Herr, "The New in the 'New Normal' for the Post-COVID Pacific Islands," *Asia-Pacific Bulletin*, no. 510, https://www.east-westcenter.org/publications/the-new-in-the-%E2%80%9Cnew-normal%E2%80%9D-the-post-covid-pacific-islands. Copyright © 2020 by East-West Center. Reprinted with permission.

Notwithstanding that the pandemic is first and foremost a health crisis, the PICTs' success with containing the health threat has made the collateral damage to their economies vastly more significant on the ground. Whereas extra regional actions tended to reinforce the region's health security, these same actions were significantly less supportive economically.

Travel and quarantine restrictions impacted on remittances and trade income while the pandemic-induced economic cutbacks undermined the demand for the region's exports. Reduced trade even threatened food security as many islands depend on imports for basic food stuffs.

The PICTs, Economic New Normal

The pandemic has hit the Island economies hard due to their high reliance on grants, tourism, and international trade. Job losses in the tourism sector are devastating for Fiji, Palau, and Vanuatu and significant for many others, especially states like Samoa and Tonga where "friends and relatives" visits help to keep the small connecting airline routes viable.

Virtually all PICTs have been obliged to pursue fiscal stimulus packages to address the domestic hardships of lost external income. Consequently, the IMF estimates that average public debt against GDP across the region has risen to a level that has undone three years of debt decline.

A new economic normal is the specific aid arrangements for meeting the cost of Covid. Bilateral sources including especially Australia and New Zealand and multilateral sources such ADB, IMF, and World Bank have made special pandemic financial support available to help maintain the Island economies. The G20 have announced a debt standstill to reduce the burden of loan repayments for this year. However, this is only transitional support as post-Covid support is far from guaranteed. Rising levels of debt in traditional aid sources are expected to make financial assistance tighter in future. A new post-Covid transitional normal will likely involve reprioritizing regional development goals.

An emergent transitional new economic normal is the search for a secure, contagion-free "bubble." This would enable eligible states to travel and trade almost as fully "as before." Australia and New Zealand have plans to create one between themselves, and Fiji has been lobbying for inclusion. Their current Covid status could make virtually all the other PICTs eligible. There are constraints on an Oceanic bubble, however. Samoa has put conditions on joining, which Fiji has found unacceptable. Other states may want reservations not acceptable to other participants in the proposed bubble. An economic question hangs over how large a bubble would have to be for viability.

The PICTs, Health New Normal

Covid-19 is the fifth virus epidemic this century (Zika-2015; MERS-2012; swine flu 2009 and SARS 2002). Medical authorities in the Pacific Islands therefore will hope inter alia there is a new normal in wider public appreciation of sanitation and social responsibility in dealing with disease. Other consequences may be less clear.

To date, Covid has not fully tested the medical resilience or the existing health security of the region. Despite initial concerns, major benefactors were able to rush medical equipment and supplies to the region to meet critical shortages. Donors were able to address the regional health crisis in a standard way notwithstanding the transport difficulties and closed borders. Use of the Pacific Islands Forum's 2018 Boe Declaration to establish "The Pacific Humanitarian Pathway on COVID-19" has been innovative. This project to provide aid "in a timely, safe, effective and equitable manner" could be a welcome transformational new normal especially were it necessary to triage priorities in a future overwhelming medical disaster. Clearing the backlog of deferred medical needs will be, unfortunately, a short-term post-Covid continuing normal. Regrettably, the important voluntary contributions NGOs such as Interplast make toward addressing regional needs will not necessarily restart immediately due to pent-up demand in their home countries. The pandemic may hasten upgrading the region's internet system to improve telehealth capacity and, ultimately, telemedicine. Rapid sharing of diagnostic information and advice across all the remote clinics and nursing stations in almost exclusively archipelagic region is vital at any time but essential in a pandemic. This would be a transformational new normal if the opportunity is seized.

Western fears that the PRC is using Covid-based "mask diplomacy" to shape a new geopolitical normal has been allayed substantially by the limited need for this aid. Sadly, by reinforcing local perceptions that no country gives humanitarian aid without an agenda, the debate itself diminishes the political returns from medical diplomacy for every donor.

Regardless of transitional and transformational "new normals," the pandemic has not changed the PICTs' view that the region's existential threat still remains climate change. That is not a new normal.

Reading 3.3

FIJI Water, Water Everywhere
Global Brands and Democratic and Social Injustice

Catherine Jones, Warwick E. Murray, and John Overton

O**VER RECENT DECADES, THE DEMAND FOR** bottled water has grown exponentially at the global scale. In the marketing of such products, discourses of purity and paradise have often been invoked. Marketed as a 'Taste of Paradise', FIJI Water has gained enormous international success as an ostensibly clean and green product. Celebrity endorsements—reaching as high as US President Barack Obama—have abounded, driven in part by the belief that the corporation is both environmentally and socially responsible. This paper describes and analyses the rise of FIJI water and critically assesses the sources and impacts of its economic success. It goes on to explore its local social and environmental impacts in the context of a country that has been subject to waves of democratic crises where the fate of the polity has been influenced by FIJI Water's actions. FIJI Water has come to assume the role of development trustee in the villages most affected by the growth in exports. The democratic crises in Fiji has given FIJI Water profound developmental influence, and this has brought both costs and benefits at the local socio-environmental scale.

Bottled water has become established as a global product associated with purity, health and, in many cases, prestige. Following on from the established success of European brands such as Perrier, Evian and San Pellegrino, FIJI Water[1] has gained much international success, especially in the US market. Celebrity endorsements—reaching as high as US President Barack Obama—have abounded, driven in part by the belief that the product originates from a tropical paradise and is produced in both environmentally and socially responsible ways. FIJI Water is regarded as a luxury bottled water product, commanding higher prices on the global market alongside European brands such as Perrier, well above less 'exotic' and geographically undefined bulk water products. At the macro-economic scale, the rapid and substantial growth of FIJI Water has brought undoubted substantial economic benefits to Fiji itself. This has occurred during a period of profound political, social and economic disruption and transformation. Achieving its most rapid growth in the 2000s, FIJI Water has become a central component in the Fijian export economy, providing much needed diversification away from traditional products including sugar and minerals. In the midst of political uncertainty, FIJI Water has risen to a position of significant influence economically and politically. The fate of the Fijian polity and economy has, at various points, been considerably influenced by the actions of this private corporation.

If the growth of FIJI Water has exacerbated the concentration of political and economic power at the national level, this is amplified substantially when analysis at the local scale is undertaken. This paper analyses the socio-economic and environmental impacts of the operation of FIJI Water in the Vatukaloko area. The corporation has gained a reputation for practising social responsibility and its presence in the area has had a range of positive impacts. The programmes it has put in place have seen it adopt a position akin to that of local authority or development trustee. However, a detailed analysis of these undertakings reveals dissatisfaction with their impacts at the local level and reveals significant tensions affecting the local political ecology and economy of productive and labour relations.

This paper is based on field research conducted in 2011 and interviews with members of the local communities (Farrelly and Nabobo-Baba, [14]). It also draws upon some of the critical public comment concerning FIJI Water that has appeared on a variety of online and published outlets. It argues that FIJI Water is an example of a Transnational Corporation (TNC) producing a niche product that thrives on the opportunities and spaces neoliberalism offers. Although the corporation has prospered in the global market and a range of positive outcomes have been felt in Fiji as a whole and the Vatukaloko villages in particular, a plethora of problems at a local scale have also been created. FIJI Water draws upon the 'exotic' nature of Fiji to differentiate its product in a competitive global market. Yet the places its imagery is founded upon appear to have received proportionally low benefits. The exploitation of local society and environment has both perpetuated and been perpetuated by contextual democratic crises.

Through this case study, we investigate the implications and impacts of and for democracy in the creation and appropriation of surplus value through the exploitation of the geographical provenance of water (its geographical source) and its putative exotic origins. Furthermore, we ask what are the different roles and interactions amongst private capital, the state, and customary owners of the resource? And, what processes build or undermine democratic participation in the use and exploitation of this water resource? The paper begins with an outline of both the economic and political context of the rise of the company and product. It then assesses the local impacts, both socio-economic and environmental, before returning to analyse the relationship between neoliberalism and democracy.

Neoliberalism and Bottled Water: The Rise of FIJI Water

FIJI Water is derived, bottled and shipped from Fiji. The water is extracted from an artesian aquifer in the Yaqara Valley on Fiji's main island, Viti Levu. FIJI Water has promoted its water as 'untouched', 'every drop is green' and 'unspoiled by the compromised air of the 21st century'. Bottles of the product tell a story of how the water 'fell as rain hundreds of years before the Industrial Revolution ... filtering through volcanic rock ... This natural process added silica, a mineral which contributes to FIJI Water's unique soft mouth feel'. Therefore, a relatively basic commodity has been 'linked to an "exotic" place, and sold to elite consumers, as a form of cultural capital' (Connell [10]: 342). FIJI Water has emerged successfully in the 'designer water wars' and has been hailed as the 'vogue' product of the bottled water industry (Niman, [27]).

The company began in 1995 when Canadian hotelier David Gilmour founded and established Natural Waters of Viti Ltd (Kaplan, [22]). Gilmour began the operation when he noticed that clients at his hotels were often drinking imported water when he believed that a unique local source could be found in Fiji that would provide a marketable variety (Connell, [10]; McMaster and Nowak, [24]). With geologists from his mining company (Barrick Gold), Gilmour located a borehole in the Yaqara Valley in the Ra province. Gilmour managed to convince the Fijian government to turn the borehole into a business venture and in 1995 was granted a 99-year lease of 20 acres (Connell, [10]). To further entice Gilmour, Fiji offered favourable business conditions in line with the country's neoliberal framework that included 'access to cheap and temporary labour, corporate-friendly laws and policies such as tax breaks, tax-holidays and subsidies, and unregulated access to abundant natural resources' (Ulrich, [39]: 9). Gilmour then sold the company for a reported US$63 million to American billionaires Stewart and Lynda Resnick (owners of Roll International Corporation) who also owned other water-based industries in New Zealand and USA in addition to large businesses such a Teleflora and POM Wonderful (*The Sydney Morning Herald*, [37]).

FIJI Water has since grown to become a recognised international brand in the highly competitive bottled water industry and has been valued at over US$35billion (Reddy & Singh, [33]). Figure [NaN] illustrates the growth of this export trade which began in the late 1990s.

Mineral water has become one of Fiji's leading exports. In 2014, exports of mineral water amounted to F$186.3 million, second behind sugar at $F201.4 million and ahead of both garments, gold and timber products. Sugar and tourism still account for a much greater share of national income, but mineral water has clearly risen in influence. FIJI Water itself experienced a brief decline in sales in 2009 following the global financial crisis but has now recovered (Lenzer, [23]). Elite pricing has played a role in this. In 2013, in the UK, litre sold for £1.95 a litre, in Australia AUS$5, in the USA at US$3.90 and in Fiji at FJD$3.50—'significantly more than you would pay for the same amount of milk, beer, petrol or even Evian' (Daye and Van Auken, [11]). Such premiums on price in Fiji and internationally communicate exclusivity, amplifying brand equity and delivering large operating profits (Ritson, [34]).

The USA is the company's dominant market. In 2008 alone, the USA collectively consumed US$8.6 billion worth of bottled water, with FIJI Water taking part of this ever-growing water industry (Royte, [35]). Connell ([10]) noted that over 97% of FIJI Water was exported internationally with 90% of this figure sent to the USA. FIJI Water was launched in the US market at an opportune time, coinciding 'with the rapidly changing consumer preferences' (McMaster and Nowak, [25]: 5).

Over the past 10 years, new markets for FIJI Water have been evolving. The product is now exported to over 40 countries worldwide (FIJI Water, [15]). Following the success in the U.S., 'FIJI Water has expanded to Canada and the Caribbean, where the brand's iconic square bottle is increasingly visible at leading on-premise and retail establishments' (Ely, [13], n.p.). Asia is a relatively new market for FIJI Water. In recent years, the company designed new bottles to appeal specifically to the Asian market. Instead of the cascading waterfall feature, the bottles for this new market featured a silhouette of a fern with single a hibiscus flower. Today, the product can be found in cafes, restaurants and supermarkets in Taiwan, Singapore, Hong Kong and Japan (Tabureguci, [38]). In the United Kingdom, FIJI Water is now a common sight in high-end department stores such as Selfridges, Waitrose, and Harrods. Yet FIJI Water received negative publicity in the United Kingdom particularly through BBC ([1]) documentary *Panorama: Bottled Water—Who Needs It?* Partly, as a consequence, the company increased its promotional campaigns in the United Kingdom, partnering with organisations such as London Elite Model Management and Le Cool London. By 2009 the company had regained its position and was exporting over 1.1 million litres to the UK (FIJI Water, [15]).

Thus, the success of FIJI Water in a macroeconomic sense is hard to refute. It has brought employment, export returns and global visibility to the Fijian economy. It has assisted in diversifying that economy away from sugar, tourism and minerals, and latterly remittances. Supported by the government, through generous tax packages (see below), this private company has branded, packaged and promoted a niche product and extracted considerable surplus value from the supposed unique environmental characteristics and water quality of a particular location in Fiji. Because of its apparent unique qualities, and the creation of a fictive place by the company (Overton and Murray, [30]), the brand has been able to compete on the basis of quality as opposed to price or economies of scale.

Democracy, Land and Bottled Water: The Rise of FIJI Water

The story of FIJI Water reveals a complex interplay of political factors behind the economic success identified in the previous section. Here, it is necessary to explain and analyse the various roles of three key parties: local landowners, the state and FIJI Water itself.

Some 87% of Fiji's land (and arguably the natural resources contained therein) is vested in customary collective ownership, primarily in clans known as mataqali. Mataqali ownership is strictly protected by law, and land cannot be alienated into private ownership, although leasing arrangements do allow individuals and companies to gain use rights to land and resources for periods of between 33 and 99 years. This system of customary ownership has been contentious and heavily politicised. Neoliberal advocates have argued that such land should be opened and privatised, allowing for a new land market and the wider use of rural credit (using individualised land titles as collateral). On the other hand, Fijian nationalists have strongly asserted indigenous land rights, even arguing for the end of many leases. In addition, there is friction between state and customary owners over the management of 'native lands' and between the chiefly elite and ordinary mataqali owners over the distribution of rent incomes (Ward and Kingdon [40]; Overton, [28]; Tokelau, [8]). Yet despite these conflicts and disagreements, customary land tenure provides a recognised mechanism for sharing the benefits of customary land/resources exploitation: chiefs and commoners share incomes, even if disproportionately. There are protocols for negotiation (through mechanisms such as sevusevu), and there is an expectation of continued relationships (Ravuvu, [32]). Such protocols are relatively participatory, even if chiefs have most influence.

The concept of vanua underpins all this: vanua sees 'land' as an holistic concept, representing all elements of the physical environment, together with its customary inhabitants (past and present). In a cultural sense in Fiji, then, vanua and the tenure system that is associated with it provide a system for the participatory and (even if not conventionally) democratic management of resources that, in theory, is sustainable and collective (Batibasaqa et al. [3]).

In the case of FIJI Water's operation, the underlying ownership of the artesian water is clear: members of the local mataqali located in three villages in Ra 'own' the land and its water. This is protected by law and inalienable, but the customary owners have the right to negotiate use rights. In this context, David Gilmour, as the early founder of FIJI Water, proved to be sensitive to local ownership and protocols and took time to establish a relationship with local communities. He promised continuing contact, employment, and a range of local projects and funding in addition to rental payments. Even after the lease was granted, it seemed that he kept largely to his word, and relations with the villages were more or less harmonious. They were not to remain so after the new owners—who had no experience of living and working in Fiji—took over in 2004.

Whilst customary tenure and protocols provide one layer that enables people to participate in the control and use of resources in Fiji, the state provides another layer, which has proved to be more contestable. Fiji was a British colony from 1874 to 1970. Its independence, and complex constitutional arrangements, led to the development of a political system that attempted to balance the interests of its two main ethnic groups (indigenous Fijians, and Fijians of Indian origin). In practice, there was early political dominance by indigenous Fijians (despite being roughly equal in size to the Indian population) and also effective control by a Fijian elite who combined customary chiefly status with economic activity and wealth.

What had seemed a reasonably stable and successful political system following independence in 1970 fell apart in the 1980s. When the ruling party, led by Ratu Mara, was defeated in an election by a coalition of a new left-leaning Labour Party and the established (largely Indian) National Federation Party in 1987, a military coup was staged. This toppled the new government and largely returned the old Fijian guard. During the following 20 years, there was considerable instability, involving a second coup in 1987 (to stymie a partial restoration of democratic government), a new constitution in 1997 (which further entrenched the indigenous Fijian political dominance established in the 1990 constitution), a Fijian-dominated government, followed by a change and a further coup in 2000. This coup eventually led to another election and a government led by Laisenia Qarase. The Qarase government, as with most regimes in Fiji during the 1990s, embraced neoliberal reform, with deregulation, incentives for foreign investment and active promotion of an export-led economy. Yet the democratic credentials of the Qarase government were questioned. It was elected under a constitution which gave preference to indigenous Fijians, it sought to pardon the perpetrators of the 2000 coup who had overthrown the previous (democratically elected) Fiji Labour government and there are frequent accusations that the government was mired in corruption and cronyism.

It was in this political environment that FIJI Water developed, following its founding in 1997. The Fijian state encouraged and supported the granting of a lease to the company, and it further granted it a 13-year tax holiday. Clearly, the Fijian state was keen to promote this icon of its neoliberal strategy. The Fijian state, however, soon changed. Following a long-simmering dispute between Qarase and the leader of the Fijian military forces, Commodore Frank Bainimarama, the latter eventually staged a coup, dismissing Qarase and installing himself as Prime Minister in December 2006. Bainimarama sought to make major constitutional changes, such as reversing ethnic Fijian hegemony, but he proved reluctant to hand back power to a civilian government until 2014 when his party won the election. He also proved unwilling to accept many of the agreements made by the previous regime. One of these involved FIJI Water. The Bainimarama government targeted the tax-free status of the company and soon moved to impose export duties. The company resisted and laid-off staff at the end of 2008. Although the government backed down, it tried again in 2010 to impose a 15% per litre duty and it also deported the company's director of external affairs. The company responded by shutting down its operations but the government and held firm. The company eventually accepted the new tax and reopened (Gino et al., [17]).

This episode revealed an interesting aspect of the non-democratic nature of the Fijian state between 2006 and 2014. The Qarase government had been elected but was clearly pro-business and, although ostensibly pro-indigenous Fijian, was content to see local land-owners do deals with foreign capital and grant long leases. On the other hand, the military regime, patently undemocratic, was not a strong champion of local customary ownership (although it has not dismantled it and the associated legal framework), but its battles with the company have shown that it has a key role in preserving local interests and controlling corporate capital. In a perverse way, it secured a more even distribution of the benefits of the highly profitable FIJI Water operation, through much increased taxes, than the previous supposed democratic state. In 2014, Fiji returned to democracy with a new constitution and Bainimarama as Prime Minister heading the Fiji First party to a clear majority in an election that was deemed free and fair by a range of external observers.

Thus, we have seen a complex interplay of political relationships and interactions amongst indigenous customary landowners, the Fijian state and FIJI Water. The FIJI Water has changed from the early Gilmour days of a locally connected and communicative operation to one that is characterised by remote overseas control, insistence on contracts rather than relationships, and a willingness to confront the state. In turn, the Fijian state has swung from one regime to another, none fully democratic, and from strong neoliberalism to more assertive economic nationalism and a willingness to confront capital. Yet whilst capital and the state have been in conflict, the local mataqali owners have been increasingly marginalised, both from participation in the company and its promised benefits, and from control over their resources, as we will see below.

The Local Social, Economic and Environmental Impacts of FIJI Water

Because FIJI Water is in rural Fiji, its everyday operations have had a direct impact on the dynamics of local communities that surround the plant, in particular on the Vatukaloko villages. On balance, the effects the outcomes have been primarily negative; here, we focus on the social and economic tensions.

Local Social Impacts

As Banks ([2]: 48) suggests: 'one of the most destructive social processes for local communities associated with large-scale resource extraction is in-migration of workers, contractors and others to the areas around the projects'. This has been the scenario in Vatukaloko. FIJI Water has increasingly hired outsiders to work in the water-bottling plant, commonly from urban centres such as Suva or, in the case of white-collar employees, expatriates from the USA, Australia and New Zealand. These outsiders live within or on the fringes of the Vatukaloko villages. The bottling plant itself presents a physical manifestation of the separation of Fijians and outsiders.: although on the road to the villages, it is surrounded by high fences and security gates. Visitors do not appear to be welcome. Not only have 'outsiders' restructured the social geography of the Vatukaloko, but the new wealth injected into the communities through employment and charity initiatives has arguably transformed traditional social hierarchies. In the Vatukaloko villages, the traditional Fijian custom of communalism—kerekere (sharing, giving and reciprocity)—is the foundation of the village's social framework. Because of the communal nature of the villages, those who receive benefits from FIJI Water are expected to contribute more to society, but one interviewee claimed that FIJI Water has arguably targeted an elite circle outside of these traditional bounds 'who do not share their income' (Pers. Comm. June, 2011). By facilitating this divide according to wealth, FIJI Water has indirectly facilitated the infusion of individualism into the Vatukaloko villages, as prior to FIJI Water, the Vatukaloko villages relied on subsistence farming and the kerekere system to sustain and frame their livelihood.

In an attempt to improve the welfare and development of the Vatukaloko villages, FIJI Water has provided assistance via through two main channels: the FIJI Water Foundation and Vatukaloko Trust Fund (VTF). Project aid in the Vatukaloko villages primarily came in the form of physical materials. Accordingly electricity infrastructure and water tanks were funded and built by FIJI Water. Yet, whilst such 'development' was well intentioned, there appeared to be little thought given to long-term sustainability. The projects required local responsibility for on-going maintenance and the up-skilling of the Vatukaloko residents. As local skills and associated financial costs to sustain these services were unavailable, residents have relied on FIJI Water for the costs of up-keep. Whilst in some ways this situation is a bonus for the village, it also perpetuates a dependent rellationship.

Local Economic Impacts

Most explicitly FIJI Water's economic presence has been felt through the VTF. FIJI Water, in its 'effort to secure the traditional blessing and support of the Vanua Vatukaloko, verbally agreed with the former Tui Vatu and Elders in 1996 that it will (i) contract for paid ancillary services and (ii) grant a royalty to assist with village developments' (Pers. Comm. June, 2011). However, this arrangement ceased in 2006, despite FIJI Water publically claiming that the fund was regionally active until 2008 (FIJI Water, [15]). Since the fund's termination, it has become controversial. On one hand, a local legal representative suggested: FIJI Water thought it appropriate, again without consulting the Vanua, to cancel the business contract that was granted to the Vatukaloko Trust Fund ab initio. This led to the company becoming bankrupt and all its assets repossessed by the Merchants Bank of Fiji and sold to pay for its debts. However, there is still balance in the debts (Pers. Comm. June, 2011).

Conversely, it was also argued that the Vanua 'misused the fund which caused FIJI Water to back out of the agreement' (Pers. Comm. June, 2011). Therefore, it was suggested that the fund had 'gone bankrupt' and 'the committee, they misused the money [...] they robbed' (Pers. Comm. June, 2011). There is clearly a deeply rooted and unresolved tension created by this infusion of wealth.

The local labour pool has become dependent on FIJI Water for employment. In 2008 and 2010, this vulnerability was highlighted when the company made the majority of staff redundant as a result of disputes with the Fijian government. When the company made many Vatukaloko locals redundant, it also promised to re-hire them once the recession eased and production increased again. However, Fiji Water 'never recruit[ed] them back'; instead, the company decided to seek more educated individuals from outside the Vatukaloko communities (Drauniivi Tagane Focus Group, Pers. Comm. June, 2011). Despite FIJI Water claiming that they provide 'sustainable business enterprises' for locals, the villages have often been the first to bear the consequences of the rift. With such rapid and extreme changes in employment, lifestyle pressures in the local villages are inevitable. During these two episodes of redundancies, many local employees who lost their income, and thus their ability to provide for their families, and reverted to subsistence livelihoods or working as manual harvesters for Indo-Fijian sugar farmers. Loss of employment was not the only problem for the villagers. The work itself did not seem to offer a high degree of skills enhancement, as locals employed by the company primarily carried out manual labour with limited opportunities for capacity building.

FIJI Water's success has prompted the Vatukaloko people to open their own bottled water plants. Local residents have discovered that they can access the same aquifer used by FIJI Water, which is outside the land leased by the company. Since this discovery, there has been increased interest from Chinese and Japanese companies. Indeed, the ability to tap into the same aquifer as FIJI Water has caused concern for the company. In 2010, David Roth (Director of External Affairs of FIJI Water) was expelled from Fiji, accused of interfering with Fiji's domestic affairs and suppressing investment by other companies (Pers. Comm. June, 2011).

Democratic Crisis and Social Injustice—the Broader Scalar Impacts of FIJI Water

There is no need for us to have bottled water, there is no need there, it somehow represents a distortion of needs, the manufacturing of wants, the illustration of gross inequalities in the world (BBC, [1]).

Beneath the glamorous image of the company promoted by its advertising, studies have increasingly questioned several activities by FIJI Water. Niman ([27]) argued that FIJI Water optimises the auto-destructive logic of consumerism. Despite FIJI Water's CEO Lynda Resnick claims that her brand is 'transparent, authentic and honest', criticisms of the company fall into five categories: the environment, advertising, tax recall, support for a dictatorship, and local ethical concerns.

An 'Environmental Nightmare'?

FIJI Water's environmental management has been questioned (Gino et al [16]; Bloxham [6]). The principle area of concern relates to the 'environmental nightmare' embedded into the production of each bottle of FIJI Water (Quraishi, [31]). High-grade plastic is used to make the bottles and is transported from China to Fiji. When the empty plastic bottles reach Fiji, they are filled with water at the company's bottling plant in the Yaqara Valley, which relies on diesel electricity generation. The bottles are then packed into cardboard boxes, loaded onto trucks, and transported to a sea cargo terminal in Lautoka. On reaching the port, the bottled water is shipped to the US Pacific Coast. On arrival the bottles are trucked to consumers across the continent. Thus, the image of a clean, pure and natural product is tarnished by a reality of heavy fossil fuel use in bottling, packaging and transport to market. In total: Fiji Water's carbon footprint (a measure of the exclusive global amount of carbon dioxide (CO_2) and other greenhouse gases emitted over the full life cycle of a product or service) was 85,396 tonnes CO_2eq in the base year 2006–2007 for all bottles produced. 72 percent of those emissions came from manufacturing raw materials, bottling and ocean freight. Overall, the average energy cost to make the plastic, fill the bottle, transport it to market and then deal with the waste would be like filling up a quarter of every bottle with oil (Lenzer, [23]).

FIJI Water's annual water extraction rate has also come under scrutiny from environmentalists. It has been estimated that the level of extraction is 'around 55 million litres of water annually' (Pers. Comm. May 2011). FIJI Water claims that this extraction rate is sustainable (FIJI Water, [15]). Despite this assurance, environmentalists argue that the company's extraction rate is 'environmentally degrading' and 'ethically questionable' (Lenzer, [23]). The BBC ([1]) documentary *Panorama: Bottled Water* revealed that the Fijian government was also concerned about FIJI Water's scale of operation, with government official Malaka Finau expressing concern over the potential loss of the aquifer. Accordingly, FIJI Water's mass extraction has been accused of being an: unsustainable business model because this water is an almost non-renewable resource, I say almost because while groundwater is theoretically replaceable it would take centuries to replenish the supply. And whose problem will it be once the fresh water is inevitably depleted? (Justine, [20], n.p.).

In a 2003 interview FIJI Water's past CEO, David Gilmour, advised the London Times that: 'the world's water is being trashed day by day' (Lenzer [23]). Yet, Gilmour also owned Barrick Gold, a Fijian mining company that uses billions of gallons of water to produce gold via a toxic cyanide leaching process (Lenzer, [23]). The company's practices are so damaging that after an environmental review, the Norwegian government announced in 2012 that it would divest itself of approximately US$200 million in Barrick stock. These activities and Gilmour's past neglect for the environment have generated many questions pertaining to FIJI Water's green ethic: We're being sold a fantasy. A moment in Fiji. A Taste of Fiji. But the insane reality is we're shipping water across an ocean and continent, to a region that already has the world's most abundant reserves of some of the best water on the planet. This behaviour is killing the planet. And the places our designer water comes from, such as Fiji [...] are among the most vulnerable environments susceptible to the ravages of global warming (Niman, [27], n.p.).

Since the above accusations have been made, FIJI Water has scrambled to reinvent its image for the environmentally conscious. In addition to its environmental charity work, in 2008 FIJI Water launched a US$5 million promotional campaign to become carbon negative by 2010 through reducing its packaging size and exploring various recycling opportunities (FIJI Water, [15], Lenzer, [23]). To achieve this, FIJI Water committed to meeting three specific targets: reduce CO_2 emissions by 25%, source 50% of its energy from renewable sources by 2010, and invest in reforestation and renewable energy projects (Ulrich, [39] and FIJI Water, [15]). FIJI Water hoped that these techniques would silence an ever-growing network of protests against the company. However, environmentalists and critics have seen this tactic as a rather egregious example of greenwashing.

This accusation of greenwashing was further heightened in a lawsuit against the company's deceptive 'carbon-negative' strategy. The lawsuit, headed by American Desiree Worthington, accused FIJI Water 'of using a practice known as "forward crediting": essentially giving yourself credit for carbon reductions that haven't happened yet' (Quraishi, [31], n.p.). Worthington argued that she paid more for the product because she expected the company to already be carbon-negative. However, under the 'forward crediting model, the offsets do not need to be currently occurring; they can simply be anticipated actions' (ibid). Scott J. Ferrell, who led the counsel for the class-action suit said: We want Fiji Water to stop distorting its environmental record to push sales of overpriced bottled water. It is unconscionable for Fiji Water to charge double the price of its competitors by convincing consumers that drinking Fiji Water helps the environment, when in reality the opposite is true (Quraishi, [31], n.p.).

Advertising

FIJI Water plays heavily on tourism stereotypes of Fiji. Whilst some elements of Fiji fit FIJI Water's clichéd tropical theme, the company is actually located in the Fijian highlands. The company suggests that it's location is far from 'farms [that would] compromise our water's purity'; however, FIJI Water is not from a source surrounded by a tropical rainforest or the sort of coastal or floral environments evident on their packaging; rather it is located on an old pastoral farm, surrounded by the Kauvadra mountain range which has experienced years of deforestation. Consequently, FIJI Water's glamorous packaging bears little resemblance to the environmental reality that at its source point.

FIJI Water has also pursued rival bottlers who use the country's name (Fiji) for marketing purposes. The FIJI (in capitals) name along with its associated pristine imagery has been trademarked by FIJI Water in numerous countries, including the United States (Deskins, [12]). Aqua Pacific owner Mohammed Altaaf has been vocal regarding this suppression, suggesting: 'it would have cost too much money for us to fight in court [over the brand]; it's just like branding a water 'American Water' and denying anyone else the right to use the name America' (Lenzer, [23]). FIJI Water has trademarked the 'FIJI' name and ironically 'We are FIJI' appears on their advertisements and posters across the island.

'Puts Lipstick on a Junta'

FIJI Water has come under criticism from Lenzer ([23]), who alleged that the company assisted in legitimising Fiji's military-led government that ruled the country from 2006 to 2014. FIJI Water has argued that it has no responsibility for the political situation in Fiji. The company was established in 1990s, long before the coups, and it has affirmed that it 'cannot and will not speak for the government and we [FIJI Water] will not back down from our commitment to the people, development, and communities of Fiji' (Bauerlein and Jeffery, [4], n.p.).

Other critics, however, have slated Lenzer's ([23]) allegation, and in turn have suggested that the relationship between the company and the government is unpredictable. Such debates have been centred on FIJI Water's US Executive David Roth being deported from Fiji in 2010 for allegedly interfering in the nation's domestic affairs. Callick ([9], n.p.) reported on the issue noting: Speaking from China, Commodore Frank Bainimarama said American

David Roth 'had been acting in a manner prejudicial to good governance and public order by interfering in the domestic affairs and governance of Fiji [...] It is unfortunate that David Roth saw it fit to engage in activities outside of his work-permit conditions,' he said, but he did not explain the nature of such actions (Callick, [9]).

Thus, the charge that FIJI Water has supported the military dictatorship in Fiji is questionable at best. Indeed, the opposite seems to have been the case. Friction between the company and the Fiji state, however, has arisen not because of any moral or democratic stance on the part of the company with regard to politics, but rather because the Fiji authorities have sought to regulate the company and renegotiate its concessions.

Tax Recall

A factor behind the early profitability of FIJI Water was its 13-year tax-free status granted by the Fijian government. Keen to attract direct foreign investment, the Fijian government granted FIJI Water a 13-year tax-free period from 1995 to 2008. [It was a fair deal] as far as I'm concerned, especially with the corporate tax arrangements, a policy that was to boost foreign investment into the country, and David Gilmour started up FIJI Water and FIJI Water became big, they have fixed market which is great for them, they got tax concession here, the only tax to our government was with duties and shipping duties and so forth, the levies are also laid-off when they bring in the large equipment, they really facilitated FIJI Water to go global (Pers. Comm. June 2011).

Therefore, FIJI Water was granted relatively free and unregulated access to one of Fiji's purest water sources. Once the tax-free deal terminates, companies are expected to conform to a normal taxation regime. For FIJI Water, this exclusive deal was scheduled to expire in 2008, and the Fijian government planned to increase FIJI Water's export duty from FJD$0.008 to FJD$0.20 per litre. However, FIJI Water refused to comply (Lenzer, [23]). The company called the tax a 'draconian' measure, and this resulted in various legal cases, impounded shipments and an industry-wide shutdown of FIJI Water. To generate animosity towards the government's decision, the company took out advertisements in national media suggesting that local communities would be badly impacted. The government relented. But in December 2010 it imposed a duty, less than the original figure, at FJD$0.15 per litre for all companies extracting over 3.5 million litres of water per annum (Government of Fiji, [18]). Bottlers who extract less than 3.5 million litres are only expected to pay FJD$0.011 per litre, a move intended to incentivise smaller bottlers. FIJI Water felt discriminated against and decided, once again, to close production: This new tax is untenable and, as a consequence, FIJI Water is left with no choice but to close our facility in Fiji, effective Monday, Nov. 29, 2010. We are saddened that we have been forced to make a business decision that will result in hardship to hundreds of Fijians who will now be without work. We consider the government's current action as a taking of our business, and one that sends a clear and unmistakable message to businesses operating in Fiji or looking to invest there: The country is increasingly unstable, and is becoming a very risky place in which to invest (Schwartz, [36], n.p.).

In the wake of the 'closure announcement, Bainimarama issued a stinging statement—and his first public attack on the company—as usual, Fiji Water has adopted tactics that demonstrate that Fiji [sic] Water does not care about Fiji or Fijians' (Lenzer, [23], n.p.). Consequently, 'an interesting game of chicken' ensured between the government and FIJI Water (Kahn, [21]). The Resnicks threatened to shift production to their backup hydration source in Tai Tapu, New Zealand, whilst Bainimarama threatened to sell the acquifer to another company, and 'international tenders [would be invited] credible and reputable private sector companies [based in China and Japan] to extract this valuable resource' (Lenzer, 2010, n.p.). In response to this threat, FIJI Water soon announced its intention to resume operations and accept the new tax levy: FIJI Water will re-open its bottling plant, effective Wednesday morning, Dec. 1 2010, at its regular start up time of 8 a.m. Through our discussions, we have also agreed to comply with Fiji's new water tax law. Moving forward, FIJI Water is committed to working with the Fijian government, and remains dedicated to helping the country's economy and its people (FIJI Water, [15], n.p.).

With the Water Resource Tax imposed, Fiji earned over FJD$78 million in revenue within the first four months of 2011 from local bottled water companies (Jones [19]). In comparison, the total amount in water taxes collected in 2009 and 2010 was only FJD$ 295000 and FJD$469000, respectively.

Conclusions

They don't have a tonne of options for economic development, but bottled water is one of them. When someone buys a bottle of FIJI Water, they're buying prosperity for the country. Without FIJI Water, Fiji is kind of screwed (Thomas Mooney, Senior Vice Present of FIJI Water in Lenzer, [23], n.p.).

FIJI Water, it has been argued, is operating a 'Reverse Robin-Hood effect' (Borg and Borg, [7]) where the company has reaped the rewards of its economic success at the expense of Fiji's local economy, society and environment. This paper has argued that, on balance, FIJI Water's impact on the Vatukaloko villages has been primarily negative. Whilst there have been benefits, the narratives of Vatukaloko residents attest to problems concerning Westernisation, greenwashing, aidwashing, vulnerability and dependency. These problems have overtones of neocolonialism whereby FIJI Water has indirectly occupied the local space and pursued its own interests. In some ways, it has replaced the functions of the Fijian government. But as Banks ([2]: 44) suggests, the triple relationship between the government, the private company and local communities' is 'massively complicated' (see also Bebbington et al, [5]). As such, it involves a rescaling of democracy and an erosion of social justice

The global success of FIJI Water can be traced back to Fiji's adoption of export orientation as recommended in the 1990s and adopted by the Rabuka regime of the late 1980s and early 1990s as a means of attracting foreign investment (Murray, [26]; Overton [29]). Fiji reduced trading barriers, accepted privatisation and embraced free trade. In this context, FIJI Water was offered a 13-year tax amnesty and unregulated access to the aquifer in the Yaqara Valley to support the growth of its business. These benefits in combination with the company's lucrative marketing campaign created the springboard for FIJI Water's global success. This campaign incorporated four main elements: endorsements, tropical discourses, health benefits and philanthropy. With these marketing strategies, FIJI Water has successfully capitalised on the natural topography and character of the Fijian Islands, portraying an image of purity, luxury and ethicality. This marketing strategy has been a key driver for FIJI Water's global success, enabling the product to be available and consumed across the world. Evidently, unlike previous niche market export endeavours from the Pacific region that failed to gain international recognition and economic success, FIJI Water has thrived.

Whilst FIJI Water has achieved global economic success, simultaneously considerable public commentary and literature has emerged critiquing the ethical nature of the company. Although FIJI Water has prospered in the global market and a range of positive outcomes with some positive economic benefits have been felt in the villages, a plethora of problems at a local scale have also been created. FIJI Water draws upon the constructed 'exotic' nature of Fiji to differentiate its product in a competitive global market. Yet, the places its imagery is founded upon appear to have received proportionally low benefits. As a consequence, there has been an erosion of social justice and rescaling of democracy which has seen power shift away from local labourers and residents.

Note

1   FIJI Water (capitalised FIJI) is a registered trademark.

References

1   BBC (2008) *Bottled water—Who needs it*? Panorama, documentary. London: BBC One.
2   Banks, G. (2009) Activities in extractive industries in Asia and the Pacific: Implications for development, *Transnational Corporations* 18 (1): 43–60.

3   Batibasaqa, K., J. Overton and P. Horsley (1999) Vanua: Land, people and culture in Fiji, in J. Overton and R. Scheyvens (eds.), *Strategies for sustainable development: Experiences from the Pacific*, pp. 100–108. London and New York: Zed Books.

4   Bauerlein, M. and C. Jeffery (2009) Mother Jones responds to Fiji Water. Retrieved 11 September 2015 from http://www.motherjones.com/mojo/2009/08/mother‐jones‐responds‐fiji‐water

5   Bebbington, A.J., J. Bury, N. Cuba and J. Rogan (2015) Mining, risk and climate resilience in the 'other' Pacific: Latin American lessons for the South Pacific, *Asia Pacific Viewpoint* 56 (2): 189–207.

6   Bloxham, A. (2011) Fiji Water accused of environmentally misleading claims. Retrieved 23 September 2011, from http://www.telegraph.co.uk/earth/earthnews/8585182/Fiji-Water-accused-of-environmentally-misleading-claims.html.

7   Borg, J. and M. Borg (2007) The Reverse Robin Hood Effect: The distribution of net benefits from the Florida Bright Futures Scholarship, *Florida Political Chronicle* 18 (1): 1–16.

8   Tokelau, J.J. (2014) Urban squatters and the poor in Fiji: Issues of land and investment in coastal areas, *Asia Pacific Viewpoint* 55 (1): 54–66.

9   Callick, R. (2010) Banished Fiji Water boss was "interfering", says Bainimarama. Retrieved 22 September 2011, from http://www.theaustralian.com.au/news/nation/banished‐fiji‐water‐boss‐was‐interfering‐says‐bainimarama/

10 Connell, J. (2006) The taste of paradise: Selling Fiji and FIJI Water, *Asia Pacific Viewpoint* 47 (3): 342–350.

11 Daye, D. and B. Van Auken (2008) Great brands can afford the elitist touch. Retrieved 20 July 2012, from http://www.brandingstrategyinsider.com/2008/03/great‐brands‐ca.html.

12 Deskins, M. (2011) FIJI Water misrepresents its sustainable image. Retrieved 15 October 2011, from http://sustainabilityandlaw.com/2011/03/30/fiji‐water‐misrepresents&#x-2010;its‐sustainable‐image‐by‐mike&#x201

13 Ely, L. (2009) Benihana partners with Best Buddies and FIJI Water to kick-off a season of giving. Retrieved 11 September 2015 from http://www.bestbuddies.org/press/news‐releases/282‐pressrelease.

14 Farrelly, T. and U. Nabobo-Baba 2014) Talanoa as empathic apprenticeship, *Asia Pacific Viewpoint* 55 (3): 319–330.

15 FIJI Water (2011) Natural artesian water: Artesian bottled water: FIJI Water. Retrieved 1 May 2011, from http://www.fijiwater.com/.

16 Gino, F., M.W. Toffel and S. van Sice (2011) FIJI Water: Carbon negative? Harvard Business School Technology & Operations Management Unit Case: 611–049.

17 Gino, F., M.W. Toffel and S. van Sice (2012) Fiji versus FIJI: Negotiating over water, Harvard Business School NOM Unit Case: 912–030.

18 Government of Fiji (2011) Water resource tax budget (budget amendment) decree 2011: To amend the water resource tax promulgation. Government Printing: Suva.

19 Jones, C.L. (2012) Weaving niche production in Pacific economies: The social, economic and environmental impacts of FIJI Water. Unpublished Masters of Development Studies thesis. Wellington: Victoria University of Wellington.

20 Justine (2011) What's going down in Fiji. Retrieved 11 October 2011, from http://www.bluegranola.com/tag/groundwater/.

21 Kahn, B. (2010). Fiji Water's CSR climate change issues. Retrieved 22 October 2011, from http://www.justmeans.com/Fiji‐Water‐s‐CSR‐Climate‐Change‐Issues/39333.html.

22 Kaplan, M. (2007) Fijian water in Fiji and New York: Local politics and a global commodity, *Cultural Anthropology* 22 (4): 685–706.

23 Lenzer, A. (2009) Fiji water: Spin the bottle. Retrieved 28 August 2011, from http://motherjones.com/politics/2009/09/fiji‐spin‐bottle.

24 McMaster, J. and J. Nowak (2002) Natural waters of Viti Limited—Pioneering a new industry in the Fijian Islands, *Journal of Management and Organisation* 9 (2): 37–45.

25 McMaster, J. and J. Nowak (2009) *FIJI Water and corporate social responsibility: Green makeover or 'Greenwashing'?* London, Ontario: University of Western Ontario, Richard Ivey School of Business.

26 Murray, W.E. (2000) 'Neoliberal globalisation, 'exotic' agro-exports and local change in the Pacific Islands: A study of the Fijian kava sector', *Singapore Journal of Tropical Geography* 21 (3): 355–363.

27 Niman, M.I. (2007) Bottled insanity. Retrieved 15 September 2011, from http://artvoice.com/issues/v6n6/bottled%5finsanity.

28 Overton, J. (1994) Land tenure and cash cropping in Fiji, in R.C. Rocombe and M. Meleisea (eds.), *Land issues in the Pacific*, pp. 117–131. Christchurch: MacMillan Brown Centre for Pacific Studies, University of Canterbury pp.

29 Overton, J. (2000) Vakavanua, vakamatanitu: Discourses of development in Fiji, *Asia Pacific Viewpoint* 40 (2): 121–134.

30 Overton, J. and W.E. Murray (2016) Fictive place. *Progress in Human Geography* doi: 10.1177/0309132515625464

31 Quraishi, J. (2011) Fiji Water sued for greenwashing. Retrieved 10 August 2011, from http://motherjones.com/blue‐marble/2011/01/fiji‐ water‐ sued‐ greenwashing.

32   Ravuvu, A. (1983) *Vaka i taukei: The Fijian way of life*. Suva: Institute of Pacific Studies of the University of the South Pacific.

33   Reddy, M. and G. Singh (2010) Branding of Fiji's bottled water: Edging into sustainable consumption, *International Journal of Entrepreneurship and Small Business* 9 (4): 448–460.

34   Ritson, M. (2006) Fiji Water. Retrieved 16 September 2011, from http://marketingblogged. marketingmagazine.co.uk/2006/08/01/fiji‐water/#0%5fundefined,0.

35   Royte, E. (2008) *Bottlemania: Big business, local springs and the battle over America's drinking water*. New York: Bloomsbury.

36   Schwartz, A. (2010) Fiji Water playing chicken with Fiji (updated). Retrieved 28 October 2011, from http://www.fastcompany.com/1706114/fiji‐ playing‐chicken‐ with‐fiji

37   *The Sydney Morning Herald* (2004). Hollywood couple buys Fiji Water for $63 m, The Sydney Morning Herald. Retrieved 25 August 2010, from http://www.smh.com.au/news/Business/ Hollywood‐couple‐ buys‐ Fiji‐bWater‐ for‐63m/2004/11/29/1101577419156.htm

38   Tabureguci, D. (2007) Asia, newest slant in FIBT's optimism. Retrieved 10 October 2011 from http://www.islandsbusiness.com/fiji%5fbusiness/indexdynamic/containerNameToReplace=MiddleMiddle/focusModuleID=19500/overideSkinName=issueArticle-full.tpl.

39   Ulrich, J. (2009) It is a strange thing for us to see water being sold: Local perceptions of the Fijian Bottled Water Industry. Missoula: Unpublished Masters of Arts Thesis, University of Montana.

40   Ward, R.G. and E. Kingdon (1995) Land, law and custom: Diverging realities in Fiji, in R.G. Ward and E. Kingdom (eds.), *Land, custom and practice in the South Pacific*, pp. 198–249. Cambridge: Cambridge University Press.

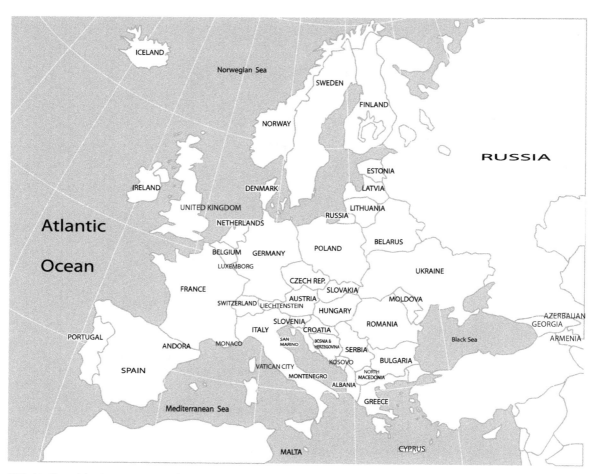

FIG. 4.1: Copyright © 2010 Depositphotos/jelen80.

Chapter IV

Europe

List of countries included in the world region of Europe:

- Albania
- Andorra
- Armenia
- Austria
- Azerbaijan
- Belarus
- Belgium
- Bosnia and Herzegovina
- Bulgaria
- Croatia
- Cyprus
- Czech Republic
- Denmark
- Estonia
- Finland
- France
- Georgia
- Germany
- Greece
- Hungary
- Iceland
- Ireland
- Italy
- Kosovo
- Latvia
- Liechtenstein
- Lithuania
- Luxembourg
- Malta
- Moldova
- Monaco
- Montenegro
- Netherlands
- North Macedonia
- Norway
- Poland
- Portugal
- Romania
- Russia
- San Marino
- Serbia
- Slovakia
- Slovenia
- Spain
- Sweden
- Switzerland
- Ukraine
- United Kingdom
- Vatican City (Holy See)

Introduction

The term **worldview** corresponds to the distillation of the overarching collective values, narratives, and views that are inherited and shared by the members of a culture. Among other things, the characteristics of worldview include that it endures, or transcends time. It expresses what a culture considers beautiful, ugly, palatable, distasteful, right, wrong, good, and bad. It is a kind of cultural filter or lens through which members experience and make sense of the world. Until we encounter a different worldview, often through travel or study abroad, we tend to assume everyone else thinks, values, and acts in the world as we do. In theory, anthropologists have studied over 3,800 distinct cultures in the world, and, based on this definition, each has its own worldview. Yet, in practice, the concept of worldview tends to be applied in broad strokes, often in terms of a continent (e.g., Asian or African), region (e.g., Eastern, Western, Mesopotamian), or ethnicity (e.g., Kayapo, Jewish, Tibetan). While there are obvious exceptions, in general, each of the six regions examined in this book tend to have their own corresponding worldview, which is continually contested and reinforced amid the forces of globalization.

The region of Europe is the birthplace of the Western worldview, the dominant ideas that continue to shape much of what the 21st-century world thinks, value, and believes. Currently, the dominant global economic system (capitalism), political system (democracy), language and writing system (English), and concepts of state sovereignty (Peace of Westphalia) originated in Europe. For example, English is often considered the language of business and the **lingua franca**, or common language used by those whose native languages are different. In addition, the **Anglosphere**, with the United Kingdom at its epicenter, includes Australia, Canada, New Zealand, and the United States. These are developed countries that speak English primarily but not exclusively; share close historical, cultural, and political ties and values with *Anglia* (the Latin word for England); and endorse international liberal democracy and human rights.

The prosperity and development of Europe can be attributed to a range of factors, including advantageous geographical, historical, cultural, and economic conditions. Among its unique geographical characteristics, Europe is recognized as a region and a continent covering approximately 10 million square kilometers, or 3.9 million square miles. While a relatively small part of the Eurasian landmass, Europe includes its most northern, eastern, and western points. Europe has multiple climate zones and fertile soil. Its landforms include plains, uplands, mountains, peninsulas, and islands.

For more than two thousand years, Europeans have achieved extraordinary cultural, economic, and political expansion due in part to their maritime vantage points and skills. For example, Europe's extensive navigable river and canal systems link multiple countries and allow sea access to otherwise landlocked countries. Moreover, Europe has approximately

38,000 kilometers, or 24,000 miles, of coastline, providing direct access to the Arctic and Atlantic Oceans as well as the Mediterranean, Black, and Caspian Seas. Its top 10 busiest container ports, located on the North Sea and Mediterranean Sea, include port cities in the Netherlands (known informally as Holland), Belgium, Germany, Spain, Greece, Italy, and the United Kingdom. Among the busiest European ports, in descending order, are Rotterdam (NL), Antwerp (BE), Hamburg (GER), Bremerhaven (GER), Valencia (ES), Pireaus (GR), Algeciras (ES), Gioia Tauro (IT), Felixstowe (UK), and Barcelona (ES) (Eurostat, 2008–2018; Windley, 2020).

Regions are human constructions, and there is no universal agreement on which countries each contains. To illustrate, consider that some sources include in Europe all or part of Russia and Turkey. Sometimes the entire country of Russia is shown on a map of Europe, but perhaps only a portion of Russia is included. It may be hard to figure out if such a representation is for practical reasons or some other cartographic purpose. For example, to make a map of Europe fit on a page, does the map cut off a portion of Russia? If a map shows only part of Russia, should we assume that a fraction of Russia is in Europe and the rest is in Asia? Indeed, some sources consider only the western, more populous area of Russia as a part of Europe, and the rest in Asia. Similarly, only Western Turkey may be considered a part of Europe, with the Turkish city of Istanbul as the gateway between Europe and Asia. Some sources may include Turkey in Europe, Asia, and/or the Middle East. To clarify, for our purposes, all of Russia is included in the region of Europe, but Turkey is among the countries that do not fit any of the global regions delineated in this text.

Among its distinct political qualities, Europe is home to the largest and smallest countries in the world. Russia is the largest and most populous European country, with nearly 146 million people. The smallest country in terms of area, the Holy See, also has Europe's smallest population, about 800 people. Determining the oldest country in Europe depends on your criteria, considering Greece has existed for thousands of years, but Portugal is the country with the oldest defined political borders and San Marino is the first republic with its own constitution. It may be easier to define the newest European country, Kosovo, which declared independence from Serbia in 2008. Kosovo has obtained bilateral official state recognition from the majority of United Nations member states. Kosovo is not universally recognized as a state. It seeks multilateral support, which is necessary to join the United Nations and enjoy a host of international economic and political benefits as a full-fledged sovereign state.

Europe, the third most populous global region (after Asia and Africa, respectively), is home to just over 500 million people, or almost 7% of the world's population (European Parliamentary Research Service, 2019). Europe is home to a diverse **cultural heritage**. This somewhat redundant term refers to tangible objects (artifacts) and intangible ideas, beliefs, values, and expressions that a culture produces, safeguards, and transmits from generation to generation within a community. Among other things, cultural heritage corresponds to the collective memory of a community, including its traditions, narratives, social practices, rituals, architecture, holidays, music, dances, foods, recipes, and languages. The culturally vibrant and linguistically varied region of Europe is home to approximately 160 ethnic groups and 200 languages, 24 of which are the official languages of the European Union. International cooperation in the promotion of intercultural understanding as well as the protection and preservation of cultural heritage are central to the mission of international governmental organizations (IGOs), including the European Union and the United Nations Educational, Scientific, and Cultural Organization (UNESCO).

The European Union

The region of Europe contains multiple subregions including the **European Union** (**EU**), an economic and political partnership between 27 European countries. It was established by the Maastricht Treaty on November 1, 1993, by the EU founding countries, or **EU-6**: Belgium, France, Germany, Italy, Luxembourg, and the Netherlands. The EU seeks to achieve the post–WWII goal of making war obsolete and creating peace and prosperity in Europe. It advances the economic, cultural, and political integration of EU states and is predicated on the "Four Freedoms" guaranteed by EU law, which are to protect the free movement of goods, services, capital, and people. It is an **international governmental organization** (**IGO**), a multilateral organization of countries working to advance their common goals and interests. Among other things, these organizations work to solve global or regional economic, cultural, and/or political issues of mutual concern. The EU addresses regional and international issues, such as climate change and COVID-19, and promotes democracy and human rights. In 2019, the EU was the world's largest economy, trade bloc, or single market. It was top trading partner of 80 countries and led the world in trading manufactured goods and services as well as importing (excluding oil) from developing countries (European Commission, 2019a). The EU did not want to lose the **United Kingdom** (England, Scotland, Wales, and Northern Ireland), which resigned from the EU in 2019. It remains to be seen if, and by what measures, its departure will serve the short- and long-term best interests of the UK.

Europe's Aging and Migrant Populations

Zero population growth (**ZPG**) indicates that a population is not increasing or decreasing. Some European countries have experienced ZPG for decades. Multiple factors may limit human population growth, such as demographic shifts, the availability of birth control, and fewer births as well as increases in longevity and women earning postsecondary education degrees. Even with the increase of inward migration in Europe in the mid-2010s, in 2019 the fertility rates of all of the countries of Europe were below ZPG (Lutz & Samir, 2011).

In 2018 in the European Union (EU), the median age was 43.1 years and nearly 20% of the population was age 65 or older (Eurostat 2019; Eurostat Statistics Explained, 2019). The European countries with 20% or more of their populations over the age of 65 include Italy (with 27% of its population over age 65); Portugal (23%); Bulgaria, Finland, and Germany (21%); and Croatia, Denmark, France, Greece, Latvia, and Sweden (20%) (Haider, 2017). By 2050, the UN expects the world population to reach 9.7 billion, yet population declines are expected in 55 countries. Of those 55, nine out of 10 are in Europe (the other is Japan). Further, of the 55 countries, 26 expect a population decrease of at least 10%, but 11 expect a 15% decline. Moreover, in 2019, five of the top 10 countries where people, on average, live the longest are in Europe, including Monaco, the country with the world's highest life expectancy, 89.32 years (geoba.se, 2020). The share of older persons relative to the total population is increasing. By 2050, 11% of the population of the EU is expected to be over age 80.

The term **migrants** is an imprecise term that refers to people who change their country of residence as well as refugees, asylum seekers, and displaced persons. Migrants may be voluntarily or involuntarily escaping armed conflicts, political instability, human rights abuses, unemployment, and poverty. Migrants and their descendants often form diasporic communities in their new homeland. Europe, one of the primary destination regions for international migrants, hosted 82 million international migrants in 2019 (International Organization for Migration, 2019; United Nations Department of Economic and Social Affairs, 2019). The European countries who hosted the most migrants in 2019 include Germany, the Russian Federation, the United Kingdom, and France (International Organization for Migration, 2019).

Diaspora refers to a transnational community based on their migrant experience and background as well as connections to their homeland. While hundreds of thousands of migrants have been granted citizenship in European countries, currently thousands languish in camps, particularly in Greece and Turkey, hoping to gain entry into Europe and avoid deportation.

Immigration is a divisive political topic in Europe. Particularly since 2015, as armed conflicts escalated in Syrian and Ukraine, deep divisions erupted between and among European countries over the unprecedented influx of migrants. The anti-immigration rhetoric of Europe's nationalist, right-wing populist, euroskeptic, and ultra-right-wing political parties have intentionally and purposefully scapegoated migrants as the source of domestic problems, ranging from high unemployment and crime rates to declining social services. Interestingly, despite its influx of migrants, from 2009 to 2019, Europe had less than a 2% proportional change in its population, the smallest shift compared to other world regions, indicating that the arrival of migrants offset Europe's declining birth rates (International Organization for Migration, 2019). Evidence suggests that migrants contribute to economies and thereby help to maintain the "cradle to grave" social services in European countries experiencing aging and declining populations. Further:

> migrants provide a source of dynamism globally and are overrepresented in innovation and patents, arts and sciences awards, start-ups and successful companies. Such historical and contemporary contributions have become increasingly overlooked or ignored in recent discussions on international migration." (International Organization for Migration, 2019, p. 161)

There are immeasurable ways that migrants enrich societies and economies as well as civic-political and cultural life (e.g., sports and the arts), and too often their contributions are unrecognized, underrated, and taken for granted.

The Paris Agreement and Climate Change

Paris Climate Change Conference, held on December 12, 2015, produced **The Paris Agreement**, the first international agreement to address climate change. The Paris Agreement is an international treaty that was signed by 185 states and the EU (197 countries total). This pact acknowledges the global threat posed by climate change and strengthens the global response to climate change, namely to reduce GHG emissions and keep temperatures from rising. The goal is to reach net-zero emissions, or climate neutrality, by 2050. Currently, global temperatures are 1 degree Celsius (1.8 degrees Fahrenheit) above pre–Industrial Age levels. The goal is to keep global temperatures from rising 2 degrees Celsius (3.6 degrees Fahrenheit) above pre–Industrial Age levels. The Paris Agreement, sponsored by the United Nations Framework Convention on Climate Change (UNFCC), went into effect on November 4, 2016. The United States ratified the agreement, but under the direction of President Trump, the United States withdrew from the Paris Agreement on June 1, 2017.

The Paris Agreement includes legally binding rules for the states involved. Among the commitments, every participant country agreed to develop and implement their own nationally determined contributions (NDCs), which is their plan to achieve the Paris Agreement goals. Further, countries agreed to initiate their NDCs in 2020 and report their post-2020 emissions and progress on climate change initiatives. Moreover, countries agree to be reevaluated every 5 years to reduce emissions and achieve the temperature goals. In addition, the Paris Agreement ensures that starting in 2020, developed countries will provide developing countries with at least $100 billion per year and other forms of public and private assistance to combat the impacts of climate change, namely to reduce greenhouse gas

(GHG) and anthropogenic emissions, as well as adapt to a sustainable low carbon future (United Nations Climate Change, n.d.).

A priority of the Paris Agreement is to abate the greenhouse effect. As solar radiation and energy reaches Earth's lower atmosphere, most of it is absorbed by the land and oceans. Yet, **greenhouse gas emissions** (GHG) are gases and substances that trap the sun's energy in the lower atmosphere, or troposphere, a process that generates heat and causes temperatures to rise, thereby producing the greenhouse effect, which contributes to global warming. Greenhouse gases include but are not limited to water vapor, carbon dioxide, methane, nitrous oxide, ozone, and some artificial chemicals like chlorocarbons (CFCs). Some of the major sources of GHGs are airlines and power stations as well as in manufacturing and industry (Larkin, 2019). Burning fossil fuels (for electricity, heat, and transportation) is the greatest source of GHG (U.S. EPA, 2017).

Although Europe is the world's third largest emitter of GHG and is responsible for 10% of the world's GHG emissions, this region is doing much to lead the world in addressing climate change and utilizing renewable energy. In particular, the Nordic or Scandinavian countries (Denmark, Finland, Norway, and Sweden) are leading by example, as they have already established net-zero policies and laws. Moreover, in 2017, the European countries making use of the greatest share of renewable energy were, in descending order, Sweden (53.9%), Finland (39.3%), Latvia (37.6%), Austria (33.0%), and Denmark (30.8%) (Gray, 2017). By 2020, the EU goal was to cut 20% of carbon dioxide and other greenhouse gas (GHG) emissions (compared to 1990), produce 20% of total energy consumption from renewable energy, and increase energy efficiency by 20%. By 2050, the EU plans to cut emissions by 80 to 95% compared to 1990 levels. As part of a "green deal" for the European Union, the president of the European Commission, Ursula von der Leyen, pledged in 2019 to commit to carbon neutrality by 2050 (European Commission, 2019b; Gray, 2017; Larkin, 2019). A major goal is **carbon neutrality**, or *net zero emissions*. This refers to balancing carbon emission with carbon absorption as well as strategies to reduce or remove carbon and carbon dioxide from the environment.

The EU climate-protecting initiatives are expected to cost approximately 180 billion euros, or at least 20 % of the EU's budget, from 2014 until 2020. The EU plans to finance initiatives in part by selling emission certificates and using that revenue to finance technologies, such as carbon capture and storage (CCS), that need to be developed to remove carbon dioxide from the atmosphere. The benefits include creating new jobs and saving existing jobs, becoming more resource efficient and significantly reducing oil and gas imports, and dramatically reducing air pollution. For years, government officials have feared a voter backlash if they commit to climate neutrality. However, from 1990 until 2018, the EU has had an average annual growth of 2.818, as Europe experienced a 22% reduction in carbon dioxide emissions (World Bank Group, 2019; Europa.org). Therefore, the EU has demonstrated that GDP growth is possible while significantly reducing carbon dioxide emissions, which should encourage all countries to meet their Paris Agreement obligations as if the world depends upon it. It does.

While several European states plan to achieve 100% renewable energy by 2030, the world has yet to figure out how to reduce GHG emissions, keep global temperatures from rising, accomplish carbon neutrality, and decarbonize Earth's atmosphere. The world demand for power continues to outweigh the growth in clean energy, as developing countries consume more energy each year. Addressing climate change and global warming will likely require a multi-prong approach that includes but is not limited to reducing industrial emissions, utilizing alternative fuel sources to coal and other fossil fuels, growing woodlands (which absorb carbon dioxide), and providing tax incentives for affordable electric cars and renewable energy.

References

European Commission. (2019a, February 18). *EU position in world trade.* https://ec.europa.eu/trade/policy/eu-position-in-world-trade/

European Commission (2019b, September 10). *The European Union continues to lead the global fight against climate change.* https://ec.europa.eu/commission/presscorner/detail/en/IP_19_5534

European Environment Agency. (2019, December 19). Total greenhouse gas emission trends and projections in Europe. https://www.eea.europa.eu/data-and-maps/indicators/greenhouse-gas-emission-trends-6/assessment-3

European Parliamentary Research Service. (2019). Demographic outlook for the European Union 2019. European Parliament. https://www.europarl.europa.eu/RegData/etudes/IDAN/2019/637955/EPRS_IDA(2019)637955_EN.pdf

Eurostat. (2017, March 16). *1.2 million asylum seekers registered in 2016.* https://ec.europa.eu/eurostat/documents/2995521/7921609/3-16032017-BP-EN.pdf/e5fa98bb-5d9d-4297-9168-d07c67d1c9e1

Eurostat. (2019a). Ageing Europe: Looking at the lives of older people in the EU. https://ec.europa.eu/eurostat/documents/3217494/10166544/KS-02-19%E2%80%91681-EN-N.pdf/c701972f-6b4e-b432-57d2-91898ca94893

Eurostat. (2019b). Migration and migrant population statistics. https://ec.europa.eu/eurostat/statistics-explained/index.php/Migration_and_migrant_population_statistics#Migrant_population:_22.3_million_non-EU_citizens_living_in_the_EU_on_1_January_2018

Eurostat. (2019, March). *Migration and migrant population statistics.* https://ec.europa.eu/eurostat/statistics-explained/index.php/Migration_and_migrant_population_statistics#Migrant_population:_22.3_million_non-EU_citizens_living_in_the_EU_on_1_January_2018

Eurostat Statistics Explained. (2019, July). *Population structure and ageing.* https://ec.europa.eu/eurostat/statistics-explained/index.php/Population_structure_and_ageing

Eurostat. (2020). Top 20 ports handling contains, 2008–2018 (thousand TEUs).png. https://ec.europa.eu/eurostat/statistics-explained/index.php?title=File:Top_20_ports_handling_containers,_2008–2018_(thousand_TEUs).png

Geoba.se (2020). *The world: life expectancy (2020) – top 100+.* http://www.geoba.se/population.php?pc=world&type=15

Gray, A. (2017, April 3). The best countries in Europe for using renewable energy. *World Economic Forum.* https://www.weforum.org/agenda/2017/04/who-s-the-best-in-europe-when-it-comes-to-renewable-energy/

Haider, F. (2017, April 25). Countries with the largest aging population in the world. *WorldAtlas.* https://www.worldatlas.com/articles/countries-with-the-largest-aging-population-in-the-world.html

International Organization for Migration. (2019). *World migration report 2020.* United Nations. https://www.un.org/sites/un2.un.org/files/wmr_2020.pdf

Larkin, M. (2019, July 18). How can the EU hit net-zero emissions? *World Economic Forum.* https://www.weforum.org/agenda/2019/07/how-can-the-eu-hit-net-zero-emissions/

Lutz, W., & Samir, K.C. (2011). Global human capital: Integrating education and population. *Science* 333 (58), p. 587–592. https://science.sciencemag.org/content/333/6042/587

UN Climate Change. *What is the Paris Agreement?* https://unfccc.int/process-and-meetings/the-paris-agreement/what-is-the-paris-agreement

UN Department of Economic and Social Affairs (2019, September 17). The number of international migrants reaches 272 million, continuing an upward trend in all world regions, says UN. https://www.un.org/development/desa/en/news/population/international-migrant-stock-2019.html

U.S. Environmental Protection Agency. (2019). *Sources of greenhouse gas emissions.* https://www.epa.gov/ghgemissions/sources-greenhouse-gas-emissions

Windley, B. F. (2020). Europe. *Encyclopaedia Brittanica, Inc.* https://www.britannica.com/place/Europe

World Bank. (2019). *GDP growth (annual %) – European Union.* https://data.worldbank.org/indicator/NY.GDP.MKTP.KD.ZG?end=2018&locations=EU&name_desc=false&start=1990

Europe's Populist Surge
A Long Time in the Making

Cas Mudde

T HE YEAR 2015 WAS A DREADFUL one for Europe in general and for the EU in particular. It started with the terrorist attack against the magazine *Charlie Hebdo* in Paris and ended with an even more deadly jihadist assault in the same city. In between, the EU battled an economic crisis in Greece, which threatened the entire eurozone, and endured a staggering inflow of refugees from the Middle East and other war-torn regions.

The year 2016 has not been much better. More terrorist attacks have shaken the continent. The refugee crisis has abated slightly, but only because the EU has outsourced the problem to Turkey—a country that is itself experiencing a bout of instability. And for the first time, the EU is set to lose a member, the United Kingdom, as a result of the so-called Brexit referendum.

All these developments have helped push populist movements to the center of European politics. The threat of terrorism and anxiety about a massive wave of immigrants from the Muslim world, coupled with the widespread belief that the EU hinders rather than helps when it comes to such problems, have created a perfect storm for populists, especially enhancing the standing of right-wing populists in many countries. Chief among them is Hungarian Prime Minister Viktor Orban, who has taken advantage of public fears to rally opposition to German Chancellor Angela Merkel and her belief that Europe should embrace a *Willkommenskultur*, a "culture of welcoming." Meanwhile, the eurozone crisis has aided the rise of left-wing, anti-austerity populists in Greece and Spain.

But although the threats to security and economic stability that have rattled Europe in the past few years may have spurred the current populist surge, they did not create it. Its origins lie further back, in the structural shifts in European society and politics that began in the 1960s. Because so much commentary on contemporary populism overlooks its deep historical sources, many observers fail to appreciate the durability of today's populist appeals and the likely staying

Cas Mudde, "Europe's Populist Surge: A Long Time in the Making," *Foreign Affairs*, vol. 95, no. 6, ed. Gideon Rose, pp. 25–30. Copyright © 2016 by Council on Foreign Relations, Inc. Reprinted with permission.

power of the parties built around them. It's true that populists have often struggled to hold on to power once they've obtained it. But today's social, political, and media landscapes in Europe favor populists more than at any time since the end of World War II. To reverse the populist tide, today's floundering, hollowed-out mainstream European parties and the entrenched elites who guide them will have to respond with far more dexterity and creativity than they have shown in recent decades.

The Pure People

As with any "ism," definitions are crucial. A useful one goes like this: populism is an ideology that separates society into two homogeneous and antagonistic groups, "the pure people" and "the corrupt elite," and that holds that politics should be an expression of "the general will" of the people. With a few exceptions, that kind of thinking remained on the margins of European politics throughout the nineteenth century and much of the twentieth century. Aspects of populism could be found in the communist and fascist movements, particularly during their oppositional phases. But both of those ideologies (and the regimes that embraced them) were essentially elitist, placing a small group of powerful insiders above the masses.

In the first decades of the postwar era, Western European politics was defined by a broad consensus on three key issues: alignment with the United States in the Cold War, the need for more political integration on the continent, and the benefits of maintaining a strong welfare state. Deep and wide support for those positions left little space for ideological alternatives, and populism was no exception. It wasn't until the 1980s that populist thinking truly began to make its mark, with the arrival of radical right-wing parties such as France's National Front, which rose to prominence in the wake of mass immigration and growing unemployment by promising to return France to the monocultural glory of its past.

Today, populist parties are represented in the parliaments of most European countries. The majority are right wing, although not all are radical. Others are left wing or espouse idiosyncratic platforms that are difficult to place on a left-right spectrum: for example, the Italian Five Star Movement, which has found success with a combination of environmentalism, anticorruption rectitude, and antiestablishment rage. In national elections held in the past 5 years, at least one populist party earned 10% or more of the vote in 16 European countries. Collectively, populist parties scored an average of 16.5% of the vote in those elections, ranging from a staggering 65% in Hungary to less than 1% in Luxembourg. Populists now control the largest share of parliamentary seats in six countries: Greece, Hungary, Italy, Poland, Slovakia, and Switzerland. In three of those (Hungary, Italy, and Slovakia), populist parties collectively gained a majority of the votes in the most recent national elections, although in Hungary and Italy the main populist parties are rivals. The situation in

Hungary is most striking, where the governing party (Fidesz) and the largest opposition party (Jobbik) are both populist. Finally, in three other countries—Finland, Lithuania, and Norway—populist parties are now part of the governing coalitions.

TINA Politics

Most conventional explanations of this trend emphasize the importance of two factors: globalization and the economic crises in Europe that resulted from the financial meltdown of 2008 and the subsequent Great Recession. But the current populist moment is part of a longer story and is rooted in the post-industrial revolution that led to fundamental changes in European societies in the 1960s. During those years, deindustrialization and a steep decline in religious observance weakened the support enjoyed by established center-left and center-right parties, which had been largely dependent on working-class and religious voters. In the quarter century that followed, a gradual realignment in European politics saw voters throw their support to old parties that had become virtually nonideological or to new parties defined by relatively narrow ideological stances.

Later, during the last two decades of the twentieth century, mainstream European parties increasingly converged on a new elite consensus—a common agenda that called for

To Viktor go the spoils: Orban at an Austria-Hungary soccer match, June 2016. Copyright © Reuters/Sergio Perez.

integration through the EU, multiethnic societies, and neoliberal economic reforms. The embrace of a vision of Europe as a cosmopolitan, business-friendly technocracy was particularly pronounced among parties that had traditionally been social democratic, many of which were inspired by British Prime Minister Tony Blair's concept of a "New Labour" party and German Chancellor Gerhard Schröder's move toward a "new center" (*neue Mitte*). The traditional center-right parties also shifted away from their historical identities, as leaders such as Merkel and David Cameron of the British Conservative Party adopted more centrist and pragmatic approaches to economic and cultural issues.

This convergence created a fertile breeding ground for populism, as many voters began to see political elites as indistinguishable from one another, regardless of their party affiliations. To many Europeans, mainstream elites of all parties also seemed to share an essential powerlessness, owing to two massive transfers of authority that took place in the second half of the twentieth century: from national governments to supranational entities such as the EU and the International Monetary Fund and from democratically elected officials to unelected ones such as central bankers and judges. In many EU member states, vital issues such as border control and monetary policy were no longer the exclusive responsibility of the national government. This led to the emergence of so-called TINA politics—"TINA" being short for "There is no alternative," the line political elites often used as a shorthand for the argument that their responsibility to the EU or the IMF outweighed their duty to be responsive to the demands of voters.

At the same time, the advent of the internet produced electorates that were more plugged in to political debates and more independent-minded (although not necessarily better informed), which made them more critical of and less deferential toward traditional elites. In particular, voters became more aware of the fact that elected officials often blamed agents or factors outside their control—the EU, globalization, U.S. policy—for unpopular policies but claimed to be fully in control and took credit whenever policies proved popular.

The internet also severely limited the gatekeeping function of mainstream media. With far more stories and voices finding an audience, populist narratives—which often contained a whiff of sensationalism or provocation—became particularly attractive to media organizations that were chasing eyeballs as revenue from subscriptions and traditional advertising plummeted. These subtle but profound shifts set the stage for short-term triggers, such as the global financial crisis and the spillover from Middle Eastern conflicts, to turbocharge populism's growth.

Power Hungary

The rise of populism has had important consequences for the state of liberal democracy in Europe. Although populism is not necessarily antidemocratic, it is essentially illiberal, especially in its disregard for minority rights, pluralism, and the rule of law. What is more, as the case of Hungary demonstrates, populism is not merely a campaign strategy or a style of political mobilization that leaders shed as soon as they achieve political power. Since 2010, Orban has openly set about transforming his country into what he described in a 2014 speech as "an illiberal new state based on national foundations," in which the government purposely marginalizes opposition forces by weakening existing state institutions (including the courts) and creating new, largely autonomous governing bodies and packing them with Fidesz loyalists.

Although the situation in Hungary is exceptional, Orban's success has inspired and emboldened many other right-wing populists in the EU, from Marine Le Pen in France to Jaroslaw Kaczynski in Poland. Most distressing, the rise of populist illiberalism is facing less and less opposition from embattled mainstream parties, which have fallen silent or have even applauded the trend.

Left-wing populists have been nowhere near as successful as their right-wing counterparts. In Greece in 2015, Syriza's amateurish attempt to challenge EU-imposed austerity policies backfired, and Prime Minister Alexis Tsipras was ultimately forced to accept precisely the kinds of spending cuts and structural reforms that he had pledged to prevent. Since then, no other left-wing populist parties have managed to succeed at the national level, with the exception of Podemos (We Can) in Spain. And although left-wing populists are generally less exclusionary than their right-wing counterparts, political polarization in Greece has increased significantly since Syriza came to power in January 2015. Many opponents of the government feel vilified by official rhetoric portraying them as members of a fifth column doing the bidding of Berlin or Brussels. And Tsipras has proposed several laws that could limit the space for political opposition by increasing state control of education and the media.

Even in countries without populist governments, a populist Zeitgeist has taken hold. In many cases, populists now set the agenda and dominate public debate, while mainstream politicians merely react, sometimes even adopting elements of populist rhetoric, peppering their speeches with references to "the people" and condemnations of "elites." Consequently, even traditionally pro-European Christian democrats and social democrats now use "Brussels" as a derogatory term, evoking a distant elite, removed from the concerns of the common people and posing a threat to national sovereignty.

A New Populist Era?

Many scholars contend that European populism is an episodic phenomenon—that it creates moments rather than eras—and that although populists can succeed in opposition, they inevitably fail once in power. That is wishful thinking, and those who engage in it generally put too much stock in a few high-profile populist implosions. This sanguine view overlooks the fact that Orban has been in power for 6 years and still leads the most popular party in Hungary and populism has dominated politics in Slovakia ever since the fall of communism. Meanwhile, Austria is poised to become the first European country in the postwar era to directly elect a populist radical-right president: Norbert Hofer of the Freedom Party, who leads in the most recent opinion polls.

Deep structural changes in European societies produced the current populist wave. Those changes are not likely to be reversed anytime soon, so there is no reason to anticipate that populism will fade in the near future. Moreover, populist parties are growing just as major establishment parties are becoming increasingly obsolete: in many European countries, it has become rare for any party to win more than one third of the national vote.

Mainstream parties have to develop short-term and long-term strategies to deal with the new reality of fragmented party systems that include influential populist parties. So-called *cordons sanitaires*—coalition governments, such as that in Belgium, that explicitly seek to exclude populist parties—will become increasingly difficult to sustain. In the many countries where populists now represent the third- or second-biggest party, a *cordon sanitaire* would force all the other parties to govern together, which would have the unintentional effect of re-creating many of the very conditions that led to the rise of European populism in the first place. At the same time, it will become harder for establishment parties to govern alongside populist parties. In recent years, populist parties have been willing to serve as junior partners in coalitions. Now, however, many populist parties are much bigger than their potential mainstream partners and will be far less likely to take a back seat.

Still, populist parties are ultimately subject to the same basic political laws that constrain their establishment rivals. Once they achieve power, they, too, must choose between responsiveness and responsibility—between doing what their voters want and what economic reality and EU institutions dictate. Orban has so far been successful at doing both things at the same time, in part by saying different things to different audiences. But Tsipras has learned about the pressures of responsibility the hard way and has suffered a significant drop in popularity.

This dilemma for populists presents opportunities for liberal democratic parties, be they new or old, but only if they do not simply attack the populist vision but also provide clear and coherent alternatives. Some establishment figures seem to grasp this. For example, in positioning himself for next year's national elections in France, the center-right politician Alain Juppé has cast himself as "a prophet of happiness" with a positive vision of a more harmonious country—a stark contrast to the negativity and fear-mongering of his rival within the Republicans, Nicolas Sarkozy, and a rebuke to the divisive rhetoric of Le Pen, the right-wing populist leader of the National Front. And in Germany, Merkel has mostly avoided a strong populist backlash—despite immense frustration and pushback inside and outside her own party—by acknowledging public anger while sticking to a clear policy agenda and a positive message: "*Wir schaffen das*" (We can do this).

In essence, the populist surge is an illiberal democratic response to decades of undemocratic liberal policies. To stem the populist tide, establishment politicians will have to heed the call to repoliticize the crucial issues of the 21st century, such as immigration, neoliberal economics, and European integration, bringing them back into the electoral realm and offering coherent and consistent alternatives to the often shortsighted and simplistic offerings of the populists.

Reading 4.2

The Broken Bargain
How Nationalism Came Back

Jack Snyder

NATIONALISM AND NATIVISM ARE ROILING POLITICS on every continent. With the election of President Donald Trump in the United States, the growing power of right-wing populist parties in Europe, and the ascent of strongmen in states such as China, the Philippines, and Turkey, liberals around the world are struggling to respond to populist nationalism. Today's nationalists decry the "globalist" liberalism of international institutions. They attack liberal elites as sellouts who care more about foreigners than their fellow citizens. And they promise to put national, rather than global, interests first.

The populist onslaught has, understandably, prompted many liberals to conclude that nationalism itself is a threat to the U.S.-led liberal order. Yet historically, liberalism and nationalism have often been complementary. After World War II, the United States crafted a liberal order that balanced the need for international cooperation with popular demands for national autonomy, curbing the aggressive nationalist impulses that had proved so disastrous in the interwar years. The postwar order was based on strong democratic welfare states supported by international institutions, such as the World Bank and the International Monetary Fund (IMF), that coordinated economic policy between states while granting them the flexibility to act in their own national interest. The political scientist John Ruggie has called this arrangement "embedded liberalism," because it embraced free markets while subjecting them to institutionalized political control at both the domestic and the international level—a bargain that held for several decades.

Yet over the past 30 years, liberalism has become disembedded. Elites in the United States and Europe have steadily dismantled the political controls that once allowed national governments to manage capitalism. They have constrained democratic politics to fit the logic of international markets and shifted policymaking to unaccountable bureaucracies or supranational institutions such as the EU. This has created the conditions for the present surge of populist nationalism. To contain it, policymakers will have to return to what worked in the past, finding new ways to reconcile national accountability and international cooperation in a globalized world. The proper response to populism, in other words, is not to abandon liberal internationalism but to re-embed it.

The Great Transformation

Nationalism is generally understood as the doctrine that the cultural unit of the nation, whether defined along civic or ethnic lines, should be congruent with the political unit of the state. For most of history, political loyalties did not coincide with national boundaries. This began to change in early modern Europe following the Protestant Reformation, as centralized states secured monopolies on violence and legal authority within their territory, gradually displacing the Catholic Church and transnational dynastic networks. At the same time, early commercial capitalism was shifting economic power away from rural landlords and toward the thriving urban middle classes. The state increasingly fused with its nation, a distinctive people that contributed blood and treasure to the state and that, in exchange, insisted on the right to participate in government. Over time, the nationalist claim to popular self-determination became the handmaiden of democracy.

Meeting in the middle: Viktor Orban greets Angela Merkel in Budapest, February 2015. Copyright © Associated Press/Tibor Ilyes.

During the nineteenth century, nation-states in western Europe (as well as European settler colonies such as the United States) developed strong civic institutions, such as universalistic legal codes and national educational systems, that could assimilate diverse groups into a shared cultural identity. (In eastern European countries and other late-developing states, however, different ethnic groups gained political consciousness while still living together in multinational empires—there, homogeneity was achieved not through assimilating civic institutions but through war, ethnic cleansing, and expulsion.) One of the most widely invoked theorists of nationalism, Ernest Gellner, argued that this process of internal cultural homogenization was driven by the requirements of industrial capitalism. In order to participate in national economies, workers needed to speak the national language and be fully integrated into the national culture. In countries with a strong civic state, these pressures transformed the nation-state into a culturally, politically, and economically integrated unit.

By the early decades of the twentieth century, however, tensions had begun to emerge between liberal capitalism and nationalist democracy. Nineteenth-century capitalism relied on automatic market controls, such as the gold standard, to regulate financial relations between states. Governments lacked both the will and the ability to intervene in the economy, whether by spending to counteract downturns in the business cycle or by acting as the lender of last resort to forestall bank runs. Instead, they let the invisible hand of the market correct imbalances, imposing painful costs on the vast majority of their citizens.

This laissez-faire policy became politically untenable during the late nineteenth and early twentieth centuries, as more and more people gained the right to vote. After the crash of 1929 and the Great Depression, enfranchised citizens could demand that their national leaders assert control over the economy in order to protect them from harsh economic adjustments. In some countries, such as Germany and Japan, this led to the ascent of militantly nationalist governments that created state-directed cartel economies and pursued imperial expansion abroad. In others, such as the United States under President Franklin Roosevelt, governments instituted a form of social democratic capitalism, in which the state provided a social safety net and launched employment programs during hard times. In both cases, states were attempting to address what the economic historian Karl Polanyi, in *The Great Transformation*, identified as the central tension of liberal democratic capitalism: the contradiction between democratic rule, with its respect for popular self-determination, and market logic, which holds that the economy should be left to operate with limited government interference.

During the interwar years, the world's leading liberal powers—France, the United Kingdom, and the United States—had made tentative efforts to create an international order to manage this tension. U.S. President Woodrow Wilson's Fourteen Points called for a world of independent national democracies, and his proposal for a League of Nations promised a peaceful means for resolving international disputes. In practice, the United States refused to join the League of Nations, and the British and the French ensured that the Treaty of Versailles humiliated Germany. But despite these shortcomings, the interwar liberal order functioned, for a time. The 1922 Washington Naval Treaty initially helped prevent a naval arms race between Japan and the Western allies. The 1925 Pact of Locarno guaranteed Germany's western border. And the 1924 Dawes Plan and the 1929 Young Plan provided the Weimar government with enough liquidity to pay reparations while also funding urban infrastructure improvements and social welfare provisions. The system held until the collapse of the international economy after 1929. In both Germany and Japan, the resulting economic crisis discredited liberal and social democratic political parties, leading to the rise of authoritarian nationalists who promised to defend their people against the vicissitudes of the market and the treachery of foreign and domestic enemies.

It was only after World War II that liberal internationalists, led by those in the United States and the United Kingdom, learned how to manage the tension between free markets and national autonomy. The Marshall Plan, in which the United States, beginning in 1948, provided financial assistance to western Europe, did more than provide capital for postwar reconstruction. It also conditioned this aid on governments opening their economies to international trade, thereby strengthening liberal political coalitions between workers (who benefited from cheaper goods imported from abroad) and export-oriented capitalists (who gained access to global markets for their products). The institutions that came out of the 1944 Bretton Woods conference, including the World Bank and the IMF, offered loans and financial aid so that states could adjust to the fluctuations of the international market. As originally intended, this postwar system, which included the precursor to the EU, the European Economic Community, as well as the Bretton Woods institutions, was designed not to supersede national states but to allow them to cooperate while retaining policy autonomy. Crucially, leading democracies such as France, the United Kingdom, the United States, and West Germany decided to share some of their sovereignty in international organizations, which made their nation-states stronger rather than weaker. In more recent decades, however, these hard-won lessons have been set aside.

Disembedding Liberalism

For the first few decades following World War II, embedded liberalism—characterized by strong domestic welfare states supported by international institutions—succeeded in granting autonomy and democratic legitimacy to nation-states while curbing aggressive nationalism. Yet as early as the 1970s, this arrangement came under pressure from structural changes to the global economy and ideological assaults from libertarians and advocates of supra- and trans-nationalism. The resulting erosion of embedded liberalism has paved the way for the nationalist revival of today.

The Bretton Woods system had relied on countries fixing their exchange rates with the U.S. dollar, which was in turn backed by gold. But already by the early 1970s, chronic U.S. trade deficits and the increasing competitiveness of European and Japanese exports were making this system untenable. At the same time, the United States was experiencing "stagflation"—a combination of high unemployment and high inflation that was resistant to the traditional Keynesian strategies, such as government spending, on which postwar economic management had relied. In response, U.S. President Richard Nixon suspended the dollar's convertibility to gold in 1971, moving toward an unregulated market system of floating exchange rates. Other structural developments also put embedded liberalism under strain: the globalization of production and markets strengthened the relative power of capital, which was highly mobile, over labor, which was less so. This weakened the power of traditional labor unions, undermining the capital-labor bargain at the center of the postwar order.

These economic trends were accompanied by ideological developments that challenged both core principles of embedded liberalism: social democratic regulation of the economy and the political primacy of the nation-state. The first of these developments was the rise of free-market fundamentalism, pioneered by economists such as Friedrich Hayek and Milton Friedman and adopted by political leaders such as British Prime Minister Margaret Thatcher and U.S. President Ronald Reagan. Beginning with Thatcher's election in 1979, these leaders and their ideological backers sought to drastically curtail the welfare state and return to the laissez-faire policies of the nineteenth century. This market fundamentalism was initially used by the right as a cudgel against the social democratic left, but over time it was adopted by leaders of center-left parties, such as French President François Mitterrand, U.S. President Bill Clinton, and British Prime Minister Tony Blair, who during the 1980s and 1990s pushed through financial deregulation and cuts to the welfare state. These policies hurt members of the white working class, alienating them from the political system and the center-left parties that had traditionally protected their interests.

The other element of the ideological assault on embedded liberalism came from enthusiasts of supra- and trans-nationalism. In an influential 1997 essay in this magazine, Jessica Mathews argued that technological change and the end of the Cold War had rendered the nation-state obsolete. Its functions, according to Mathews and other, like-minded thinkers, would be usurped by supranational organizations such as the EU, coordinating institutions such as the World Trade Organization, and various transnational networks of activists, experts, and innovators. In 1993, for instance, Europe had adopted a common market and created the bureaucratic edifice of the EU to administer the resulting flows of goods, money, and people. This was followed by the adoption of the euro in 2002. Although intended to promote European integration, the euro effectively stripped its members of monetary sovereignty, greatly reducing their policy autonomy.

This transnational paradise, moreover, left little room for democracy. The gradual transfer of authority from national governments to Brussels has put considerable power in the hands of unelected technocrats. Europeans who are unhappy with EU policies have no way to vote out the bureaucrats in Brussels; their only effective way to impose democratic accountability is through national elections, creating a strong incentive for nationalist mobilization. Different European countries have different policy equilibriums based on the preferences of their voters, the needs of their national economies, and the rhetorical strategies of their national political elites. The search for nationally tailored solutions, however, is confounded by the EU's requirement that all member states agree on a policy in lockstep. After the 2015 migrant crisis, initiated by Germany's decision to briefly open its borders, Brussels began cajoling and coercing other EU member states to accept some of the migrants in the name of burden sharing. Small wonder, then, that Hungarians, Italians, and Poles who opposed immigration began flocking to nationalist politicians who promised to resist pressure from the EU. Similar policy divergences on economic austerity have also been expressed in terms of national resentments—between Germans and Greeks, for instance—and have fueled mobilization against Brussels.

Scholars debate whether populist nationalism in the United States and Europe arises mainly from economic or cultural grievances, but the most persuasive explanation is that nationalist political entrepreneurs have combined both grievances into a narrative about perfidious elites who coddle undeserving out-groups—immigrants and minorities—while treating the nation's true people with contempt. In this view, elites use bureaucratic and legal red tape to shield themselves from accountability and enforce politically correct speech norms to silence their critics. This story doesn't fit the facts—among other anomalies, residents of rural regions with few immigrants are among the most dedicated opponents of refugees—but it should not be surprising that a narrative of self-dealing elites and dangerous immigrants has resonated, given humans' well-known propensity for in-group bias. Nativistic prejudice is latent, ready to be activated in times of cultural flux or economic strain when traditional elites seem unresponsive.

A different face of the contemporary nationalist revival is the rise of authoritarian populism in developing states such as Brazil, India, the Philippines, and Turkey. Similar to older rising illiberal powers, such as nineteenth-century Germany, these countries have been able to use the so-called advantages of backwardness—cheap labor, technology transfers, and state-directed resource allocation—to grow rapidly; that is, until they reach approximately one-fourth of U.S. GDP per capita. Beyond that point, growth tends to slow markedly unless states follow in the footsteps of reformers such as Japan, South Korea, and Taiwan and adopt the full panoply of liberal institutions. Often, however, their governments eschew liberal reform. Instead, facing stagnating growth and inefficiencies from corruption, they double down on some combination of demagogic nationalism, repression, and crippling overinvestment in massive infrastructure projects, which are designed to retain the support of business elites. In such cases, it is the responsibility of these states' liberal economic partners to press for reforms—at the risk, however, of triggering even more nationalist backlash.

If It Ain't Broke, Don't Fix It

How, then, should leaders respond to the rise of nationalism? The first step is to recognize that the tension fueling contemporary nationalism is not new. It is precisely the tension identified by Polanyi, which the embedded liberal order of the postwar years was designed to manage: the contradiction between free markets and national autonomy. Illiberal nationalism has never been particularly successful at governing, but it is a temptation whenever liberalism drifts too far away from democratic accountability.

Historically, this contradiction has been resolved only through an order of democratic welfare states supported by international institutions, which grant them the policy flexibility to adjust to market fluctuations without inflicting undue pain on their citizens. Resolving today's nationalist dilemma will require abandoning laissez-faire economics and unaccountable supranationalism and returning to the principles of embedded liberalism, updated for the present day. This, in turn, calls for a revival of the basic practices of postwar liberalism: national-level democratic accountability, economic coordination through international institutions, and compromise on competing priorities.

Today, political polarization makes compromise seem unlikely. Both illiberal nationalists and cosmopolitan elites have, in their own way, doubled down on one-sided solutions, seeking to rout their opponents rather than reach a durable settlement. Trump calls for a border wall and a ban on Muslim immigration, and his opponents continue to speak as if immigration and refugee policy is a matter of abstract legal and moral commitments rather than a subject for democratic deliberation. In Europe, meanwhile, the Germans cling to austerity policies that punish countries such as Greece and Italy, and illiberal populists fume against EU restrictions on their autonomy.

Yet the very failure of these one-sided measures may open up space for a renewed embedded liberalism. In the United States, President Barack Obama's Affordable Care Act, which has mostly survived despite egregious assaults from the right, is a clear example of what a modern embedded liberal solution might look like. It strengthened the welfare state by vastly expanding access to statesubsidized health care and accommodating the needs of the private sector—an echo of the domestic capital-labor compromises that made the postwar order possible.

Similar arrangements might be sought on immigration. For instance, rich countries might agree to coordinate investment in poorer ones in order to stabilize migration flows by improving conditions in the source countries. These arrangements should be institutionalized before the next crisis hits, not improvised as they were in 2015–16, when Germany and the EU hurriedly struck a deal with Turkey, paying Ankara billions of euros in exchange for housing refugees. And although international institutions such as the EU should play a role in coordinating immigration policy, democratic states must be allowed to tailor their own policies to the preferences of their voters. Pressuring countries to accept more migrants than they want simply plays into the hands of illiberal populists. And giving the populists some of what they want now may improve the prospects for embedded liberal compromises in the future. In December 2018, Hungarians began protesting in massive numbers against their nationalist government's policy of forced overtime, which had been enacted due to labor shortages. Faced with such problems, some of the country's anti-immigration zealots may soon begin to reassess their stance.

In the essay in which he coined the term "embedded liberalism," Ruggie noted that institutionalized power always serves a social purpose. The purpose of the postwar order, in his view, had been to reach a compromise between the competing imperatives of liberal markets and national autonomy. Today's crisis of liberalism stems in large part from a loss of this purpose. The institutions of the present international order have ceased responding to the wishes of national electorates.

The evidence of the past century suggests, however, that democratic accountability is necessary for both political stability and economic welfare. And even today, nation-states remain the most reliable political form for achieving and sustaining democracy. It is likely impossible to remake them in order to better conform to the needs of global markets and transnational institutions, and even if it were possible, it would be a bad idea. Instead, defenders of the liberal project must begin adapting institutions to once again fit the shape of democratic nation-states. This was the original dream of the embedded liberal order; now is the time to revive it.

Russia as It Is
A Grand Strategy for Confronting Putin

Michael McFaul

RELATIONS BETWEEN RUSSIA AND THE UNITED STATES have deteriorated to their most dangerous point in decades. The current situation is not, as many have dubbed it, a new Cold War. But no one should draw much comfort from the ways in which today's standoff differs from the earlier one. The quantitative nuclear arms race is over, but Russia and the United States have begun a new qualitative arms race in nuclear delivery vehicles, missile defenses, and digital weapons. The two countries are no longer engulfed in proxy wars, but over the last decade, Russia has demonstrated less and less restraint in its use of military power. The worldwide ideological struggle between capitalism and communism is history, but Russian President Vladimir Putin has anointed himself the leader of a renewed nationalist, conservative movement fighting a decadent West. To spread these ideas, the Russian government has made huge investments in television and radio stations, social media networks, and Internet "troll farms," and it has spent lavishly in support of like-minded politicians abroad. The best description of the current hostilities is not cold war but hot peace.

Washington must accept that Putin is here to stay and won't end his assault on Western democracy and multilateral institutions anytime soon. To deal with the threat, the United States desperately needs a new bipartisan grand strategy. It must find ways to contain the Kremlin's economic, military, and political influence and to strengthen democratic allies, and it must work with the Kremlin when doing so is truly necessary and freeze it out when it is not. But above all, Washington must be patient. As long as Putin remains in power, changing Russia will be close to impossible. The best Washington can hope for in most cases is to successfully restrain Moscow's actions abroad while waiting for Russia to change from within.

Red dawn: Russian and Syrian soldiers outside eastern Ghouta, Syria, February 2018. Copyright © Reuters/ Omar Sanadiki.

Ups and Downs

At the end of the Cold War, both U.S. and Russian leaders embraced the promise of closer relations. So what went wrong? Russia's renewed international power provides part of the explanation. If Russia were too weak to annex Crimea, intervene in Syria, or interfere in U.S. elections, Moscow and Washington would not be clashing today. But not all rising powers have threatened the United States. Germany and Japan are much stronger than they were 50 years ago, yet no one is concerned about a return to World War II rivalries. What is more, Russia's relations with the United States were much more cooperative just a few years back, well after Russia had returned to the world stage as a great power.

In Russian eyes, much of the blame falls on U.S. foreign policy. According to this argument, the United States took advantage of Russia when it was weak by expanding NATO and bombing Serbia in 1999, invading Iraq in 2003, and allegedly helping overthrow pro-Russian governments in Georgia in 2003 and Ukraine in 2004. Once Russia was off its knees, it had to push back against U.S. hegemony. At the 2007 Munich Security Conference, Putin championed this line of analysis: "We are seeing a greater and greater disdain for the basic principles of international law. ... One state, and, of course, first and foremost the United States, has overstepped its national borders in every way."

There is some truth to this story. The expansion of NATO did exacerbate tensions with Moscow, as did Western military interventions in Serbia and Iraq. Democratic upheavals in Georgia and Ukraine threatened Putin's ability to preserve autocracy at home, even if Putin grossly exaggerated the U.S. role in those so-called color revolutions.

Yet this account omits a lot of history. After the end of the Cold War, U.S. presidents were truly committed to, in Bill Clinton's words, "a strategic alliance with Russian reform" and Russia's integration into the international system. Just as the United States and its allies helped rebuild, democratize, and integrate Germany and Japan after World War II, the thinking went, so it would rebuild Russia after the Cold War. It is true that the United States and Europe did not devote enough resources or attention to this task, leaving many Russians feeling betrayed. But it is revisionism to argue that they did not embrace Moscow's new leaders, support democratic and market reforms, and offer Russia a prominent place in Western clubs such as the G-8.

The most powerful counterargument to the idea that U.S. foreign policy poisoned the well with Russia is that the two countries managed to work together for many years. The cooperative dynamic of U.S.-Russian relations established after the fall of the Soviet Union survived not only U.S. provocations but also two Russian military operations in Chechnya and the 1998 Russian financial crisis, after which foreign governments accused the Kremlin of wasting Western aid. And even the U.S. withdrawal from the Anti-Ballistic Missile Treaty, in 2002, and another, larger round of NATO expansion, in 2004, did not end the cooperative dynamic that U.S. President George W. Bush and Putin had forged after the 9/11 attacks. Russia's invasion of Georgia in 2008 pushed U.S.-Russian relations to a low point in the post–Cold War era. But even this tragedy did not permanently derail cooperation.

How It All Went Wrong

Even after all these ups and downs, U.S.-Russian relations experienced one last spike in cooperation, which lasted from 2009 to 2011. In 2009, when U.S. President Barack Obama met for the first time with Russian President Dmitry Medvedev and Putin, who was then serving as Russia's prime minister, the U.S. president tried to convince the two Russians that he was a new kind of American leader. He had opposed the Iraq war long before it was popular to do so, he explained, and had always rejected the idea of regime change. At least at first, Medvedev seemed convinced. Even Putin showed signs of softening. Over the next few years, Russia and the United States signed the New Strategic Arms Reduction Treaty (or New START), worked through the UN to impose tough new sanctions on Iran, managed Russia's entry into the World Trade Organization, coordinated to defuse violence in Kyrgyzstan after the collapse of the government there, and arranged a vast expansion of the network used to transport U.S. soldiers and supplies to Afghanistan through Russia. In 2011, in perhaps the most impressive display of renewed cooperation, Russia acquiesced in the Western intervention in Libya. At the height of the so-called reset, in 2010, polls showed that around 50 percent of Americans saw Russia as a friendly country and that some 60 percent of Russians viewed the United States the same way.

This period of relative harmony began to break down in 2011, owing primarily to the way that Putin reacted to popular democratic mobilizations against autocracies in Egypt, Libya, Syria—and Russia itself. The Libyan uprising in 2011 marked the beginning of the end of the reset; the 2014 revolution in Ukraine marked the start of the hot peace.

Popular mobilization inside Russia was especially unnerving to Putin. He had enjoyed solid public support during most of his first eight years as president, thanks primarily to Russia's economic performance. By 2011, however, when he launched a campaign for a third term as president (after having spent three years as prime minister), his popularity had fallen significantly. The implicit bargain that Putin had struck with Russian society during his first two terms—high economic growth in return for political passivity—was unraveling. Massive demonstrations flooded the streets of Moscow, St. Petersburg, and other large cities after the parliamentary election in December 2011. At first, the protesters focused on electoral irregularities, but then they pivoted to a grander indictment of the Russian political system and Putin personally.

In response, Putin revived a Soviet-era source of legitimacy: defense of the motherland against the evil West. Putin accused the leaders of the demonstrations of being American agents. Obama tried to explain that the United States had not prompted the Russian demonstrations. Putin was unconvinced. After his reelection in the spring of 2012, Putin stepped up his attacks on protesters, opposition parties, the media, and civil society and placed under house arrest the opposition leader he feared the most, the anticorruption blogger Alexei Navalny. The Kremlin further restricted the activity of nongovernmental organizations and independent media outlets and imposed significant fines on those who participated in protests that the authorities deemed illegal. Putin and his surrogates continued to label Russian opposition leaders as traitors supported by the United States.

Putin's anti-American campaign was not just political theater intended for a domestic audience: Putin genuinely believed that the United States represented a threat to his regime. Some pockets of U.S.-Russian cooperation persisted, including a joint venture between the Russian state-owned oil giant Rosneft and ExxonMobil, an agreement brokered by Obama and Putin in which Syria pledged to eliminate its chemical weapons, and Russian support for the international negotiations that produced the Iran nuclear deal. But most of these ended in 2014, after the fall of the pro-Russian Ukrainian government and the subsequent Russian invasion of Ukraine. Once again, Putin blamed the Obama administration, this time for supporting the revolutionaries who toppled Ukrainian President Viktor Yanukovych.

Putin was never inclined to believe in Washington's good faith. His training as a KGB agent had led him to distrust the United States along with all democratic movements. But in the early years of his presidency, he had held open the possibility of close cooperation with the West. In 2000, he even suggested that Russia might someday join NATO. After the 9/11 attacks, Putin firmly believed that Russia could work with the United States in a global war on terrorism. In 2008, after he stepped aside as president, he allowed Medvedev to pursue closer ties with Washington. But the Western intervention in Libya confirmed Putin's old suspicions about U.S. intentions. Putin believed that the United States and its allies had exploited a UN resolution that authorized only limited military action in order to overthrow the Libyan dictator Muammar al-Qaddafi. In Putin's view, Obama had turned out to be a regime changer, no different from Bush.

Confronting the Kremlin

Four years after Russia annexed Crimea, the United States has still not articulated a bipartisan grand strategy for dealing with Russia. Such a strategy is necessary because Washington's conflict with the Kremlin doesn't revolve around mere policy disagreements: rather, it is a contest between Putinism and democracy. No tweaking of U.S. policy on Syria or NATO will influence Putin's thinking. He has been in power for too long—and he is not likely to leave in the foreseeable future. U.S. policymakers must dispense with the fantasy that Putin's regime will collapse and democracy will emerge in Russia in the near term. The United States and its allies must continue to support human rights and democracy and embrace people inside Russia fighting for those values. But real political change will likely begin only after Putin steps down.

The United States also has to give up on the idea that Russia can or should be integrated into multilateral institutions. The theory that integration would moderate Russian behavior has not been borne out by events. The United States must dig in for a long and difficult confrontation with Putin and his regime. On most issues, the aim should be to produce a stalemate, as preserving the status quo will often be the best the United States can hope for.

Containment must start at home. Limiting Putin's ability to influence U.S. elections should be priority number one. The Trump administration should mandate enhanced cybersecurity resilience. If the federal government can require all cars to have seat belts, then federal authorities can require elementary cybersecurity protections such as dual authentication for all processes related to voting during a presidential election. Those who operate the systems that maintain voter registries must be required to receive training about how to spot common hacking techniques, and an even more rigorous set of standards must be adopted for the vote count. In a dozen states, including large battlegrounds such as Florida and Pennsylvania, at least some precincts lack paper trails for each ballot cast. These sloppy practices have to end. Every precinct must be able to produce a paper record for every vote.

Congress should also pass laws to provide greater transparency about Russian media activities inside the United States, including a requirement for social media companies to expose fake accounts and disinformation. Foreign governments should not be allowed to buy ads anywhere to influence voter preferences. Beyond elections, the federal government must devote more time and money to blocking Russian threats to all national electronic infrastructure.

To further counter Putin's ideological campaign, the United States should organize democracies around the world to develop a common set of laws and protocols regulating government-controlled media. Through regulation, Washington should encourage social media platforms to grant less exposure to Kremlin-created content. Algorithms organizing search results on Google or YouTube should not overrepresent information distributed by the Russian government. When such material does appear in searches, social media companies should make its origins clear. Readers must know who created and paid for the articles they read and the videos they watch.

On their own, without government intervention, social media platforms should provide sources from more reliable news organizations; every time an article or video from the Kremlin-backed news channel RT appears, a BBC piece should pop up next to it. Social media companies have long resisted editorial responsibilities; that era must end.

In Europe, Putin's success in courting Hungarian President Viktor Orban and nurturing several like-minded political parties and movements within NATO countries underscores the need for a deeper commitment to ideological containment on the part of Washington's European allies. Those allies must pay greater attention to combating Russian disinformation and devote more time and resources to promoting their own values. NATO members must also meet their defense spending pledges, deploy more soldiers to the alliance's frontline states, and reaffirm their commitment to collective security.

No theater in the fight to contain Russia is more important than Ukraine. Building a secure, wealthy, democratic Ukraine, even if parts of the country remain under Russian occupation for a long time, is the best way to restrain Russian ideological and military aggression in Europe. A failed state in Ukraine will confirm Putin's flawed hypothesis about the shortcomings of U.S.-sponsored democratic revolutions. A successful democracy in Ukraine is also the best means for inspiring democratic reformers inside Russia and other former Soviet republics. The United States must increase its military, political, and economic support for

Ukraine. Washington should also impose new sanctions on Russians involved in violating Ukraine's sovereignty and ratchet them up until Putin begins to withdraw.

In the Middle East, the United States needs a more aggressive strategy to contain Russia's most important regional ally, Iran. It should continue to arm and support Syrian militias fighting Iranian soldiers and their allies in Syria and should promote anti-theocratic and pro-democratic ideas in the region, including inside Iran. Abandoning the fight in Syria would deliver a tremendous victory to Moscow and Tehran. The goals of U.S. policy toward Iran must remain denying Tehran a nuclear weapon, containing its destabilizing actions abroad, and encouraging democratic forces inside the country, but not coercive regime change from the outside.

The United States must contain the Kremlin's ambitions in Asia, as well. Strengthening existing alliances is the obvious first step. Putin has sought to weaken U.S. ties with Japan and South Korea. To push back, the United States should make its commitment to defend its allies more credible, starting by abandoning threats to withdraw its soldiers from South Korea. It should also begin negotiations to rejoin the Trans-Pacific Partnership. A harder but still important task will be to divide China from Russia. In 2014, Putin suffered a major setback when China did not support his annexation of Crimea at the UN. But today, putting daylight between the two countries will not be easy, as Putin and Chinese President Xi Jinping have forged a united front on many issues. When opportunities do arise, such as working with Beijing toward North Korean denuclearization, Washington must act.

Western countries must also develop a coherent strategy to contain the Russian government's economic activities. Europe must reduce its dependence on Russian energy exports. Projects such as the planned Nord Stream 2 natural gas pipeline from Russia to Germany are no longer appropriate and should be discontinued. Putin uses government-owned and supposedly private companies to advance his foreign policy interests; the United States and Europe must impose greater financial sanctions on the activities those firms undertake in the service of Kremlin interests abroad if Russia continues to occupy Ukraine or assault the integrity of democratic elections. At a minimum, the West must adopt new laws and regulations to require greater transparency around Russian investments in the United States, Europe, and, as far as possible, the rest of the world. Russian officials and businesspeople tied to the Kremlin cannot be allowed to hide their wealth in the West. Genuine private-sector companies inside Russia should be encouraged to engage with Western markets, but authorities must expose the ill-gotten financial assets that Putin and his cronies have parked abroad. The goal should be to underscore the economic benefits of free markets and access to the West while highlighting the economic costs of state ownership and mercantilist behavior.

On the other side of the equation, Western foundations and philanthropists must provide more support for independent journalism, including Russian-language services both inside and outside Russia. They should fund news organizations that need to locate their servers outside Russia to avoid censorship and help journalists and their sources protect their identities.

More generally, the United States and its democratic allies must understand the scope of their ideological clash with the Kremlin. Putin believes he is fighting an ideological war with the West, and he has devoted tremendous resources to expanding the reach of his propaganda platforms in order to win. The West must catch up.

How Do You Solve a Problem Like Putin's Russia?

Containing Russia does not mean rejecting cooperation in every area. The United States selectively cooperated with the Soviet Union during the Cold War; it should do so with Russia now. First on the list must be striking new arms control deals or at least extending existing ones, most urgently New START, which is set to expire in 2021 and contains crucial verification measures. Combating terrorism is another area for potential partnership, as many terrorist organizations consider both Russia and the United States to be their enemies. But such cooperation will have to remain limited since the two countries have different ideas about what groups and individuals qualify as terrorists, and some of Russia's allies in the fight against terrorism, such as Iran, Syria, and Hezbollah, are at odds with the United States. U.S. and Russian officials might also seek to negotiate an agreement limiting mutual cyberattacks. Yet Washington should not pursue engagement as an end in itself. Good relations with Russia or a friendly summit with Putin should be not the goal of U.S. diplomacy but the means to achieve concrete national security ends.

Some might argue that the United States cannot pursue containment and selective cooperation at the same time. The history of the Cold War suggests otherwise. President Ronald Reagan, for example, pursued a policy of regime change against Soviet-backed communist dictatorships in Afghanistan, Angola, Cambodia, and Nicaragua while negotiating arms control deals with Soviet leaders.

On global issues in which Russia does not need to be involved, the United States should isolate it. Since the end of the Cold War, U.S. presidents have been eager to give their counterparts in the Kremlin symbolic leadership roles as a way to signal respect. Those days are over. Conversations about Russia rejoining the G-8 must end. Western governments should boycott sporting events held in Russia. Let the athletes play, but without government officials in the stands. Given Moscow's politicization of Interpol arrest requests, Interpol must suspend Russian participation. Even Russia's presence at NATO headquarters must be rethought. The more the United States can do without Russia, the better.

Even as the United States isolates the Russian government, it must continue to develop ties with Russian society. By canceling exchange programs, banning U.S. civil society organizations, and limiting Western media access to Russian audiences, Putin has tried to cut the Russian people off from the West. The United States and Europe need to find creative ways to reverse this disturbing trend. Happily, far more opportunities exist to do so today than did during the Cold War. Washington should promote student and cultural exchanges, dialogues between U.S. and Russian nongovernmental organizations, trade, foreign investment, and tourism.

Strategic Patience

But no matter how effective a containment strategy U.S. policymakers put in place, they must be patient. They will have to endure stalemate for a long time, at least as long as Putin is in power, maybe even longer, depending on who succeeds him. In diplomacy, Americans often act like engineers; when they see a problem, they want to fix it. That mentality has not worked with Putin's Russia, and if tried again, it will fail again.

At the same time, American leaders must say clearly that they do not want endless conflict with Russia. When the current confrontation winds down, most likely because of political change inside Russia, future U.S. presidents must stand ready to seize the moment. They will have to do better at encouraging democracy within Russia and integrating Russia into the West than their predecessors have done. Past politicians and the decisions they made created today's conflict. New politicians who make different decisions can end it.

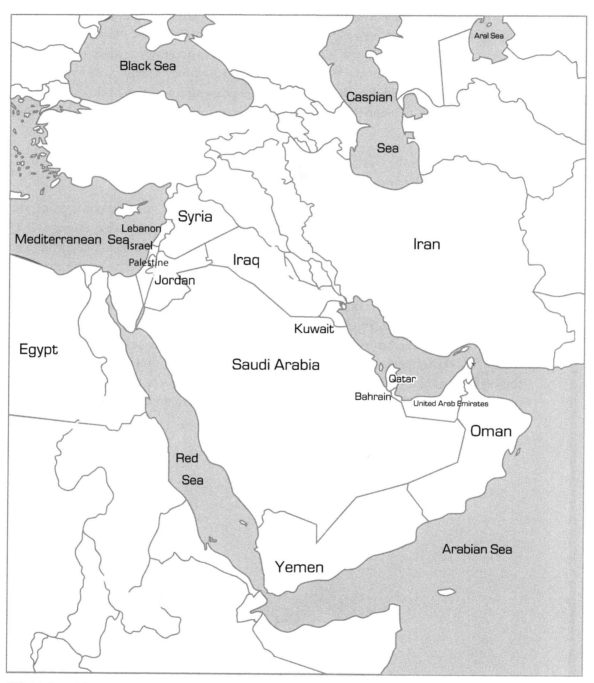

Chapter V

The Middle East

List of countries included in the world region of the Middle East:

- Bahrain
- Egypt
- Iran
- Iraq
- Israel
- Jordan
- Kuwait
- Lebanon
- Oman
- Palestine
- Qatar
- Saudi Arabia
- Syria
- United Arab Emirates
- Yemen

Introduction

Over millennia, the Middle East has been renamed and its map has been redrawn repeatedly, often by outsiders. For example, centuries ago, Europeans delineated their proximity to the rest of the Eurasian landmass in terms of the Near, Middle, and Far East. By some accounts, the *Middle East* was coined by a British military officer in the mid-1800s and adopted widely after World War I to refer to the land between Europe and India. Think about the implications of an area that was not named by its own inhabitants. The term *Middle East* can correctly be understood as a **Eurocentric** construct, or a label generated from a European perspective. It can also be considered **anglocentric**, or from a British perspective, because it was invented and used by the British to indicate the location of this territory (much of which they have, at one point or another, occupied and controlled) in relation to Great Britain. The term, the *Middle East*, endures while the *Near East* and *Far East* have fallen into disuse and in general should not be used. Today the Middle East is delineated variously. This region, spanning at least 2.4 million square miles with a population of about 411 million people, may be referred to as the Middle East and North Africa, or its acronym MENA. It is also called the Greater Middle East, Eastern Mediterranean, Southwest Asia, and Western Asia. Despite such a lack of consensus on delineating this region, this book uses the term *Middle East*, so that contemporary statistical and other data on the world regions, the majority of which refer to this area as the Middle East, may be cited.

To continue this largely semantic exploration of conceptualizing the Middle East, many people equate this region with the *Arab World* or *Islamic World*. The Arab World can describe the region where the Arabic language originated and is predominantly, but not exclusively, spoken in many derivations and dialects. Arabic is the official language of all but two Middle Eastern countries. The exceptions are Iran and Israel, where the official languages are Persian (or Farsi) and Hebrew, respectively. The Arab World corresponds to Arab-speaking countries that are members of the Arab League. Yet, the Arab World can also refer to the over 100 million people worldwide who identify as Arab, based generally on one or more common linguistic, ethnic, national, or cultural connections. These points raise sets of questions about what constitutes and unifies the Arab World. Further, the *Islamic World* does not accurately describe the Middle East. Although the Middle East is home to countries with the largest percentages of their populations that are Muslim (in descending order: Iran, Iraq, Turkey, and Algeria), currently the majority of Muslims in the world live in Asia, not the Middle East. Of the more than two billion Muslims in the world, approximately 62% live in Asia, whereas less than 20% live in the Middle East (World Population Review, 2020). Further, while the Middle East is the birthplace of the world's three major monotheistic religions—Judaism, Christianity, and Islam—it is a region that includes people who are non-Muslims or profess other faiths. While the Arabic language and religion of Islam originated in the Middle East, it is problematic to refer to this region as the Arab or Islamic World, since Arab and Islam are global phenomena.

Fertile Crescent: Then and Now

One of the sub regions of the Middle East is the **Fertile Crescent**, considered the "Cradle of Civilization" because it is the ancient birthplace of the first human farms and urban areas. Located primarily between the Euphrates and Tigris river systems, this abundant agricultural region was also the locus of the first complex societies. It marked the beginning of trade and organized religion as well as a range of technological innovations, including writing, the wheel, and irrigation (Mark, 2018).

Since 1931, the Fertile Crescent has been drying up as the result of increasing and extreme heat and drought conditions marked by significant declines in vegetation, livestock, and wildlife (Kelley, Mohtadi, Cane, Seager, & Kushnir, 2015). Less rain and unsustainably mining groundwater have drastically depleted **aquifers**, which are geologic formations for containing and transmitting groundwater. These and other aspects of climate change are linked to armed conflicts over water access, one of the factors that initiated the civil war in Syria that began in 2011. Currently in this sub region, a network of hydropower dams, facilitating Turkey's agricultural production and hydropower capabilities, is causing deluge and drought in Iraq. Increasingly, many global regions face climate change issues, such as water insecurity and sustainability as well as water-related conflict and migration.

Foreign Labor Force in the Middle East

Particularly since the late twentieth century, millions of individuals and families have migrated, mostly from Asia and Africa, seeking economic opportunities in the burgeoning economies of many wealthy Gulf States. Foreign workers outnumber nationals in the U.A.E., Qatar, and Kuwait, where approximately 90% of their population have been guest workers. In 2019, the Middle East hosted more than 32 million international migrants, mostly migrant workers who earned billions of dollars in income (ILO, 2019). Foreign workers, often temporary contract workers, have been essential in building the infrastructures and economies of the Middle East, a region with has experienced severe labor shortages, particularly in construction, petroleum production, retail, and other service industries (Workforce numbers in the UAE 2019, by sector, 2020). Middle Eastern companies and private citizens tend to prefer hiring foreign workers who are willing to work for low wages doing what is often considered to be menial or demeaning labor. The work tends to be gender stratified, with men dominating construction, clerical, domestic, and service economic sectors, whereas women usually work as domestics, nannies, nurses or nurse assistants, and caregivers for the elderly and disabled.

It is helpful to know the following terms associated with guest workers in the Middle East. An **expat**, short for an expatriate, is someone living outside their country of origin, often because it enables them to earn more income and pay little or no taxes to their home country. It can also refer to a person who has given up their citizenship to become the citizen of another country. A **migrant worker** is someone who moves from home to another location or country, usually for seasonal, temporary, and low-wage work. Generally, the term expat is associated with those who work in a more professional or managerial capacity compared to migrants, a word that tends to correspond to low-skill menial laborers. A **remittance worker** is someone who works abroad temporarily and sends all or part of their earnings to a spouse or family member who usually lives in the worker's country of origin. In many of the workers' countries of origin, remittances are a major economic sector and total in the billions of dollars annually. In 2019, there was a record $554 billion in global remittances to low- and middle-income countries (LMICs). In 2019, the top remittance recipient countries were India (83.1 billion), China (68.4 billion), Mexico (38.5 billion), the Philippines

(35.2 billion), and Egypt (26.8 billion). In 2020, the global pandemic significantly impacted global remittances (Migration and Development, 2020; Ong, 2020).

Although the point of origin and destination countries have generally supported the sustained development of the foreign labor force in the Middle East, hundreds of thousands of these workers have been victims of exploitation, discrimination, and physical and emotional abuse as well as extreme violence, homicide, and other human rights violations. Middle Eastern employment recruitment and placement agencies often engage in coercive practices, contract substitutions, and ineffective complaint procedures as well as exorbitant brokerage, travel visa, and other fees (International Labour Organization and Walk Free Foundation, 2017). Frequently, migrants are subjected to substandard working and living conditions, long working hours without breaks or days off, forced confinement, deplorable living conditions, and food deprivation, as well as physical and sexual abuse (Human Rights Watch, 2018). Moreover, workers are not compensated for working overtime or long shifts or paid on time. Further, migrants are often inadequately protected from income loss due to injury, sickness, maternity leave, disability, or old age. Sick or injured migrants frequently do not receive treatment and as the result work-related injuries have led to deaths. There are limited investigations and accountability for migrant homicides and "disappearances." While it is illegal to do so, employers routinely confiscate workers' passports and residency permits, essentially holding laborers "hostage" and prohibiting them from leaving their employ (International Labour Organization and Walk Free Foundation, 2017).

Labor law protections for workers are limited or nonexistent in many Middle Eastern countries. For example, there is no minimum wage for all workers in most Middle Eastern countries. A few operate a two-tiered national minimum wage that pays migrants significantly less than what nationals earn. One of the most significant labor law issues centers on the ancient **kafala** employment system, the legal basis of visa-sponsorship laws in many Middle Eastern countries. The rules of this employment system binds a worker to one employer and sets the rules for work contracts and termination. Under these rules, migrant workers cannot resign, switch jobs, or return home without their employer's permission (Meaker, 2018). If workers attempt to leave without their sponsor's consent, the workers face stiff penalties, including fines, imprisonment, or deportation. Moreover, guest workers often lack legal representation and voice in the host country's judicial system. In fact, migrants who press charges against an employer risk fines and imprisonment for leveling "false" accusations, since the courts typically rule in favor of the nationals' counterclaims. The Arabic word *kafala* translates to mean "take care of," yet the kafala system is exploited to effectively trap workers and force them to remain in the employ of abusive sponsors (Human Rights Watch, 2018).

Saudi Arabia and Iran Wars: Cold, Sectarian, and Proxy

A **cold war** is a type of political hostility, just short of open warfare, between two or more countries. While the Cold War between the United States and USSR (and their respective allies) lasted from 1947 until 1991, Saudi Arabia and Iran began their ongoing cold war in 1979. In that year, the Shah (Emperor) of Iran, Mohammad Reza Pahlavi, a Western-backed monarch, was deposed in the Iranian Revolution.

The Shah's regime was replaced by an Islamic **theocracy**. In this case, a theocracy is a system of government in which clergy members observe Shia religious law, exert religious and political control over major state functions, and defer to the authority of the ruling cleric. At the top of Iran's political power structure is a strict Shiite Muslim cleric, the **Ayatollah**, or Supreme Leader, who is the head of state and commander-in-chief of the military. He is a direct bloodline descendant of Ali (the cousin and son-in-law of the Islamic prophet Muhammad), considered to be the rightful caliph and first imam (leader) of Shia Islam (Esposito, 2010). In addition, the second highest ranking official in Iran is the president. He is elected by the people to head the government, do what the Ayatollah decrees, and represent Iran at meetings with heads of state from around the world. From its earliest days, the Islamic Republic of Iran, the world's first Islamic democracy, began exporting in earnest its revolutionary ideology as well as its domestic and international political goals, which included undermining its chief regional adversary, Sunni Saudi Arabia (National Foreign Assessment Center, 1980).

Much of the animosity between Saudi Arabia and Iran is rooted in the sectarian differences between Sunni and Shia, the two major denominations, or sects, of Islam. **Sectarian** refers to a group or person who ascribes to a particular set of religious beliefs. Conversely, a **nonsectarian** does not belong to a religious sect and/or is equally welcoming of all religions. Of the 1.9 billion Muslims worldwide, the majority, or approximately 1.5 billion, are Sunni Muslims and 240 to 340 million are Shia Muslims. In other words, about 85% of Muslims are Sunni and 15% are Shia. The population of Saudi Arabia is at least 90% Sunni and Iran is about 90% Shia (Desilver & Masci, 2017; Council on Foreign Relations, 2014). Saudi Arabia is predominantly Sunni and home of the two holiest sites of Islam (Medina and Mecca). It also professes to be the leader of the Sunnis. On the other hand, Iran, the epicenter of Shia Islam, claims a similar dogmatic position in the Islamic world as well as the majority population of the world's Shiites. The sectarian divide between Sunni and Shia, and by extension Saudi Arabia and Iran, stems from two competing principles of political legitimacy that emerged during the establishment of the **caliphate**, an Islamic state based on Islamic principles and law. Upon the death of the prophet Mohammed in 632 A.D., the Sunnis asserted that leadership should be determined by the community, whereas the Shiites believed Mohammed's successor, the caliph (head of the caliphate) must be his direct bloodline descendants. Despite this central disagreement, for centuries Sunni and Shia have managed to peacefully coexist in terms of recognizing each other as Muslims, sharing many religious beliefs and practices, and adhering to **Sharia**, or Islamic jurisprudence.

Yet, as the theological split between the Sunni and Shia intensified politically, fierce sectarian antagonisms spread through the Middle East with the Saudi and Iranian governments engaged in proxy war. A **proxy war** typically involves two or more powerful protagonist countries that fight each other using intermediaries and militias in a third, weaker country. Saudi Arabia and Iran exert their considerable influence in interstate and intrastate conflicts throughout the Middle East. Covertly and overtly, they have provided weapons, military advice, troops, and direct military attacks to support their respective regional proxies and allies. The Saudi Arabian–Iranian rivalry has had a devastating effect on the region, making it nearly impossible for politically and economically fragile states to function. It has escalated and protracted violence, resulting in millions of civilian injuries, deaths, and displacements as well as some of the worst humanitarian crises of our time, namely in Syria and Yemen.

References

Council on Foreign Relations (2014). The Sunni-Shia divide. https://www.cfr.org/interactives/sunni-shia-divide#!/sunni-shia-divide

Datta, M. (2019, January 14). How many people are enslaved in the world today? *World Economic Forum*. https://www.weforum.org/agenda/2019/01/fact-check-how-many-people-are-enslaved-in-the-world-today/

Desilver, D., & Masci, D. (2017, January 31). World's Muslim population more widespread than you might think. Pew Research Center. https://www.pewresearch.org/fact-tank/2017/01/31/worlds-muslim-population-more-widespread-than-you-might-think/

Esposito, J.L. (2010). *Islam: The straight path* (4th ed.). New York, NY: Oxford University Press.

Human Rights Watch. (2018). *World Report 2018*. New York, NY: Seven Stories Press.

International Labour Organization & Walk Free Foundation. (2017). Global estimates of modern slavery: Forced labour and forced marriage. http://www.ilo.org/wcmsp5/groups/public/---dgreports/---dcomm/documents/publication/wcms_575479.pdf

International Labour Organization. (2019). Labour migration. https://www.ilo.org/beirut/areasof-work/labour-migration/lang--en/index.htm

Kelley, C. P., Mohtadi, S., Cane, M. A., Seager, R., & Kushnir, Y. (2015). Climate change in the Fertile Crescent and implications of the recent Syrian drought. *Proceedings of the National Academy of Sciences of the United States of America, 112*(11), 3241–3246.

Mark, J. J. (2018, March 28). Fertile Crescent. *Ancient History Encyclopedia*. https://www.ancient.eu/Fertile_Crescent/

Meaker, M. (2018, October 1). *The Middle East's kafala system imprisons millions of women*. Medium. https://medium.com/s/powertrip/the-middle-easts-kafala-system-imprisons-millions-of-women-172d191a1fa1

Migration Data Portal. (2020, June 10). Remittances. https://migrationdataportal.org/themes/remittances#:~:text=In%202019%2C%20in%20current%20USD,(World%20Bank%2C%202020).

Minderoo Foundation (2019). Measurement, action, freedom: An independent assessment of government progress towards achieving UN sustainable development goal 8.7. Global Slavery Index. https://www.ilo.org/beirut/areasofwork/labour-migration/lang--en/index.htm

National Foreign Assessment Center. (1980) Iran: Exporting the revolution: An intelligence assessment. CIA.gov. https://www.cia.gov/library/readingroom/docs/CIA-RDP81B00401R000500100001-8.pdf

Ong, R. (2020, April 22). World Bank predicts sharpest decline of remittances in recent history. Press release no. 2020/175/SPJ. World Bank. https://www.worldbank.org/en/news/press-release/2020/04/22/world-bank-predicts-sharpest-decline-of-remittances-in-recent-history

Pew Research Center. (2019, March 31). 10 countries with the largest Muslim populations, 2015 and 2060. https://www.pewresearch.org/fact-tank/2019/04/01/the-countries-with-the-10-largest-christian-populations-and-the-10-largest-muslim-populations/ft_19-03-29_muslimchristianpopulations_muslim/

Statistica. (2020, June 15). Workforce numbers in the UAE 2019, by sector. *Statista.com*. https://www.Statistia.com/statistics,638515/uae-total-number-of-workforce-by-economic-sector/

World Bank. (2019, April 8). Record high remittances sent globally in 2018. https://www.worldbank.org/en/news/press-release/2019/04/08/record-high-remittances-sent-globally-in-2018

World Population Review. (2020). Muslim population by country 2020. http://worldpopulationreview.com/countries/muslim-population-by-country/

Reading 5.1

The Challenge of Iran

Robin Wright

I RAN, PROUD AND PASSIONATE, HAS BEEN a conundrum since its 1979 revolution. It stunned the world by introducing Islam as a form of modern governance, in turn altering the balance of power across the Middle East. It rattled the region by exporting its zealous ideology and siring or sponsoring militant allies elsewhere. And it unnerved both East and West by defiantly challenging international norms and charting its own course. All three factors complicated dealing with the Islamic Republic.

But Iran looms even larger today. The confluence of challenges—defiance over its nuclear program, rising repression, support for extremists, and menacing rhetoric—has created a sense of impending crisis both at home and abroad.

Political volatility at home was reflected in six months of tumultuous protests after the disputed 2009 presidential election. For millions of Iranians in many cities, the issue quickly escalated from alleged voter fraud to condemnation of the regime, its leadership and even the Islamic system. The regime, briefly, appeared on a precipice. Tehran eventually restored control. But its tactics indicated the regime's insecurity. It had to militarize to survive.

Tensions with the international community have been reflected in a series of U.N. sanctions since 2006 over Iran's refusal to convince the world it was not building a bomb. In the end, even Russia, which built Iran's first nuclear reactor, voted for a series of punitive sanctions. So did China, which has become Iran's most important big-power trading partner.

Iran now represents a far more complex challenge than other hotspots—Afghanistan, Iraq and North Korea—for several reasons:

- Its revolution was one of the three transformative events in the Middle East in the 20th century. Iran's actions will be pivotal to global events in the early 21st century because of its resources, ideology, weaponry, allies and location.

- Strategically, Iran's frontiers and coastline have for millennia been central to political, military and commercial developments. Today, it spans three of the world's most volatile regions and its most vital shipping lanes for oil. Iran has the potential to help stabilize or destabilize all four.

- Politically, Iran has been the most dynamic and controversial experiment in blending Islam and democracy—and the experiment is far from over. It continues to play out in the domestic political crisis. The outcome could affect the wider Islamic world as profoundly as the revolution.

- Militarily, Iran has the largest armed forces in the Middle East and, with the exception of Israel, Egypt and increasingly Saudi Arabia, the largest arsenal, although much of its weaponry is of low quality, aging or obsolete. It has also armed militant allies from Lebanon to Afghanistan.

- Economically, Iran is one of the world's largest and most valuable properties, rich with oil and natural gas. Its assets in turn give it leverage and political leeway globally.

The Revolution

The Islamic Republic still has to prove the long-term viability of its zealous ideology and hybrid political system, the issues at the heart of its domestic crisis. Yet Iran's 1979 revolution was clearly one of the three most innovative revolutions of the Modern Age. Like two other upheavals, it introduced a new ideology and redefined the world's political spectrum.

In toppling the Bourbon monarchy, the French revolution introduced equality and civil liberty as the basis of modern democracy. The Russian revolution overthrew the Romanov dynasty in the name of classless egalitarianism, the foundation of communism. By ousting the last in a string of dynasties dating back more than 2,000 years, the Iranian revolution sought to demonstrate that Islam was an effective idiom of political expression, opposition and governance.

For the Middle East, the revolution was one of the three most important turning points of the 20th century. The collapse of the five-century-old Ottoman Empire after World War I and Israel's creation in 1948 were the other two. In many ways, Iran was a logical place for sweeping political innovation because of its own rich history, religious tenets, two earlier attempts at reform, and struggle to end foreign influence.

Historically, Iran has more independent political experience than virtually any other modern Muslim state. Most were created or gained independence from European colonial powers only in the 20th century. But Iran had a long, if somewhat varied, history of sovereignty. Persia also had long exposure to ideas from the outside world, as a crossroads between East and West and a target of invading armies from ancient Greece to contemporary Britain.

And with more than five millennia of civilization, Iranians have a sense of historic importance and a role in shaping the world.

Political Islam

Shiite Islam was also a logical force for change. In Sunni Islam, clerics are advisers; a believer's relationship with God is direct. In Shiite Islam, the clergy is empowered to interpret God's word for the faithful. Their fatwas have absolute authority in telling a believer what is right or wrong, what to do or not do. Shiite clerics also have a leadership hierarchy. And central to the original schism, Shiite Islam demands that the faithful fight against injustice, even if it means certain death. In tapping into strong Shiite traditions, revolutionary leader Ayatollah Ruhollah Khomeini became the most credible authority to mobilize disparate Iranian factions against the last shah.

Islam also provided a framework for an alternative to the monarchy. The new Islamic Republic was the first grand experiment in blending Islam and democracy. Iran's 1979 constitution borrowed heavily from French and Belgian law. It called for separation of powers between the three branches of government. It stipulated that the president and legislature, as well as provincial and local councils, should be popularly elected by men and women, originally as young as 15. It imposed a two-term limit on the presidency. And it continued the monarchy's practice of allocating seats in parliament for Christians, Jews and Zoroastrians—at least token acknowledgement of individual or minority rights.

But the constitution then added a provision that all laws must be compatible with Islamic law, or Sharia. It also established a set of parallel Islamic institutions that mirrored each of the republican branches of government—and often had more power. And on top of it all, the constitution imposed a supreme leader, who had absolute powers. The supreme leader became the equivalent of an infallible political pope.

Revolution within Shiism

The Islamic Republic also represented a revolution within Shiism. More than any branch of Islam, Shiites historically were wary of political power. They viewed the state as imperfect, corruptible and a source of persecution. They deliberately distanced themselves from politics. After Iran's revolution, however, they became the political power, changing the role of the clerics as well a central tenet of the "quietist" Shiite faith. Tehran's Shiite theocracy is the only time Muslim clerics have ever ruled a state.

Iran has in turn put Shiism—Islam's so-called second sect, making up between 10 percent and 12 percent of the world's 1.3 billion Muslims—on the political map. In its first three decades, the Islamic Republic fostered a network of Shiite allies in neighboring states stretching from Lebanon to Afghanistan. Sunni governments began to fear the so-called Shiite crescent, anchored by Iran, that stretched west across Iraq, into Syria and Lebanon, and south through Shiite minorities in the oil-rich sheikhdoms.

Political Phases

Iran's revolution has passed through at least four phases:

Phase one: The first phase was the Khomeini decade from 1979 until the ayatollah's death in 1989. It was a tumultuous period of revolutionary extremes that included killing off supporters of the *ancien regime*, taking foreigners hostage, and fostering its zealotry across the Islamic world. The turmoil was exacerbated by an eight-year war with Iraq that proved to be the Middle East's bloodiest modern conflict. It produced more than one million casualties.

Phase two: The second phase coincided with the two terms of President Akbar Hashemi Rafsanjani, from 1989 until 1997. The revolution's early passions were replaced by a hard-earned pragmatism, produced in part by excesses that backfired against the clerics and exhausted the population. Under Rafsanjani, arrogance gave way to a conservative realism. The government of God increasingly ceded to secular statecraft.

Phase three: The third phase between 1997 and 2005 coincided with the reformist era of President Mohammad Khatami, a dark horse former cabinet minister who tapped into the groundswell of interest in political openings. The government soon improved relations with its own people as well as the outside world. Iran had, temporarily, a freer press, freer speech, wider debate, relaxed social restrictions and a burgeoning civil society. But parliament failed to legislate reforms. And by the end of Khatami's two terms, a political schism had developed between the regime headed by the supreme leader and the government headed by the president.

Phase four: The fourth phase began in 2005 with the upset election of the little-known mayor of Tehran, Mahmoud Ahmadinejad, over Rafsanjani. The emergence of hardliners reflected three broader shifts: Disillusionment with politics led many, especially young Iranians and women, to boycott the poll. Public anger swelled against the clergy, especially Rafsanjani, for corruption and failing to improve the average Iranian's life in a quarter century. And a second generation of revolutionaries hardened by the Iran-Iraq War, largely laymen, began to challenge the clerics who ended the monarchy.

Domestic Crisis

Through each phase, Iranian politics increasingly splintered. In the early 1980s, Iran was a virtual one-party state. The Islamic Republic Party dominated all branches of government.

But the infighting quickly became so serious that Khomeini publicly rebuked its officials, "Stop biting one another like scorpions." The divisions became a chasm; the party was dissolved in 1987.

Three decades later, Iran had more than 200 parties, factions and political groups—many of them still squabbling. A common political axiom in Tehran joked: "Where there are five Iranian Shiites, there are six political factions."

The depth of the divide among the original revolutionaries was witnessed after the 2009 presidential election. Mir Hossein Mousavi, the prime minister who led Iran throughout the Iran-Iraq War, charged the regime with massive fraud in his loss to Ahmadinejad. He also warned that it was turning into a dictatorship—the dictator being Supreme Leader Ayatollah Ali Khamenei, who as president had been his colleague in running the government during the 1980s.

The post-election protests were the biggest threat to the regime since the revolution. Beyond the immediate election issue, they reflected the degree of public daring, the diversity of political thought, and the growing unease about the system, even among those inside it. And the internal turmoil did not end with the regime's crackdown. The splintering continued, as conservatives began to turn on Ahmadinejad's core of hardliners for abuse of power.

People Power

The more dynamic part of the domestic crisis, however, was the spontaneous display of people power. Since the mid-1990s, the Iranian public—rather than any specific politician—had spurred the movement for political change. It was always an amorphous, leaderless body in search of a head that tapped into the limited number of candidate choices allowed to run after vetting by the Guardian Council. The embryonic reform movement first put Mohammad Khatami into the presidency in 1997 and then turned to Mousavi in 2009. Both men were adopted by the movement; neither was the original inspiration for reform.

The demonstrations were in some ways a logical next step in a longstanding debate over Iran's political system. After the shah's ouster, the revolutionaries were divided between ideologues and realists on the shape of a new government. Ideologues argued that the first modern theocracy should be a "redeemer state" championing the cause of the world's oppressed; restoring Islamic purity and rule in the 57-nation Islamic world; and creating a new Islamic bloc to defy both East and West. Realists argued that Iran should seek legitimacy by creating a capable Islamic state and institutionalizing the revolution. They, too, wanted a new political and social order independent of the outside world, but they also wanted to be realistic about Iran's need to interact economically and diplomatically with the world.

For 30 years, the bottom line issue had been variations on the same theme: whether to give priority to the revolution or to the state. Put another way: whether the Islamic Republic is first and foremost Islamic or a republic. The same theme had played out in the 2009 election. Ahmadinejad championed the revolutionary clerics' original vision of helping the oppressed, while Mousavi campaigned on the need for a viable and practical state. The same issues were also central to the post-election turmoil. Mousavi warned that the alleged vote-rigging was killing the idea that Islam and republicanism were compatible.

In 2009, the public became immersed in the debate too—first by turning out to vote and then in protesting alleged fraud. The newly named Green Movement also launched the most imaginative civil disobedience campaign in the Islamic world. It included a commercial boycott of goods advertised on state-controlled television. It featured anti-regime slogans and caricatures printed on the national currency—from a green V to signify the Green Movement's election victory to a stamped picture of Ahmadinejad with the caption "people's enemy." And it painted imaginative graffiti—usually in green—on public walls, the back of buses, bridge underpasses, university buildings and fences.

The public political energy was admired among reformers in other Muslim countries, including Sunni societies that had disdained the revolution or distanced themselves from Shiite Iran. Despite the government crackdown, the sheer magnitude of participation assured that the debate started shortly after the revolution was still far from over.

Fear of Foreigners

Historically, many of Iran's most tumultuous times have been caused by foreign invasions, meddling or influence. From the Persian prism, the showdown with the outside world in the 21st century is only the latest round. Long experience has bred deep suspicion and xenophobia.

Ancient Persia was pivotal to Alexander the Great's drive into India in the 4th century B.C. Its conquest by Arab armies in the 7th century gave the then new Islamic Empire access to central and eastern Asia. Persia was invaded by Turks in the 11th, 16th and 18th centuries. It was conquered by Genghis Khan's Mongol army in the 13th century and by Tamerlane in the 14th century. The Safavid dynasty actually converted to Shiism in the 16th century—some 900 years after Shiism's birth in Islam's great schism—to create a separate identity and prevent the encroachment of Sunnis in the neighboring Ottoman Empire. Persia was then challenged by the Afghans in the 18th century.

In the 20th century, Iran was occupied by Britain and the Soviet Union. The Persian Corridor was also the most viable supply route for U.S. Lend Lease aid to the Soviet Union during World War II. Some 40,000 American soldiers were deployed in Iran to keep the train link open. After the war, Iran was the first crisis of the new United Nations when the

Soviets refused to leave. In 1946, the U.N. Security Council passed a resolution calling on Moscow to pull-out its forces from northern Iran. President Harry Truman's ultimatum to Joseph Stalin on Iran spawned a new U.S.-Iran friendship that steadily deepened until the revolution. But the subsequent Cold War arguably also had its origins in this confrontation.

Rejecting Encroachment

The fight against foreign influence has also been central to the Iranian campaign for empowerment over the past century. The 1905–1911 Constitutional Revolution erupted after the monarchy doled out political and economic concessions to Britain and Russia. The backlash sparked prolonged instability and forced the Qajar dynasty in 1906 to accept demands for a constitution and parliament, both of which limited the king's powers. Iran had only the second constitution and parliament in Asia, after the Ottoman Empire. The first round of political reforms ended when an army colonel seized power in 1925, crowned himself Persia's new king, took the name Pahlavi, changed the country's name to Iran, and launched rapid modernization. He was forced to abdicate for pro-Nazi sentiments in 1941.

In 1953, Iran went through a second burst of democratic activism. An elected government led by Prime Minister Mohammad Mossadegh challenged the second and last Pahlavi shah, who was also heavily influenced by foreign powers. Mossadegh's four-party coalition advocated constitutional democracy and limited powers for the monarchy. It also wanted to nationalize Iranian oil after the Anglo-Iranian Oil Company refused a 50–50 profit-sharing deal. The shah's attempt to have Mossadegh dismissed backfired; the backlash forced the monarch to flee to Rome. Foreign powers restored the monarchy. The CIA and British intelligence orchestrated riots that forced Mossadegh to resign and allowed the young king to return to the Peacock Throne for another quarter century.

In many ways, the 1979 revolution was an extension of the two earlier challenges. In the 21st century, the struggle against foreign influence still defines Iran's current stand-off with the world. When the outside world today calls for cooperation, many Iranians see it as an attempt to co-opt or coerce them into conformity—to Western ways, morals and influence.

U.S. Relations

Since the revolution, Iran's showdown with the world has pivoted most of all on the United States. The shah's ouster transformed a country that for three decades had been one of two pillars—along with Israel—of U.S. policy in the Middle East. After the United States took in the ailing shah, Tehran began to view Washington as the ultimate enemy. The revolutionaries suspected another CIA plot to put the monarch back on the throne.

Defying international law, Iranian students responded by seizing the U.S. Embassy in a drama that dragged out for 444 days. The ordeal of 52 American hostages was largely responsible for ending the presidency of Jimmy Carter after one term. In the mid-1980s, Iran's double-dealing during the covert arms-for-hostage swap—in which Iran helped free three American hostages in Lebanon, only to have three more picked up—was the biggest scandal for the Reagan administration. Iran has been a consistent thorn for all six American presidents who tried to figure out how to deal with Tehran.

The two sides shouted at each other. In 1979, Iran dubbed the United States the "Great Satan." In 2002, the Bush administration called Iran part of an "axis of evil." Both countries occasionally tried outreach, although they were never on the same page at the same time. Their counterparts often suspected that the other would not or could not deliver; opportunities to at least explore rapprochement were missed. The most significant effort by Iran was President Khatami's call to bring down "the wall of mistrust." But it went largely unheeded in Washington until it was too late to salvage the effort.

American presidents also singled out Iran for mention in important speeches. In his 1989 inaugural address, President George H.W. Bush offered "new engagement" to the world, but made a special offer to Iran. "There are today Americans who are held against their will in foreign lands, and Americans who are unaccounted for. Assistance can be shown here, and will be long remembered. Good will begets good will. Good faith can be a spiral that endlessly moves on."

After the announcement of his 2009 Nobel Peace Prize, President Obama said it had to be "shared with everyone who strives for justice and dignity—for the young woman who marches silently in the streets on behalf of her right to be heard even in the face of beatings and bullets." He did not name her, but Iranians knew he was referring to Neda Agha Soltan, the aspiring 26-year-old musician who was shot on a Tehran street during the 2009 election protests. The cell phone video capturing her bloodied death was transmitted around the world.

By the end of 2010, tensions between Washington and Tehran had reached new heights because of suspicions about Iran's long-term nuclear intentions, support for Iraqi and Afghan militias targeting U.S. troops, Ahmadinejad's denial of the Holocaust and Israel's right to exist, and human rights abuses.

Nationalism

Tehran's policies and world perspective today are also rooted in a past rich with accomplishments. Iranians are notoriously proud, as is their right. Persia produced some of history's greatest scientists, physicians, astronomers, mathematicians, philosophers, architects, artists and poets. Iranians believe their contributions are not over—if only the outside world will give them a chance.

Zoroaster founded the first monotheistic religion, which introduced the ideas of good and evil and a day of judgment even before Judaism. Avicenna, or Ibn Sina, was an 11th century philosopher and physician whose medical texts were taught in Europe until the 17th century. A crater on the moon is named after him. In the 11th century, Omar Khayyam was one of the world's leading mathematicians and astronomers as well as a poet famed for more than 1,000 quatrain verses. Rumi, a 13th-century philosopher, is the world's most popular poet in the 21st century. Hafez, Saadi, and Ferdowsi were other great medieval poets whose works are still admired today. The list goes on and on.

Iran's intellectual culture has been evident even in the current political infighting. Some of the most modern and democratic ideas in the Islamic world today have emerged among Iranian philosophers, reformers and dissidents. Iranian philosopher Abdulkarim Soroush was the intellectual father of the reform movement. A former revolutionary, he turned on the regime. In the mid-1990s, he began to challenge the theological justification for a supreme leader and called for separation of mosque and state. He also declared that freedom always had precedence over religion, because Muslims could only be true believers if they embraced the faith with their own free will.

Given their past, Iranians see only greatness in their future; they view their current status as only a blip on the screen of history. The quest for nuclear energy, which dates back to the shah, is viewed as a key to modern development. For many ordinary Iranians, the right to enrich uranium to fuel nuclear reactors is first and foremost an issue of sovereignty. As they modernize, they want to avoid any further dependence on the outside world. To understand Iranian nationalism, think of a proud, chauvinistic Texan—then add 5,000 years.

Strategic Value

The outside world has always valued Iran because of its location. Today, no nation can afford to ignore Iran, regardless of who is in power, for several reasons:

- It holds some 10 percent of the world's oil reserves. Iran is OPEC's second largest oil producer. It also has the world's second largest reserves of natural gas.

- Iran's vast resources provide enormous leverage in an oil-hungry world. Since World War II, petroleum has been essential to the movement of modern armies and for development of modern industry. Free access to oil has also been essential to both political and economic power.

- Iran's geo-strategic location bridges the world's most volatile blocs of countries—the Middle East to the west, the Asian subcontinent to the east, and the Caucuses and Central Asia to the north. Peaceful relations with Iran are pivotal to the stability of more than one dozen countries.

- Iran's position and the traditions of its Aryan people, the Indo-European race whence Iran gets its name, have long made Iran the crossroads of culture and geography.

- Iran's population is now among the world's top twenty. In the first decade after the revolution, it almost doubled from 34 to 62 million when the clerics called on Iranian women to breed an Islamic generation.

Neighborhood Geography

Iran stands apart geographically because of two great mountain ranges, the Alborz and the Zagros, and three great bodies of water, the Caspian Sea, the Persian Gulf and the Indian Ocean. In terms of territory,

- Iran is roughly one-fifth the size of the United States.

- It ranks 18th among the world's nations in geographic mass.

- Neighboring Afghanistan, by comparison, is 41st.

- Neighboring Iraq is 58th.

- Iran is more than twice as large and twice as populated as both countries.

Iran's nine other frontiers are important for more than trade and transit.

Iraq: To the West, Iran's 910-mile border with Iraq is an entry point into the Arab world's Fertile Crescent.

Turkey: To the northwest, Iran shares a 312-mile border with Turkey, a vital member of NATO.

Afghanistan: To the east, Iran shares a 585-mile border with Afghanistan; the two countries share one of the world's most active routes for trafficking narcotics.

Pakistan: To the southeast is the 570-mile border with Pakistan. The father of Pakistan's nuclear bomb provided pivotal equipment to Tehran.

Gulf states: Iran's frontier along the Persian Gulf, through which more than 40 percent of the West's oil passes daily, is the longest of the six countries that rim the strategic waterway. Iran effectively controls the Strait of Hormuz, the so-called chokepoint for Gulf oil exports.

Turkmenistan: To the north, Iran has a 620-mile border with the former Soviet republic, the most autocratic of the Central Asian nations.

Azerbaijan: To the north, Iran shares a 270-mile border with Azerbaijan. About one quarter of Iran's population is ethnic Azeri.

Armenia: To the north, Iran's smallest frontier is the 22-mile border with Armenia. Armenians are among the Christian minorities represented by specially allocated seats for Christians in Iran's parliament.

Azerbaijan-Nakhchivan exclave: To the north, Iran shares a 112-mile border.

Ethnically, Iran is also a geographic crossroad mirroring most of its neighbors. Only 51 percent of Iranians are pure Persians. The rest are Azeris in the northwest and Turkoman in the northeast. Kurds live along the western border with Iraq. Baluchis (or "wanderers") straddle the arid and unruly southeast border with Pakistan. Arabs live on the southern coast. The Lors, an Arab-Persian mix, live mainly in the mountains, while nomadic herding tribes live in the south.

The Future

- In the 21st century, Iran's unique version of God's government must prove its viability on earth—and that it can deliver what its people want—or risk the same fate as other utopian ideologies.

- No Islamic country is likely to replicate the Iranian experience. The costs are too high, the results too controversial. The Shiite character of the revolution also makes it unlikely to be repeated among Sunni-dominated societies.

- Yet Iran's Shiite alliance remains a major power bloc capable of heavily influencing the outcome of elections and conflicts—and sparking tensions with Sunni communities.

- Iran's resources create a huge cushion against punitive actions such as economic sanctions. In an oil-hungry world, they also undermine international cooperation.

- Iran's labyrinthine political system—and competing sources of power—complicate all forms of diplomacy. Engagement, especially with the United States, has become a domestic political issue—unrelated to the merits of rapprochement.

Reading 5.2

The Next Arab Uprising
The Collapse of Authoritarianism in the Middle East

Marwan Muasher

TWO PERFECT STORMS HAVE STRUCK THE Arab world in the past decade. In 2011, in what was at first optimistically called "the Arab Spring," popular uprisings unseated autocrats across the region. Hopes ran high that these peaceful protest movements would usher in a new era of democracy in the Middle East. But except in Tunisia, they ended in turmoil or deadly civil wars. Then, in 2014, the region's leaders were dealt another blow when the price of oil plummeted, threatening the basic model of governance on which their power rested. Low oil prices since have made it difficult for regimes to fund bloated budgets, buy off elites, and hold up long-postponed reforms. This is not a temporary aberration: it is unlikely that the price of oil will ever again rise to its pre-2014 levels.

On the surface, many Arab states appear to have weathered these two storms—however shakily. But there is more turbulence ahead. The shocks of 2011 and 2014 were just the first symptoms of a deeper transformation under way in the region: the fundamental bargain underpinning stability in Middle Eastern states is coming undone, and unless regional leaders move quickly to strike new bargains with their citizens, even larger storms will come.

For more than half a century, Middle Eastern governments have used oil wealth to fund a system of economic patronage. Known as "rentier states," these governments derive a substantial portion of their revenue from selling off national resources or bargaining for foreign backing rather than extracting taxes from citizens. In some countries, such as Saudi Arabia and the United Arab Emirates (UAE), the revenue has come from the sale of domestic oil resources; in others, such as Egypt and Jordan, they have come in the form of transfers from regional patrons with oil wealth. Throughout the Middle East, governments have used oil resources to fund stable jobs, education, and health care, and in return, leaders have received political submission. But as oil prices have remained low and the region's demographics have shifted, that basic tradeoff has

Marwan Muasher, "The Next Arab Uprising: The Collapse of Authoritarianism in the Middle East," *Foreign Affairs*, vol. 97, no. 6, ed. Gideon Rose, pp. 113–124. Copyright © 2018 by Council on Foreign Relations, Inc. Reprinted with permission.

begun to seem unsustainable. Without the revenue necessary to continue feeding bloated, inefficient systems, governments are struggling to hold up their end of the bargain. Their primary source of political legitimacy is slipping away.

If they respond to these shifting fortunes by tightening their grip on power and failing to implement meaningful reforms, Middle Eastern governments risk unleashing social unrest on a scale beyond anything they've seen before. The only way around such a disruption will involve economic and political reforms that create a fundamentally new social contract in the Middle East, one negotiated from the bottom up. Without the rentier model to lean on, governments must build productive economies that are based on merit rather than loyalty and dominated by the private sector rather than the state. Because such large structural changes will create pushback and problems of their own, they will be impossible without the buy-in of the public. Economic adjustments will not succeed without political changes that are at least as dramatic. If Middle Eastern governments embrace economic reforms in conjunction with greater political accountability and participation, they may have a fighting chance at long-term stability. If they do not, the next, larger storm will arrive before long.

The Broken Bargain

The social contracts binding Middle Eastern governments and their citizens have traditionally been imposed from the top down. These authoritarian bargains, in which rulers secure legitimacy and support through public spending rather than participatory political processes, have been predicated on a rentier system. Using oil wealth, governments would provide economic patronage, acting as the main purveyors of jobs, subsidies, and basic health care and education. The oil-producing states—Algeria, Bahrain, Iran, Iraq, Kuwait, Libya, Oman, Qatar, Saudi Arabia, and the UAE—used revenue from the sale of their own oil. Oil-importing states— Egypt, Jordan, Morocco, and Tunisia—relied on large grants from their flush oil-producing neighbors and remittances from their citizens working abroad in the oil industry. The Gulf states supported oil-importing countries, especially Egypt and Jordan, for political reasons (to ensure that these countries' positions were largely in line with their own) and economic ones (Egypt and Jordan provided cheap, educated labor). By the turn of the century, grants and remittances accounted for, on average, over ten percent of Egypt's and Jordan's GDPs. Rentierism took different forms in different states, but in one way or another, oil revenues long allowed many oil-importing Middle Eastern countries to live beyond their means.

In return for their patronage, states expected citizens to leave governing to a small elite, which, over time, became more and more isolated from the general population. Meanwhile, oil rents helped regimes buttress themselves with political, economic, and bureaucratic circles whose loyalty was ensured and whose interests were tied to their own. The more jobs

We're not gonna take it: during protests in Amman, Jordan, June 2018. Copyright © Reuters/Ammar Awad.

and subsidies governments could provide, the better. But rather than creating jobs through productive systems based on merit and led by the private sector, they found that providing public-sector jobs, whether or not they were useful, was the best way to ensure allegiance and dampen demands for accountability. The ratio of public-sector jobs to private-sector jobs in the Middle East and North Africa was the highest in the world.

Social contracts predicated on rentierism functioned throughout the second half of the twentieth century—that is, for as long as citizens considered the services provided in exchange for their acquiescence to be at least minimally satisfactory. But in the 1990s, the conditions states needed to hold up their end of the deal had begun to disappear. As governments grew, they needed the price of oil to remain high in order to fund expanding bureaucracies and the needs of elites. States were stretched well beyond their means. In Jordan, for example, the government and the army employed a whopping 42 percent of the labor force by the early years of this century. Energy subsidies provided by the government to citizens reached

11 percent of GDP in Egypt, ten percent in Saudi Arabia, nine percent in Libya, eight and a half percent in Bahrain and the UAE, and eight percent in Kuwait.

Once the size of these states' bureaucracies began to outpace the rise in oil prices at the turn of the century, something had to give. Governments could no longer afford to hire more people or pay for subsidies on commodities such as bread and gasoline. Unemployment rates in the Middle East and North Africa reached an average of 11 percent in 2000; among young people, the average was 30 percent. As governments struggled to maintain bloated states, the quality of health and educational services started to decline. But rather than offer citizens more political representation to help ease the blow, governments continued to insist that citizens uphold their end of the authoritarian bargain—refrain from demanding greater influence—even as leaders came up short on theirs.

Shock Waves

Many Middle Eastern governments tried to address the fracturing of the old social contract by introducing economic reforms without accompanying political changes. Although these reforms were largely intended to help regimes preserve their grip on power, some of them, if well implemented, could have also benefited citizens. But without the systems of checks and balances necessary to oversee economic transformations, even well-intended efforts—privatizing state-run industries, liberalizing trading systems, integrating into the global economy—ended up benefiting elites rather than the broader population.

Without proper monitoring bodies, corruption skyrocketed. Most Middle Eastern publics came to associate the economic reforms of the beginning of this century with elite self-enrichment rather than their own betterment. The ranking of several Middle Eastern countries on Transparency International's Corruption Perceptions Index declined considerably. Jordan fell from a ranking of 43 (out of 133 countries) in 2003 to 50 (out of 178) in 2010. During the same period, Egypt's ranking fell from 70 to 98, and Tunisia's from 39 to 59.

In some cases, the breaking of the old social contract proved too much for societies to bear. Although it was by no means the only factor that led to the Arab uprisings of 2011, it contributed to the collapse of several regimes, particularly those in countries where institutions were already weak. Tunisian President Zine el-Abidine Ben Ali and Egyptian President Hosni Mubarak were the first to fall. In Libya, Syria, and Yemen, where the sitting regimes had never been interested in building solid institutions, street protests overwhelmed weak states and led to the crumbling of the existing order and, ultimately, civil war. In Bahrain, antigovernment demonstrations gave way to an ongoing low-level insurgency that has irritated but not seriously threatened the monarchy. The monarchies in Jordan and Morocco faced sustained protests but survived the upheaval relatively unscathed.

In the Gulf countries, regimes had a solution at hand, at least in the short term: throw money at the problem in order to pacify the public. King Abdullah of Saudi Arabia promised an aid package of $130 billion that included higher salaries and more housing assistance for Saudi citizens. Other Gulf governments offered similar packages, all made possible by high oil prices. In February 2011, the Kuwaiti government gave every citizen 1,000 Kuwaiti dinars (about $3,560) and free staple foods for over a year. In Oman, the government funded 30,000 more jobs and 40 percent more university scholarships. In Jordan, King Abdullah responded to protests by immediately introducing ad hoc reform measures that helped temporarily stave off discontent. A $5 billion aid package put together by various Gulf states helped the country withstand the pressure from the street. But even this turned out to be only enough to quell dissent until the next storm struck, in 2014.

The uprisings of 2011 should have taught Middle Eastern governments that serious attention to governance—not just economic reforms—was long overdue. But once the initial pressure had subsided, the surviving governments reverted to their old habits almost immediately. They were bolstered in their turn back toward authoritarianism by the violence and enormous human suffering unfolding in Libya, Syria, and Yemen, as well as by the rise of Islamists in Egypt, which discouraged citizens elsewhere from pursuing further confrontations with the state.

Then came the next shock. In August 2014, the price of oil, which had reached over $140 a barrel in 2008, fell below $100 a barrel. It reached a low of $30 a barrel in 2016 before rebounding to around $70 a barrel, where it remains today. For Saudi Arabia, which needs the price of oil to stay above approximately $85–$87 a barrel to maintain a balanced budget and to fund lavish assistance to other regional governments, this decline meant that the government had to dramatically change its spending habits to avoid going into debt. Other grant-giving countries, such as Kuwait and the UAE, also had to curtail their regional assistance. Across the Middle East, oil producers could no longer afford to function as welfare states, and oil-importing countries could no longer rely on grants awarded by oil-producing ones or remittances from their citizens working in those countries to finance their patronage systems.

The end of the era of high oil prices triggered a new wave of protests. In 2018, demands for change escalated in Saudi Arabia, including by leading preachers, women, and political activists, and Jordan witnessed street protests for the first time since the Arab Spring. These two countries illustrate particularly well the repercussions of the end of rentierism in the region. The first, Saudi Arabia, is an example of an oil-producing country that can no longer act as welfare state. The second, Jordan, is an example of an oil-importing country that can no longer depend on oil money from abroad to fuel an inefficient economic and political system.

Changing Course

In Saudi Arabia, the end of high oil prices coincided with the passing of power to a new generation of leaders—most prominent among them Crown Prince Mohammed bin Salman, also known as MBS. The economic writing was on the wall for Saudi Arabia well before MBS, who is only in his early 30s, rose to prominence. Starting in 2015, large deficits meant that Saudi Arabia could no longer afford to maintain its generous internal and external subsidies. In 2017, the budget deficit reached $61 billion, or 9.2 percent of GDP. The country expects to run deficits until at least 2023. As a consequence, the Saudi government has cut subsidies and allowed the price of services to rise. Saudi Arabia's regional interventions in Syria, Yemen, and elsewhere have further strained its struggling economy. The Yemeni war alone is estimated to cost the Saudi government $6–$7 billion each month.

The Saudi government has responded to this new reality with a weak package of reforms that are unlikely to fully address the challenges. In an attempt to boost the country's stagnant economy, the government announced a radically expansionary budget for 2018 but offered no sense of how it will be financed. The Saudi government has stopped its traditional assistance to Jordan for three years and can no longer support the regime of Abdel Fattah el-Sisi in Egypt to the tune of tens of billions of dollars each year, a program the Saudis began after Sisi ousted Egypt's Islamist government in 2013. It has also embarked on an impressive social reform agenda, including allowing women to drive, reopening movie theaters, and curtailing the powers of the Islamist police force, in what is probably an effort to appease the new generation and divert attention from demands for political reform.

These social reforms have gained MBS significant popularity among young Saudis. But youth unemployment in the kingdom remains staggering: it reached almost 35 percent in 2017. Will the new generation accept austerity and the loss of privileges and subsidies without more of a voice in the running of their country in exchange? If the revolts of 2011 offer any evidence, the answer is likely no. The Jordanian example, in particular, suggests that continued economic austerity, coupled with over 30 percent youth unemployment, is likely to push the new generation to demand more of a voice. Those demands may even include calls for the introduction of an elected parliament, which would be a first in Saudi history.

Saudi Arabia is not the only Gulf country facing the challenge of low oil prices. Kuwait, which already has an elected parliament, faced a drop in its oil revenues of around $15 billion in 2014 and again in 2015. As in the Saudi case, Kuwait first relied on its massive fiscal reserves (estimated at over $600 billion) but is now introducing cuts in subsidies and a medium-term plan of economic reforms that will begin steering the Kuwaiti economy away from its reliance on oil. Oman has reacted similarly to the low oil prices: cutting subsidies, reducing benefits for public-sector workers, and hiking taxes.

Precarious Peace

In Jordan, declining financial support from neighboring oil-producing countries and a drop in remittances have challenged the government's ability to continue funding a system of economic patronage. Although Jordan is ruled by a monarchy that much of society accepts as legitimate, recent waves of protests suggest that the system is more vulnerable than many think. The monarchy has traditionally responded to demands for reform by implementing ad hoc measures that pacify the public but never result in true power sharing with the legislative and judicial branches of government. Essential to such measures has been generous financial aid from the Gulf states (and other powers, including the United States), which has allowed the Jordanian government to maintain an inefficient, patronage-based political and economic system. The government has used the money to continue buying the support of the elite and funding a bloated bureaucracy in a system that prioritizes patronage over merit.

In 2011 and 2012, large-scale protests erupted throughout Jordan in response to economic and political grievances, but they petered out after King Abdullah made a series of political reforms and regional instability directed attention elsewhere. But King Abdullah's actions—firing prime ministers, reforming the constitution, and replacing the government three times in 18 months—were quick fixes designed to appease the protesters rather than lasting, serious reforms. By 2016, Jordan's political elite was so confident that it had gotten through the Arab uprisings unharmed that it amended the constitution to give the king additional powers and further consolidate the executive branch's grip on power.

But the apparent stability concealed deeper problems. Jordan is in the grip of a slowly developing economic crisis, driven by soaring public debt, which now stands at 95 percent of GDP; low growth, now around two percent; and high unemployment, now 18.5 percent and over 30 percent among young people. The sharp reduction in financial support from oil-producing states has meant that the country can no longer rely on that aid to keep its debt in check and finance its public deficit. Saudi Arabia, which headed a Gulf initiative that provided Jordan with $5 billion after the 2011 protests, put a three-year freeze on subsidies to Jordan starting in 2015. (After more recent protests, Kuwait, Saudi Arabia, and the UAE announced a new, $2.5 billion aid package to Jordan, mostly in the form of guarantees to pay the country's loans, but that hardly replaced the lost assistance.)

Successive Jordanian governments have treated such challenges as purely technical problems. Among the public, however, demands have escalated beyond the need for economic changes. In May 2018, protests erupted throughout Jordan, particularly in affluent neighborhoods in western Amman, led by the middle class (the Islamists, who had spearheaded protests in 2011 and 2012, were conspicuously absent). In addition to calling for the withdrawal of a controversial income tax law, the protesters demanded the dissolution of Parliament and a change of government. Evidently, King Abdullah's quick fixes in 2011 and

2012 failed to address the roots of the unrest: without the rents necessary to keep funding a system of patronage, the social contract in Jordan has broken down. Durable solutions to the protesters' demands will require a new social contract, not symbolic reforms.

Egypt continues to suffer from the economic effects of its revolution and from the decrease in the massive assistance it used to receive from Saudi Arabia and the UAE. In 2016, two years after that Gulf assistance dropped, Egypt floated its currency and had to rely on a $12 billion loan from the International Monetary Fund to help it restore economic stability.

The one notable exception to the current state of affairs in the Middle East is Tunisia. After its revolution in 2011, Tunisia may not have solved its political, economic, and security issues, but its leaders understood the need for a new social contract. For three difficult years, an elected constituent assembly negotiated and ultimately agreed on a new constitution that upheld the principle of the peaceful rotation of power, gave women almost full rights, and affirmed a commitment to the collective and individual rights of all parts of Tunisian society. Tunisia is by no means out of the woods, but it has achieved a solid footing for future stability and prosperity.

A New Social Contract

If the message coming from the Arab street was lost on the region's leaders in 2011, in part due to the failure of the protests to spark serious efforts to build new institutions (except in Tunisia), the end of rentierism is giving Middle Eastern governments another chance to hear it. Economic reforms must be accompanied by political ones that give people a meaningful say in the running of their countries.

The transition to more efficient economies is sure to be slow and rocky and to face significant pushback from the forces that benefit from the status quo. Decades-old rentier systems have created vested interests with little desire to usher in merit-based structures that might rob them of their privileges.

Political will at the top will be needed to put in place gradual, serious, and participatory processes that the public can believe in. The necessary reforms will require a period of material hardship. Middle Eastern citizens will accept short-term sacrifices in the name of badly needed long-term change—but only if they are included in the process and guided by leadership they can trust.

Middle Eastern governments should begin this process by doing more to empower women. Women's participation in the work force in the region is the lowest in the world (32 percent, compared with a world average of 58 percent, according to a 2009 World Bank report). Governments must also better exploit technology to raise productivity and gear their efforts toward a more knowledge-based economy. They must rapidly diversify their sources of revenue away from oil by empowering the private sector and encouraging public-private partnerships. And they must promote the rule of law and a culture of equality among all citizens, which will help foster innovation. This will require ending legal discrimination against women and minority groups.

Critically, governments cannot remain the primary employers in Middle Eastern countries. Fostering the proper legal and financial environments to promote the private sector, particularly small and medium-sized enterprises, will help companies expand and replace public-sector jobs. This is easier said than done: outdated educational systems and inadequate health services have left large parts of the population in most Middle Eastern states ill equipped for work in the private sector. In order to minimize unemployment and hardship, transitions to economies dominated by the private sector must include big changes to educational and health-care systems. In particular, schools and universities need to shift from promoting the rote learning of absolute truths toward encouraging critical thinking, innovation, and the acceptance of diverse viewpoints.

Even if governments start now, these changes will require a generation or two to fully take effect. But the uprisings of 2011 should have already taught Middle Eastern leaders that they are short on time. They must make painful economic decisions now to avoid worse suffering down the road. And whether leaders like it or not, the consent of the governed will be a critical factor in the success of transitions from rentier economies to productive systems. Citizens and leaders will have to agree on a new social contract. This time, rather than governments imposing contracts from the top down, the ethnically, culturally, and religiously diverse communities that make up Middle Eastern countries must be allowed to negotiate them from the bottom up.

Forging this new social contract will require visionary leaders who have the will to stand up to their country's own elite, who grasp that the way to keep power is to share it, and who can persuade the populace that they are capable of guiding it to a better future. Sadly, not many such leaders exist today. (They are rare everywhere, not just in the Middle East.) But Middle Eastern governments have no choice. If they continue to ignore the need for change, the havoc to come will bring change on its own.

Reading 5.3

The Kurdish Awakening
Unity, Betrayal, and the Future of the Middle East

Henri J. Barkey

"WE'VE BEEN FIGHTING FOR A LONG time in Syria," said U.S. President Donald Trump in the last days of 2018. "Now it's time for our troops to come back home." The president's surprise call for a rapid withdrawal of the nearly 2,000 U.S. troops stationed in Syria drew widespread criticism from members of the U.S. foreign policy establishment. But it came as an even greater shock to the United States' main partner in the fight against the Islamic State (or ISIS), the Syrian Kurds. For weeks prior to the announcement, Turkish President Recep Tayyip Erdogan had been threatening to invade areas of northern Syria controlled by Kurdish militants. The only thing stopping him was the presence of U.S. troops. Removing them would leave the Kurds deeply exposed. "If [the Americans] will leave," warned one Syrian Kurd, "we will curse them as traitors."

Details about the U.S. withdrawal from Syria remain sketchy. But whatever Washington ultimately decides to do, Trump's announcement marked a cruel turn for Kurds across the Middle East. Back in mid-2017, the Kurds had been enjoying a renaissance. Syrian Kurds, allied with the world's only superpower, had played the central role in largely defeating ISIS on the battlefield and had seized the group's capital, Raqqa. The People's Protection Units (YPG), a Syrian Kurdish militia, controlled large swaths of Syrian territory and looked set to become a significant actor in negotiations to end the country's civil war. Turkish Kurds, although besieged at home, were basking in the glow of the accomplishments of their Syrian counterparts, with whom they are closely aligned. And in Iraq, the body that rules the country's Kurdish region—the Kurdistan Regional Government, or KRG—was at the height of its powers, preparing for a September 2017 referendum on independence.

By the end of 2018, many of the Kurds' dreams appeared to be in tatters. After the overwhelming majority of Iraqi Kurds voted for independence in the KRG's referendum, the Iraqi government, backed by Iran and Turkey, invaded Iraqi Kurdistan and conquered some 40 percent of its territory. Overnight, the KRG lost not only nearly half of its land but much of its international influence, too. The Turkish Kurds, despite gaining seats in parliament in the June 2018 elections, had endured relentless assaults from Erdogan and his government throughout the year, including a renewed military campaign against the Kurdistan Workers' Party (PKK), a left-wing separatist group. In Syria, Turkey invaded the Kurdish-controlled town of Afrin in March 2018, displacing the YPG and some 200,000 local Kurds. Then, in December, the Syrian Kurds learned that their American protectors might soon abandon them altogether.

These setbacks, however, belie a larger trend—one that will shape the Middle East in the years ahead. Across the region, Kurds are gaining self-confidence, pushing for long-denied rights, and, most important, collaborating with one another across national boundaries and throughout the diaspora. To a greater extent than at any previous point in history, Kurds in the four traditionally distinct parts of Kurdistan—in Iran, Iraq, Syria, and Turkey—are starting down the road of becoming a single Kurdish nation. Significant barriers to unity remain, including linguistic divisions and the presence of at least two strong states, Iran and Turkey, with an overriding interest in thwarting any form of pan-Kurdism. Yet recent events have initiated a process of Kurdish nation building that will, in the long run, prove difficult to contain. Even if there is never a single, unified, independent Kurdistan, the Kurdish national awakening has begun. The Middle East's states may fear the Kurdish awakening, but it is beyond their power to stop it.

The Lost Cause

Around 30 million Kurds currently live in Greater Kurdistan, a contiguous region stretching across southeastern Turkey, northwestern Iran, northern Iraq, and northeastern Syria. Kurdish tribes interacted with the Arab, Persian, and Turkic empires over the centuries, sometimes cooperating with them and sometimes rebelling against them. Modern Kurdish nationalism has its roots in the dissolution of the Ottoman Empire after World War I. The 1920 Treaty of Sèvres, signed between the Allies and the defeated Ottomans, called for an independence referendum in the Kurdish-majority areas of modern-day Turkey. Yet following Turkey's war of independence, the new Turkish government renegotiated with the Allies. This resulted in the 1923 Treaty of Lausanne, which guaranteed Turkish sovereignty over what could have potentially been an independent Kurdistan.

Kurdish demands for independence, however, did not go away. Throughout the twentieth century, Kurdish revolts, often backed by rival states, erupted in nearly every country that had a significant Kurdish population. Turkey put down Kurdish rebellions in 1925, 1930, and 1937. Then, in the mid-1980s, the PKK launched an armed insurgency in Turkey that has

This land is our land: Kurdish peshmerga forces in Makhmur, Iraq, August 2014. Copyright © Reuters/Youssef Boudlal.

continued off and on until the present day. In Iran in 1946, Kurds backed by the Soviet Union established the first genuine Kurdish government, the independent Republic of Mahabad, which lasted for one year before collapsing after Moscow withdrew its support. Iraqi Kurds have also frequently revolted against their central government. Supported by the shah of Iran, they fought two wars against Baghdad during the 1960s and 1970s, only to be defeated in 1975 after the shah struck a deal with the Iraqi strongman Saddam Hussein, abandoning the Kurds to their fate.

This agitation has meant that for each of the four states with a large Kurdish minority, suppressing Kurdish nationalism has been a paramount policy objective. The new Turkish state under President Kemal Ataturk banned the use of the Kurdish language in 1924 and over time introduced draconian rule in Kurdish areas, burning villages, displacing people, and confiscating their property. (Although U.S. intelligence was always confident that Turkey could handle any challenge posed by the Kurds, a 1971 CIA report conceded that Turkish policies, especially those preventing the use of the Kurdish language, were at the root of Kurdish unrest.) Iran similarly banned Kurdish dialects in the 1930s. In Syria, the central government not only prohibited the teaching and learning of Kurdish but also placed restrictions on Kurdish landownership. And beginning in the 1960s, Damascus revoked the citizenship of tens of thousands of Syrian Kurds, rendering them stateless. All across the Middle East, Kurdish areas were economically neglected and marginalized.

In the face of this repression, the Kurds have succeeded in preserving and even strengthening their identity across generations. As the Kurdish scholar Hamit Bozarslan has observed, Kurds have been treated as a minority by the governments of Iran, Iraq, Syria, and Turkey, but they do not see themselves as one. They are a majority in their homeland, Kurdistan, which only through an accident of geopolitical history has been rendered an appendage of other states. And it is the Middle East's modern state system that has, historically, been the main obstacle to Kurdish national aspirations. A prescient 1960 intelligence report by the CIA argued that the Kurds of Iran and Iraq had all the necessary elements for autonomy—military strength, leadership, and the possibility of material support from an outside power, the Soviet Union. "Only the relative stability of parent governments," the report noted, "stands in the way of active Kurdish separatism."

Two Steps Forward, One Step Back

For most of the twentieth century, the only possible path to Kurdish autonomy (or independence, for that matter) ran through state failure. And in effect, this is exactly what has transpired over the past two decades. If the Kurds today have a glimmer of hope in Iraq and Syria, it is because of the collapse of authority in Baghdad and Damascus. In particular, the actions of the United States—its support of the Kurds following the Persian Gulf War, its 2003 overthrow of Saddam and subsequent occupation of Iraq, and its more recent efforts to combat ISIS in Syria—have created the conditions for the revival of Kurdish political aspirations. Washington, unintentionally and in service of its own strategic needs, has midwifed Kurdish nationalism.

American military and political engagement with the Kurds began in earnest with the 1990–91 Gulf War. After the Iraqi army was evicted from Kuwait, it turned its guns on the Kurds and Shiites who had responded to U.S. President George H. W. Bush's call to rise up against Baghdad.

Faced with the possibility of a humanitarian crisis, the United States, with support from France and the United Kingdom, declared a no-fly zone over the Kurdish regions of northern Iraq. Protected by the no-fly zone, the Iraqi Kurds were able to carve out regional autonomy, founding the KRG in 1992. Iraqi Kurdistan became a bastion of pro-American sentiment in the country, especially after the United States' invasion in 2003, promoting further U.S.-Kurdish cooperation. Kurdish forces allied with U.S. troops in the initial war against Saddam, and in the ensuing years, Iraqi Kurdistan provided an anchor of stability as the rest of the country descended into civil war.

The founding of the KRG provided an important psychological boost to the Kurds, not just in Iraq but across the rest of the Middle East, too. It demonstrated that Kurds could govern themselves and secure international recognition. It also began to reshape Kurdish relations with other states. Although Turkey has traditionally disapproved of Kurdish demands for autonomy, the Turkish government under Erdogan chose not to confront the KRG but to build political and economic links with it instead. The landlocked Iraqi Kurds needed a channel for diplomacy and commerce—especially oil exports—and Ankara was happy to provide one. In 2010, Turkey opened a consulate in the KRG's capital, Erbil. Then, in 2012, the KRG and Turkey signed a deal to construct an oil pipeline from Iraqi Kurdistan to the Mediterranean. By 2018, some 400,000 barrels of KRG oil were reaching the Turkish port of Ceyhan every day. Ankara has provided an economic lifeline to the KRG, granting it the breathing room to consolidate itself in Iraq. For a time, Erdogan also profited domestically, as Turkish Kurds close to the KRG's president, Masoud Barzani, began voting for Erdogan's party in Turkish elections. Confident of his Kurdish bona fides, in 2009, Erdogan launched a domestic peace process with the PKK.

Yet soon, another U.S. action was to unintentionally change the Kurds' position in the Middle East. In 2014, the Obama administration began a bombing campaign to prevent Kobani, a Syrian Kurdish town on the Turkish border, from falling to ISIS. At the time, ISIS had just swept through northern Iraq and Syria, capturing large stretches of territory, including Iraq's second-largest city, Mosul. Washington's decision to protect Kobani elicited frenzied objections from Erdogan, since the United States would be directly supporting the YPG, which had close ties with the PKK in Turkey. The U.S. partnership with the YPG was a battlefield success, and the Kurds' eventual victory at Kobani became a turning point in the fight against ISIS. But this very success began to ring alarm bells in Ankara.

For Erdogan, a U.S.-YPG alliance represented a game changer for the region. What the Turkish president feared most was the emergence of a second KRG, this one in Syria. After all, the KRG itself was the product of a U.S. intervention that led to a civil war and the breakdown of central authority in Baghdad, culminating in the creation of a federal system in Iraq, with the KRG as a constituent element. With Syria already consumed by civil war, Ankara believed that Washington was on the verge of repeating what it had done in Iraq—that is, transforming Syria into a federal state in which the Kurds would gain the right to govern themselves. Erdogan could not assent to federal arrangements in two neighboring countries, much less to a Syrian-Kurdish one closely linked to the PKK. In 2014, Erdogan abandoned his negotiations with the PKK and began a policy of outright conflict with both the Turkish and the Syrian Kurds. He sought to delegitimize all Kurdish political activity by associating it with the PKK, arresting large numbers of Kurdish activists and politicians.

But if the United States inadvertently disrupted Kurdish-Turkish relations, U.S. policy in Iraq and Syria, taken as a whole, has earned the Kurds an unprecedented degree of international legitimacy. France, the United Kingdom, and the United States have all extended diplomatic recognition to the KRG, as well as providing it with economic and other forms of support. And the Syrian Kurds, previously ignored by the outside world, have been able to raise their global profile thanks to their role in the fight against ISIS. This recognition has come not only from Western powers. In a draft proposal for a new Syrian constitution, put forward in 2017 through the Astana peace process, Russia suggested two important concessions to the Kurds: dropping the word "Arab" from the name Syrian Arab Republic and creating a "culturally autonomous" region in the country's northeast, where children would be educated in both Arabic and Kurdish. These concessions were rejected by Damascus, and there is no guarantee that they will ever be granted. But their inclusion in the Russian proposal demonstrated that despite the Syrian Kurds' precarious position, outside powers are beginning to recognize them as an autonomous force to be reckoned with.

The Kurdish Renaissance

Kurds mobilized throughout the twentieth century to win cultural autonomy and some degree of self-rule from central governments. For nearly 100 years, rebellions and resistance constituted the backdrop of ordinary Kurdish life. Now, this is changing, as Kurds have acquired governing experience—not just in the KRG but also in numerous municipalities in Syria and Turkey. This, in turn, has caused Kurdish identity to begin to coalesce across national boundaries.

So far, the Kurds' experience in power has been fraught with problems. The KRG, for instance, is on the path to becoming a petrostate, dependent on oil sales and beset by corruption, patronage, and the outsize power of its two leading political families, the Barzanis and the Talabanis. The political wing of the YPG, the Democratic Union Party, has succeeded in efficiently providing services in the areas of Syria that it controls, but it has also constructed a one-party proto-state. And in Turkey, although representatives of the left-wing, Kurdish dominated Peoples' Democratic Party (HDP) won 102 municipalities in the July 2016 elections, Erdogan has since removed 94 of them from office. He has vowed to act similarly after the next round of municipal elections this March. Future HDP success may even motivate Erdogan to have the party shut down by the Constitutional Court, as Turkey's generals did to the HDP's predecessors.

But even if Kurdish self-government has not been an unalloyed success, it has been a boon for Kurdish culture and language across the region. This is especially true in Iraqi Kurdistan, which boasts its own Kurdish-language institutions, including schools and media organizations. Despite challenges such as the existence of two distinct Kurdish dialects, which roughly correspond to the KRG's political divisions—Kurmanji is spoken in areas dominated by the Kurdistan Democratic Party, whereas Sorani is spoken in those run by the Patriotic Union of Kurdistan—the KRG has established a rich Kurdish cultural environment in the territory it controls. There are now hundreds of Kurdish television channels, websites, news agencies, and other cultural products, such as novels and movies. And in Syria, where for decades Damascus banned even private education in Kurdish, the Democratic Union Party has formally introduced Kurdish-language education in the areas under its control. After nearly a century of attempting to prevent the dissemination of Kurdish language and culture, central governments have now decisively lost that battle.

Iraq's Kurdish-language renaissance has in turn stimulated a renewal of Kurdish self-awareness in transnational social media and diaspora communities. The Kurdish diaspora is especially strong in Europe, to which over one million Kurds have immigrated over the past six decades—initially as guest workers and then as refugees fleeing repression. Free to organize and collaborate with other civil society groups, Europe's Kurds have raised public awareness of Kurdish issues and put pressure on national governments in Germany, France, and the Netherlands—as well as on the EU as a whole—to change their policies toward Iran, Iraq, Syria, and Turkey. In this, they have been aided by the rise of Kurdish-language social media.

The flourishing of Kurdish has extended even to Iran and Turkey, where the Kurds have relatively little power. During Erdogan's brief opening to the Kurds between 2009 and 2014, there was a proliferation of Kurdish-language institutes, publications, and private schools. The resulting euphoria did not last long; by the end of 2017, almost all of these had been eliminated by Ankara, which went as far as systematically taking down all signs in Kurdish, traffic signals as well as signs for schools and municipal buildings. But not everything has been lost. Some Turkish universities still allow students to study Kurdish, and the Turkish state has created a TV channel dedicated to official broadcasts in Kurdish. In Iran, meanwhile, the government has, since 2015, allowed optional high school and university Kurdish-language classes in the country's Kurdish-majority regions.

Making a Nation

The increasing fluidity of physical boundaries between Kurds, the creation of Kurdish-run governments such as the KRG, the emergence of strong diaspora communities (especially in Europe), and the rise of Kurdish-language social media and cultural products—all have combined to strengthen pan-Kurdish identity. Today, Kurds from Iran, Iraq, Syria, Turkey, and the diaspora are all engaged in a common conversation. They do not speak in unison, but the days of Kurd-on-Kurd political violence, which flared up in Iraq during the 1990s, are gone, in large part because the Kurdish public will not tolerate it. The Kurds have acquired all the attributes of a nation, except sovereignty.

This newfound unity is reflected in the emergence of pan-Kurdish military units. Turkish Kurds have fought with the YPG in Syria, just as Syrian and Turkish Kurds have been integrated into the armed forces of the KRG. Diaspora Kurds have also volunteered to fight, particularly with the YPG. The PKK commands armed forces in Iraq, Turkey, and Syria and in 2004 created an affiliate in Iran. The erosion of intra-Kurdish boundaries was greatly accelerated by ISIS' advance through Iraq and Syria in the summer of 2014, which imperiled Kurds in both countries and fostered pan-ethnic solidarity. Faced with a genuine existential peril, the Kurds put their own fractious politics aside and appeared as one. And the more that they do so, the more they will begin to reshape the politics of the Middle East.

In both Iraq and Syria, the fragility of central governments provides Kurds with an opportunity for self-rule that is still unthinkable in Iran and Turkey. This process is much further along in Iraq, where the KRG's autonomy is protected by the constitution. Yet the KRG is still vulnerable, as Baghdad's reaction to the disastrous 2017 independence referendum demonstrated. In Syria, the Kurds may have an opportunity to reach a deal with the Assad regime that would grant them a degree of regional autonomy. Such a result is far from guaranteed, however, and a U.S. withdrawal from the country could leave the Syrian Kurds at the mercy of Damascus and Ankara. Even so, any Syrian or Turkish campaign to eliminate the YPG, however bloody, would engender a backlash among Kurds across the Middle East. Nothing builds national consciousness like a David taking on a Goliath.

In Turkey, the Kurds have made a great deal of progress over the past decade, despite the recent deterioration in their relations with the central government. Erdogan's efforts to sabotage the HDP's electoral chances—imprisoning candidates, imposing media blackouts, and harassing Kurdish voters—have not prevented the party from entering the Turkish parliament in three successive elections. (Many HDP politicians, including the party's leader, Selahattin Demirtas, are even now languishing in jail.) The new Turkish constitution, passed by referendum in April 2017, has transformed Turkey into a presidential system and neutered its parliament, so the HDP's influence, despite its significant number of deputies, is greatly limited.

Nonetheless, the fact that the party came in third in the June 2018 elections, behind only the ruling party and the main opposition party, is an indication that the Kurdish issue has been institutionalized in Turkish politics. The HDP's success will encourage the mobilization of Kurdish civil society and, eventually, the development of Kurdish ties with others in the Turkish opposition. And the proliferation of Kurdish organizations in Europe may help to move European attitudes toward Turkey in a more pro-Kurdish direction. It is the

Turkish Kurds who, although divided between a military wing (the PKK) and a political wing (the HDP), are in the best position to assume a leadership role for Kurds across the region. This is because they, unlike the other Kurdish communities, are part of a country embedded in Western institutions. Even if Turkey's practices diverge from Western norms, Turkish Kurds have benefited from exposure to the values and principles associated with the West.

The case of the Iranian Kurds is the most opaque, given Tehran's strained relations with the outside world and the secretive nature of the regime itself. Yet events in other parts of Kurdistan are influencing developments in Iran's Kurdish regions. Iran has always pursued a multipronged policy toward the Kurds. Domestically, it has repressed them, including through the liberal use of capital punishment against activists. At the same time, it has forged ties with the KRG in a successful effort to control Iranian Kurdish groups residing in Iraqi Kurdistan. Yet as Iran finds itself overstretched in the region, its leaders worried about regime stability and the country's worsening economy, the central government may come to see the Kurds as an even greater threat. Iranian Kurds have had little experience with self-rule, having lived for decades under a government that interferes in all aspects of daily life. But Iran, like Syria, is a brittle state. Change will start at the center. The more pan-Kurdish identity and confidence grow, the more likely it is that Iranian Kurds will be prepared for instability in Tehran.

Finally, the United States remains the single most important actor when it comes to determining the future of the Kurds, particularly in Iraq and Syria. Trump may be ending the U.S. partnership with the YPG, but the Syrian Kurds have nonetheless benefited from the relationship, as they were previously considered by outside powers to be the least important Kurdish population in the region. Now they are on the map: hours after Trump announced the United States' withdrawal from Syria, a spokesperson for the French foreign ministry claimed that France would "ensure the security" of the Syrian Kurds. Yet Washington's move will force the Syrian Kurds to negotiate with Damascus earlier than they had planned to, and from a position of relative weakness. A full U.S. withdrawal, moreover, could cause a destabilizing scramble among regional powers in Syria, with disastrous results for the Kurds.

Concerned about these repercussions, U.S. officials, including Secretary of State Mike Pompeo and National Security Adviser John Bolton, have warned Turkey not to intervene against the Kurds in northern Syria. Having stumbled into the Middle East's perpetual Kurdish conundrum, the United States is finding it hard to extricate itself. Washington will have to employ all its persuasive powers to ensure that the Kurds are not crushed by Ankara, Damascus, and other regional powers. That, in turn, will require a degree of interest and policy coherence not previously evident in the Trump administration. But to the extent that the United States values democracy, human rights, and minority rights, it should support Kurds across the Middle East within the existing nation-state system. Even if Trump is unwilling to expend much political capital to support the Kurds, there are other centers of power and influence in the United States, such as media and civil society organizations, that can do so.

Whatever happens in the near future, however, there can be no going back to the status quo that obtained only a few decades ago, before the United States' interventions in the region set the Kurds on a fundamentally new path. Despite frequent setbacks, continued repression, and over a century without a homeland, the Kurds are finally emerging as a unified people. A Kurdish state may be a long way off, but if one ever does emerge, there will be a nation there to populate it.

Chapter VI

Latin America

33 countries included in the world region of Latin America:

- Antigua and Barbuda
- Argentina
- Bahamas
- Barbados
- Belize
- Bolivia
- Brazil
- Chile
- Colombia
- Costa Rica
- Cuba
- Dominica
- Dominican Republic
- Ecuador
- El Salvador
- Grenada
- Guatemala
- Guyana
- Haiti
- Honduras
- Jamaica
- Mexico
- Nicaragua
- Panama
- Paraguay
- Peru
- Saint Lucia
- Saint Kitts and Nevis
- St. Vincent and Grenadines
- Suriname
- Trinidad and Tobago
- Uruguay
- Venezuela

Dependencies and other territories include but not limited to the following:

- Anguilla
- Bermuda
- Bonaire
- British Virgin Islands
- Caribbean Netherlands
- Cayman Islands
- Falkland Islands
- French Guiana
- Guadeloupe
- Martinique
- Montserrat
- Puerto Rico
- Turks and Caicos
- U.S. Virgin Islands

Introduction

Latin America includes 33 sovereign states and multiple territories, comprising over 12% of Earth's total land surface and a population of over 659 billion people. The region includes every country south of the United States in the Western Hemisphere, including Mexico, as well as the countries of Central America, Caribbean Islands (most of which are in the Atlantic Ocean, not the Caribbean Sea), and South America. It is a region defined by its two-fold shared history of European imperialism (when the region was dominated by Spain and Portugal), as well as ancient pre-Columbian civilizations. This region is circumscribed by the dominant religion, Catholicism (there are more Catholics in Latin America than in any other world region), and the dominant languages, Spanish and Portuguese. Ironically, the New World, "discovered" by the Spanish *conquistadores*, or conquerors, is by many measures one of the oldest, home to some of the earliest and most highly advanced human civilizations.

Why Is This Region Called *Latin America*?

The 1800s were tumultuous in Mexico's history. For example, after 300 years of Spanish rule, Mexico declared its independence from Spain on September 16, 1810. After independence, the Mexican government, run by elites who wanted to maintain power, borrowed millions of dollars from France, Spain, and England to finance the Mexican-American War (1846–1948) and the Mexican Civil War (1858–1861). These European powers became increasingly concerned that the Mexican government would not repay its debts, so in 1861, they joined forces and invaded Mexico. The Spanish and British collected their debts and went home, but the French stayed and began colonizing resource-rich Mexico.

From 1861 to 1867, Mexico was embroiled in the Franco-Mexican War, also called the Second French intervention in Mexico, when France invaded and attempted to take over Mexico. By installing Napoleon III's cousin—Maximilian of Habsburg, Archduke of Austria—as emperor of Mexico, the French established a puppet regime in Mexico. The French withdrew and the war ended in 1867 when Benito Juárez became the president of Mexico, expelled the French, and executed Maximilian I for lives lost during the Mexican civil war. In the end, France's exploits resulted in the incalculable cost of countless lives lost and France spending about $300 million to recoup a $3 million debt.

The French referred to the region by the neologism *Amerique latine* (Latin America), a term that emphasized the linguistic connection between French, Spanish, and Portuguese, which are Latin-based languages, as well as its geographic location, part of the Americas. By referring to this region as Latin America, the French hoped to forge Franco-Mexican solidarity, persuade the Mexican people to accept rule by the French monarchy, and establish French legitimacy in a region dominated for centuries by the Spanish and Portuguese.

While the French colonization of Mexico failed and their troops completely withdrew from Mexico in 1867, the name they popularized for this global region has endured.

Pre-Columbian and Indigenous Peoples of Latin America

By most measures, Latin America's **pre-Columbian** era spanned from 14,000 B.C.E. to the arrival of Christopher Columbus in 1492. At the time of the first European encounters, there were more than 350 major tribal groups, 160 linguistic stocks (parent or main languages), and 15 distinct cultural centers, including the Aztec, Inca, and Mayan empires. Like today, during the pre-Columbian epoch, Latin America was home to some of the most populous urban areas in the world. These major pre-Columbian cultural centers had characteristics common to all civilizations in that each had developed a writing system, concept of time, and stable food supply as well as urban areas, government, art, tools, religion, and social hierarchies. During the pre-Columbian period, there were approximately 60 million Indigenous Peoples in Latin America. By 1600, Indigenous populations—decimated by war, slavery, starvation, and disease—namely, measles and smallpox—were reduced from approximately 56 million to four million.

Today, Latin America is home to hundreds of groups of **Indigenous Peoples**. The descendants of the original inhabitants are often considered culturally distinct colonized communities with a land-based affiliation, who aspire for autonomy, namely in the context of maintaining their ancestral lands and ways of life (Rights and Resources, 2015). Particularly since the 1980s, ethnic identity and distinctiveness have become the basis for many social rights movements in Latin America. Such efforts often center on the collective rights of Indigenous Peoples, a range of social justice issues, and **human rights**, which are basic freedoms and protections that belong to all human beings. The **United Nations Declaration on the Rights of Indigenous Peoples** is an international agreement that establishes collective and human rights—namely the legal right to exist—of Indigenous Peoples and individuals. It was initiated in 1993 and adopted by the United Nations General Assembly in 2007, despite its rejection by Canada, New Zealand, Australia, and the United States (President Barack Obama officially endorsed this UN Declaration on December 16, 2010). Yet, by many measures, Indigenous Peoples, as well as their traditional lifestyles and ancestral territories, are increasingly terrorized by the violence and encroachment perpetuated by outsiders. Brazilian president Jair Bolsonaro seriously threatens the future of Brazil's Indigenous People. For example, he advocates ranching and mining on environmentally protected lands, threatens to weaken and dismantle environmental protection laws, and vows to confiscate their reserved territories. Further, Bolsonaro failed to protect the Amazonian rainforest from the expansive wildfires in 2019 and the Indigenous Peoples who died at a disproportionate rate during the COVID-19 pandemic (Indian Law Resource Center, 2019; Castro, 2020).

Dependencies

The majority of the world's dependencies are located in Latin America. A **dependency**—also called a dependent territory, constituent state, overseas territory, protectorate, department, or non-self-governing territory—is not an independent or sovereign state. Dependencies often began as colonies or geostrategic outposts. A dependency may appear to be its own sovereign nation, but it is part of another country and administered by it. In the 21st century, dependencies—like French Guiana, Barbados, and the Falkland Islands—have some degree of political autonomy, yet, for various reasons, have democratically chosen to maintain their status and reject independence. The Falkland Islands have been a British dependency since 1833, but possession of these islands has been contested by Argentina. In 2016, the United Nations Commission on the Limits of the Continental Shelf ruled that Argentina's maritime territory includes the Falklands and expanded Argentina's territorial waters by 35%, findings rejected by the UK.

U.S. Interventionist Policies in Latin America

The **Monroe Doctrine** (1823), a policy first expressed in a speech by U.S. President James Monroe, became the basis of U.S. foreign policy in Latin America. It established the United States as the protector of the western hemisphere and prohibited European colonization and proxy war in Latin America. The "Roosevelt Corollary" (1905) was added to the Monroe Doctrine, allowing the United States to exercise *carte blanche* interventions in Latin America whenever U.S security and economic interests are perceived to be threatened.

Over the years, the United States has invoked the Monroe Doctrine multiple times, and it continues to guide U.S. foreign policy in Latin America. For example, it provided the justification for U.S. intervention in the Mexican-American and Spanish-American Wars as well as U.S. anti-Communist policies in Central America. During the 45-year Cold War between the United States and the Soviet Union, the United States utilized the Monroe Doctrine in the Cuban Missile Crisis to prevent the Soviet Union from installing ballistic missiles in Cuba. Yet, in 1959 Cuba became a communist state and defiantly exists today as the only one of five communist states that is inside of the western hemisphere as well as outside of Asia. The United States invoked the Monroe Doctrine to keep communism out of the western hemisphere, including to fight communist forces in Nicaragua and El Salvador in the 1980s. It justified U.S. support of a coup in Honduras in 2009, Trump's revocation of the

U.S. policies to normalize relations with Cuba, and sanctions against Venezuela, Cuba, and Nicaragua in 2019. In 2019, U.S. National Security Advisor John Bolton proclaimed, "The Monroe Doctrine is alive and well" (Richardson, 2019).

For over a century, U.S. capitalist business interests and practices, as well as U.S. foreign policies, have politically and economically destabilized many Latin American countries. The United States has created and sustained **banana republics**. The term describes developing countries dependent on limited agriculture or a major cash crops (like bananas or coffee) and ruled by a corrupt government. While this term could equally fit developing countries all over the world, it refers only to those in Latin America. As President Dwight D. Eisenhower put it, a pro-U.S. banana republic was more useful than a democratically elected government that threatened U.S. economic and geopolitical interests.

Moreover, the United States has experience supporting and installing Latin American **puppet regimes**. These are corrupt and undemocratic governments ruled by an authoritarian leader who is controlled by a foreign power. In Guatemala in 1954, newly elected President Arbenz made good on campaign promises by legalizing the Communist party and planning to nationalize the land holdings of the U.S.-based United Fruit Company. But the CIA orchestrated a coup that deposed Arbenz, a democratically elected president whom the U.S. regarded as a communist threat. In the name of U.S. stability and security, the United States trained and supported the takeover of a new Guatemalan president, Colonel Carlos Castillo Armas, and his authoritarian, anti-communist regime. From 1954 until his assassination in 1957, Armas reversed Arbenz-era land reforms that benefitted impoverished farmers. He also made it illegal for illiterate Guatemalans to vote. Eventually, a toxic brew of business practices of the American United Fruit Company and the fear of communism, as well as racism against and oppression of the Indigenous peoples, were among the major factors that culminated into a 36-year civil war in Guatemala, from 1960 to 1996, leaving millions dead and most of the country in ruins.

Protecting the Amazon Rainforest

The **neotropics**, a Latin American subregion stretching millions of miles from southern Mexico to southern Brazil, receives more than 100 inches of rain annually. It includes the **Amazon rainforest**, covering two million square miles across nine countries in South America. Also known as Amazonia, or the Amazon Jungle, it is the world's largest and most biodiverse tropical rainforest, home to three quarters of the world's plants and animals. It is often called the "lungs of the planet," since it generates more than 20% of Earth's oxygen. It is also the home of the Amazon, the world's largest river by volume and second longest (nearly 4,000 miles long). This vast and intricate river system flows through seven countries, emerging from cliffs in Peru and ending in the Atlantic Ocean. The Amazon rainforest is an extraordinarily biodiverse and vital habitat on the brink of being totally destroyed by human activities. In addition to devastating wildfires, the clearing of large tracts of Amazonian rainforest for agriculture and cattle ranching—as well as legal and illegal logging, extractive, and mining operations—have increased greenhouse gas emissions, exacerbated soil erosion, disrupted the water cycle, and contributed to an array of life-threatening issues for Indigenous communities in the area. This vital jungle is severely impacted by climate change, due in part to higher temperatures, wildfires, and less equatorial rainfall. By many measures, the world is at the tipping point in addressing worldwide climate change, and global solutions must prioritize the preservation of this extraordinary ecosystem.

Passports for Cash and Tax Havens

Citizenship-by-investment programs issue passports and citizenship to individuals who must donate cash or invest in local property, businesses, and/or government bonds. In 2018, the costs ranged from $100,000 to $2.5 million. That is a considerable investment into a world region where the GDP per capita in 2018 was $12,000. In 2018, at least 24 countries worldwide offered such passport programs, yet the best known, least expensive, and most popular schemes are in the Caribbean Islands, particularly those that are tax-free or low-tax countries.

In addition, many Caribbean Islands are **tax havens**, or offshore financial centers (OFCs), with special rules that allow people, usually overseas investors, to hide their cash and assets to avoid or reduce paying taxes. With the help of private banks, the illicit financial outflows to these sunny places have not only generated tremendous wealth for individuals but also boosted the GDP rates of OFC nations, allowing corrupt government officials, terrorists, and others to "legally" evade and abuse the law (Flagtheory.com, 2016; Henley 2018). The leaked Panama Papers and Paradise Papers attest to the staggering wealth that is hidden in tax havens, which in 2012 accounted for a $21 to $32 trillion in annual loss to global tax authorities (Stewart, 2012).

Violence in Latin America

Parts of Latin America have some of the lowest crime and murder rates in the world. But in recent years rates of violent crime, mostly in urban areas, has spiked, making this region one of the world's most violent. For instance, in 2016, one third of all Latin American citizens reported being the victims of violent crime, and almost 50% of the populations of Venezuela and Mexico were victims of violent crime. In 2017, Latin America reported the highest rates of physical assaults and violent robberies in the world (Muggah & Tobon, 2018). Extremely high levels of violence persist in Central America's Northern Triangle, comprised of Guatemala, Honduras, and El Salvador (Erikson, 2018; Muggah & Tobon, 2018; Muggah et al., 2018). Violence is often linked to drug cartel, organized crime, and criminal gang illegal activities and warfare. Endemic political and police corruption, weak public institutions and criminal justice systems, and youth unemployment contribute to the high and lethal levels of violence. Such violence comes with tremendous social, psychological, and economic costs, including high rates of suicide and post-traumatic stress disorder (PTSD) among survivors. Such violence also significantly increases the likelihood of migration (Muggah & Tobon, 2018).

Latin America is home to 8% of the global population but 33% of global homicides, more than three times the global average (Erikson, 2018). In 2012, of the 20 countries with the highest murder rates, 17 were in Latin America. Four Latin American countries—Mexico, Colombia, Venezuela, and Brazil—accounted for 25% of all murders in the world (Erikson, 2018). In 2017, the Latin American countries with the highest homicide rates included, in descending order, Venezuela (89 per 100,000 citizens), El Salvador (60 per 100,000), Jamaica (55.7 per 100,000), Honduras (42.80 per 100,000), and Brazil (29.70 per 100,000) (InSight Crime, n.d.). In 2018, Mexico had more than 33,000 homicides, and in the first half of 2019 it averaged 94 murders per day (Bufkin, 2019; Romo, 2019). Moreover, in 2018, of the 50 cities in the world with the highest murder rates, 43 were in Latin America (Erikson, 2018; Martell, 2019; UN Office on Drugs and Crime, 2018). More than 141 cities in Latin America report homicide rates above the regional average (Muggah & Tobon, 2018). There is little justice, as in some parts of Latin America, and only one in 20 reported murders are solved (Erikson, 2018).

Latin America is considered the most violent world region for women. Of the 10 global countries with the highest rates of violence against women and girls, three are in Latin America. Further, the rate of violence against women in Latin America has steadily increased since the 1990s, notably in the Dominican Republic and Mexico. Moreover, of all the major world regions, Latin America has the highest rate of sexual violence and second highest rate of intimate or ex-partner violence.

The most extreme form of gender-based violence is **femicide**. While there is no consensus definition of the term, femicide can be defined as a hate crime involving the intentional murder of a woman because she is a woman. Gender-related homicides are among the most egregious international human rights violations. Femicide includes but is not limited to gender-selective abortion, homicides of ethnic and Indigenous women and girls, dowry-related deaths, honor killings, violence against sex workers, and sexual-orientation hate crimes. It also includes targeting women and girls, often due to retaliatory violence, pregnancy, criminal gang activity, or religious or ethnic group membership. Globally, in 2018, 58% of femicide victims (137 per day) were murdered by an intimate partner or family member (UNODC, 2018). Femicide is not considered an isolated incident of individual violence but a social phenomenon greatly impacted by gender norms and stereotypes (UNODC, 2018). In Latin America two of every three homicides of women are considered femicides (United Nations Development Programme and UN Women, 2017). In 2016, there were 902 reported femicides in Colombia, 466 in Honduras, and 371 in El Salvador (Statistica, 2018). In 2018, Mexico had 861 reported femicides, its highest annual rate. Moreover, the majority of femicides are not investigated or investigated properly, particularly involving cases of impoverished Indigenous women. For example, in 2016, Argentina had 254 reported femicides but only 22 convictions (Human Rights Watch, 2018). In 2019, perpetrators act with impunity as femicide laws are not uniformly applied or enforced. While femicide is criminalized in many Latin American countries, in others it is not considered a crime. In 2017, femicide reached epidemic proportions, with 87,000 women killed worldwide; such lethal levels of violence are normally seen only in war and armed conflict (UNODC, 2018).

References

Bufkin, E. (2019, July 14). Mexican murder rate soars to average 94 per day. *Washington Examiner*. https://www.washingtonexaminer.com/news/mexico-murder-rate-soars-to-average-94-per-day

Castro, M. (2020, June 23). How Bolsonaro has left Brazil's Indigenous people vulnerable in the pandemic. *Vox*. https://www.vox.com/world/21273709/brazil-coronavirus-indigenous-people-covid-19-amazonas

Erikson, A. (2018, April 25). Latin American is the world's most dangerous region. A new report investigates why. *Washington Post*. https://www.washingtonpost.com/news/worldviews/wp/2018/04/25/latin-america-is-the-worlds-most-violent-region-a-new-report-investigates-why/

Flagtheory.com. (2016, March 21). Where are the countries with no taxes? https://flagtheory.com/tax-free-countries/

Henley, J. (2018, June 2). Citizenship for sale: How tycoons can go shopping for a new passport. The *Guardian*. https://www.theguardian.com/world/2018/jun/02/citizenship-by-investment-passport-super-rich-nationality

Human Rights Watch. (2018). *World Report 2018*. New York, NY: Seven Stories Press.

Indian Law Resource Center. (2019). Indigenous Peoples in Brazil and the Amazon. https://indianlaw.org/brazil

InSight Crime (n.d.). Tools and data: 2017 homicide rates for Latin America and the Caribbean. https://www.insightcrime.org/indepth/homicides/

Martell, C. (2019, March 12). *Bulletin ranking*. Seguridad, Justicia y Paz. http://www.seguridadjusticiaypaz.org.mx/seguridad/1564-boletin-ranking

Muggah, R., Szabo de Carvalho, I., & Aquirre, K. (2018, March 14). Latin America is the world's most dangerous region. But there are signs it is turning a corner. *World Economic Forum*. https://www.weforum.org/agenda/2018/03/latin-america-is-the-worlds-most-dangerous-region-but-there-are-signs-its-turning-a-corner/

Muggah, R., & Tobon, K. (2018, April). Citizen security in Latin America: Facts and figures. Igarape Institute. https://igarape.org.br/wp-content/uploads/2018/04/Citizen-Security-in-Latin-America-Facts-and-Figures.pdf

Richardson, D. (2019, April 17). John Bolton reaffirms America's commitment to the Monroe Doctrine with new sanctions. *Observer*. https://observer.com/2019/04/john-bolton-monroe-doctrine-sanctions-venezuela-nicaragua-cuba/

Rights and Resources. (2015). *Who owns the land in Latin America?: The status of indigenous and community land rights in Latin America*. http://rightsandresources.org/wp-content/uploads/FactSheet_English_WhoOwnstheLandinLatinAmerica_web.pdf

Romo, V. (2019, January 23). Mexico reports highest ever homicide rate in 2018, tops 33,000 investigations. National Public Radio (NPR). https://www.npr.org/2019/01/23/687579971/mexico-reports-highest-ever-homicide-rate-in-2018-tops-33-000-investigations

Statistica. (2018, November). Number of registered femicide victims in selected Latin American countries in 2016. https://www.statista.com/statistics/827170/number-femicide-victims-latin-america-by-country/

Stewart, H. (2012, July 21). £13tn hoard hidden from taxman by global elite. *The Guardian*. https://www.theguardian.com/business/2012/jul/21/global-elite-tax-offshore-economy

United Nations Development Programme and UN Women. (2017). From commitment to action: Policies to end violence against women in Latin America and the Caribbean. Panama City, Panama: UN House. https://www.undp.org/content/dam/rblac/docs/Research%20and%20Publications/Empoderamiento%20de%20la%20Mujer/UNDP-RBLAC

UN Office on Drugs and Crime. (2018). Gender-related killing of women and girls. https://www.unodc.org/documents/data-and-analysis/GSH2018/GSH18_Gender-related_killing_of_women_and_girls.pdf

Teenage Mothers and Antiquated Laws
Abortion in Latin America

Sofia Rada

W HEN A 10-YEAR-OLD GIRL IN PARAGUAY became pregnant after being raped by her step-father, the local authorities prohibited her from undergoing an abortion. This month, the girl, now 11 years old, underwent a Caesarean section because natural birth was deemed too risky. The tragic new mother, whose legal pseudonym is "Mainumby," and her child have yet to experience any health complications, but the girl's story has enraged many in Paraguay.

Latin America is home to some of the world's most restrictive reproductive laws and policies, which are largely aimed at preventing abortion. In Paraguay, abortion is illegal unless the pregnancy or childbirth threaten the mother's life. Authorities decided Mainumby's case did not fall under this exception, ignoring warnings that the pregnancy posed risk to her physical and mental health. Others, however, have voiced strong disapproval of the assessment. Erika Guevara, the Amnesty International director for the Americas, said in a statement, "The fact that Mainumby did not die does not excuse the human rights violations she suffered at the hands of the Paraguayan authorities."

The Paraguayan government's refusal to authorize an abortion, or consider changing the law, earned condemnation from U.N. health officials, the Inter-American Commission on Human Rights, and women's rights groups within Paraguay. Still, the authorities refused to change their position, which is rooted in the country's staunch Catholicism. When Pope Francis visited the country in July, he avoided any mention of the young girl's case. Meanwhile, the country's most senior bishop has publically criticized outside efforts to impose what he asserted to be the results of abortion—"barbarism, dehumanization, and a culture of death"—onto the country.

Amnesty International, among other human rights groups, argue that forcing the girl to carry out the pregnancy was a serious human rights violation. The World Health Organization warns that adolescents under the age of 16 are four times more likely to die during pregnancy than women in their 20s. Moreover, babies born to adolescent mothers are much more likely to die at birth, or have a low birth weight and risk of long-term effects.

Despite these alarming findings, restrictive abortion laws are commonplace in Latin America, and many young girls have had to endure the consequences. Three years ago, a 16-year-old died of leukemia in the Dominican Republic after being refused immediate treatment because she was pregnant. Last year, an 11-year-old girl from Chile, who had become pregnant after being repeatedly raped by her stepfather, was also denied any legal option to terminate her pregnancy. Cases like these and Mainumby's have led people throughout Latin America to call for change in their respective countries' reproductive laws. In Paraguay, news of the authorities' denial of an abortion to Mainumby drew unprecedented numbers of pro-choice protesters to the streets of the country's capital, Asunción.

The Danger of Abortion Bans

Although Catholicism is quickly losing its grip on its most faithful region in the world, legacies of the religion continue to affect the politics of Latin America. In part due to the influence of Catholic dogma, Latin American law has historically limited women's access to contraception and abortion. Currently, seven countries in the region prohibit abortion in all circumstances, and most others place strong restrictions on the practice. However, these legal restrictions have not reduced the likelihood that women will seek ways to terminate pregnancy. In the face of these legal bans, women seek out clandestine abortions and risk their lives and health.

In Latin America and the Caribbean, 62 percent of women between the ages of 15 and 49 want to avoid a pregnancy. However, only 22 percent of these women—a total of 23 million in 2014—are using an effective contraceptive method. The remaining face an unmet need for modern contraception and, as such, make up 75 percent of all unintended pregnancies in the region. The lack of access to adequate contraception, therefore, is linked to unwanted pregnancies, which in turn are linked to abortions, the majority of which are unsafe.

Despite the legal restrictions on abortion, it was estimated that there were 4.4 million abortions in 2008 in Latin America, and only two out of every 1,000 abortions were safe. Unsafe procedures can be lethal; the World Health Organization estimates that 12 percent of all maternal deaths that year in Latin America were due to unsafe abortion, a higher proportion than in the rest of the world. This accounts for the deaths of an estimated 2,000 Latin American women every year.

Due to the lack of access to contraception that is associated with poverty, poor women are more likely to have unwanted pregnancies. However, poverty also makes it more likely that these women will turn to unsafe ways to terminate their pregnancies. Due to stringent abortion laws, women seeking an abortion must find ways to procure money to pay for illegal procedures or to fly out of the country to receive one elsewhere. Women without these options may turn to extreme and dangerous measures. One doctor told a *BBC* reporter about encountering a woman who put caustic soda inside her vagina. After resorting to such drastic practices, these women may still face legal repercussions.

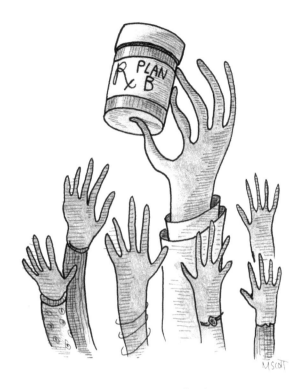

In Central America especially, abortion is both legally suppressed as well as socially stigmatized. Poor women who face problems during their pregnancy often forgo seeking medical treatment in fear that doctors at public hospitals will think they have attempted to terminate their pregnancy. This fear has arisen as countries like El Salvador have put women who suffer pregnancy complications and miscarriage in prison on abortion charges.

Poor and rural women are more likely to only have access to unsafe methods and untrained providers; therefore, they are more likely to experience severe complications. Experts estimate that in Guatemala and Mexico, of women who have abortions, 42 to 67 percent of poor women experience health complications that require medical treatment, compared to only 28 to 38 percent of wealthier women. Every year, an estimated total of 1 million women in Latin America are hospitalized for treatment of complications from unsafe abortion. These complications can range from excessive blood loss and infection to septic shock or perforation of internal organs.

The Outliers: Mexico City and Uruguay

Currently within Latin America, only Cuba, Guyana, and Puerto Rico allow abortion without restriction. Most other countries allow abortions only in special circumstances, such as to save the life of the woman, or to preserve her physical health or socioeconomic grounds. Even with these allowances, abortions can be difficult or even impossible to access, as in the case of Mainumby from Paraguay.

Of the safe abortions that occur throughout Latin America, most occur in places that have legalized the procedure, such as Uruguay and Mexico City. While abortion is not a federally protected right in Mexico, since 2007 it has been both legal and free upon request during the first 12 weeks of pregnancy in Mexico City. In 2012, Uruguay became the most recent Latin American country to liberalize its abortion laws, permitting the procedure for any reason during the first trimester.

Because Mexico City's policy on abortion does not apply to the entire country, wealthier Mexican women have disproportionate access to safe abortions. Women with economic resources can travel to Mexico City to terminate pregnancies, but disadvantaged women continue only to have access to unregulated, unsafe abortions. Additionally, the legalization of abortion in Mexico City was met with backlash in surrounding states. Some of these states enacted abortion laws that are stricter than before. Still, Mexico City's laws provide some women in Mexico with safe abortions, an option they otherwise would not have had.

Uruguay's new abortion laws have been credited as one of the reasons why the country is able to boast the third-lowest maternal death rate in the Americas after Canada and the United States. Following the legal changes, 6,676 abortions were performed—only two resulted in complications, but none resulted in death. The changes in reproductive laws in Uruguay are part of the country's prioritization of health; it was the first country in Latin American to offer an equal, guaranteed health care plan for the entire population.

Changes to the Landscape

Chile and the Dominican Republic are currently two of just a handful of countries around the world where abortion is fully criminalized. However, changes are occurring in both of these countries when it comes to reproductive laws. Last year, the Dominican Republic changed its penal code to include three exceptions to the full ban on abortion, which will take effect in December. Abortions will be allowed when the mother's life is at risk, in cases where the fetus will be unable to survive outside the womb, and in cases where pregnancy is the result of rape or incest. In Chile, a new bill could dramatically change the country's stringent abortion laws.

Abortion has been prohibited under any circumstance in Chile since 1989, when former dictator Augusto Pinochet enacted a law banning the procedure. The country made a step toward amending this strict law this month when its health commission voted to move forward President Michelle Bachelet's proposal to allow abortions in certain circumstances, such as when the pregnancy is the result of rape, when the life of the woman is at risk, or when the fetus is unviable.

The bill's success, however, is far from guaranteed. Since its introduction, it has prompted bitter feuding inside the Bachelet government, especially from the Christian Democratic Party within her coalition. For now, women seeking abortion under all circumstances in Chile could face up to five years in prison. The bill would need to win simple majorities in both the lower house and the Senate for this to change. However, advocates of abortion legalization hope that the bill's advancement represents the potential for change for women's reproductive rights in Latin America.

Many on both sides of the argument view abortion as an issue of morality—either pointing out that denying women access to abortions is a violation of human rights, or, conversely, arguing that abortions are a form of murder. Others have had some success in reframing the issue to highlight the public health concerns involved with existing restrictions on abortion. This arising argument has the potential to spread change regarding abortion throughout the region.

Reading 6.2

Venezuela's Suicide
Lessons From a Failed State

Moisés Naím and Francisco Toro

C ONSIDER TWO LATIN AMERICAN COUNTRIES. THE first is one of the region's oldest and strongest democracies. It boasts a stronger social safety net than any of its neighbors and is making progress on its promise to deliver free health care and higher education to all its citizens. It is a model of social mobility and a magnet for immigrants from across Latin America and Europe. The press is free, and the political system is open; opposing parties compete fiercely in elections and regularly alternate power peacefully. It sidestepped the wave of military juntas that mired some Latin American countries in dictatorship. Thanks to a long political alliance and deep trade and investment ties with the United States, it serves as the Latin American headquarters for a slew of multinational corporations. It has the best infrastructure in South America. It is still unmistakably a developing country, with its share of corruption, injustice, and dysfunction, but it is well ahead of other poor countries by almost any measure.

The second country is one of Latin America's most impoverished nations and its newest dictatorship. Its schools lie half deserted. The health system has been devastated by decades of underinvestment, corruption, and neglect; long-vanquished diseases, such as malaria and measles, have returned. Only a tiny elite can afford enough to eat. An epidemic of violence has made it one of the most murderous countries in the world. It is the source of Latin America's largest refugee migration in a generation, with millions of citizens fleeing in the last few years alone. Hardly anyone (aside from other autocratic governments) recognizes its sham elections, and the small portion of the media not under direct state control still follows the official line for fear of reprisals. By the end of 2018, its economy will have shrunk by about half in the last five years. It is a major cocaine-trafficking hub, and key power brokers in its political elite have been indicted in the United States on drug charges. Prices double every 25 days. The main airport is

Moisés Naím and Francisco Toro, "Venezuela's Suicide: Lessons From a Failed State," *Foreign Affairs*, vol. 97, no. 6, ed. Gideon Rose, pp. 126–138. Copyright © 2018 by Council on Foreign Relations, Inc. Reprinted with permission.

Venezuela is burning: at an anti-Maduro rally in Caracas, June 2017. Copyright © Reuters/Carlos Garcia Rawlins.

largely deserted, used by just a handful of holdout airlines bringing few passengers to and from the outside world.

These two countries are in fact the same country, Venezuela, at two different times: the early 1970s and today. The transformation Venezuela has undergone is so radical, so complete, and so total that it is hard to believe it took place without a war. What happened to Venezuela? How did things go so wrong?

The short answer is Chavismo. Under the leadership of Hugo Chávez and his successor, Nicolás Maduro, the country has experienced a toxic mix of wantonly destructive policy, escalating authoritarianism, and kleptocracy, all under a level of Cuban influence that often resembles an occupation. Any one of these features would have created huge problems on its own. All of them together hatched a catastrophe. Today, Venezuela is a poor country and a failed and criminalized state run by an autocrat beholden to a foreign power. The remaining options for reversing this situation are slim; the risk now is that hopelessness will push Venezuelans to consider supporting dangerous measures, such as a U.S.-led military invasion, that could make a bad situation worse.

Chavismo Rising

To many observers, the explanation for Venezuela's predicament is simple: under Chávez, the country caught a strong case of socialism, and all its subsequent disasters stem from that original sin. But Argentina, Brazil, Chile, Ecuador, Nicaragua, and Uruguay have also elected socialist governments in the last 20 years. Although each has struggled politically and economically, none—aside from Nicaragua—has imploded. Instead, several have prospered.

If socialism cannot be blamed for Venezuela's demise, perhaps oil is the culprit. The most calamitous stage of Venezuela's crisis has coincided neatly with the sharp fall in international oil prices that started in 2014. But this explanation is also insufficient. Venezuela's decline began four decades ago, not four years ago. By 2003, Venezuela's GDP per worker had already declined by a disastrous 37 percent from its 1978 peak—precisely the decline that first propelled Chávez into office. Moreover, all of the world's petrostates suffered a serious income shock in 2014 as a result of plummeting oil prices. Only Venezuela could not withstand the pressure.

The drivers of Venezuela's failure run deeper. Decades of gradual economic decline opened the way for Chávez, a charismatic demagogue wedded to an outdated ideology, to take power and establish a corrupt autocracy modeled on and beholden to Cuba's dictatorship. Although the crisis preceded Chávez's rise to power, his legacy and Cuba's influence must be at the center of any attempt to explain it.

Chávez was born in 1954 into a lower-middle-class family in a rural town. He became a career military officer on a baseball scholarship and was soon secretly recruited into a small leftist movement that spent over a decade plotting to overthrow the democratic regime. He exploded into Venezuela's national consciousness on February 4, 1992, when he led an unsuccessful coup attempt. This misadventure landed him in jail but turned him into an improbable folk hero who embodied growing frustration with a decade of economic stagnation. After receiving a pardon, he launched an outsider bid for the presidency in 1998 and won in a landslide, upending the two-party system that had anchored Venezuelan democracy for 40 years.

What drove the explosion of populist anger that brought Chávez to power? In a word, disappointment. The stellar economic performance Venezuela had experienced for five decades leading up to the 1970s had run out of steam, and the path to the middle class had begun to narrow. As the economists Ricardo Hausmann and Francisco Rodríguez noted, "By 1970 Venezuela had become the richest country in Latin America and one of the twenty richest countries in the world, with a per capita GDP higher than Spain, Greece, and Israel and only 13 percent lower than that of the United Kingdom." But by the early 1980s, a weakened oil market had brought the era of fast growth to an end. Lower oil revenue meant cuts in public spending, scaled-down social programs, currency devaluation, runaway inflation, a banking crisis, and mounting unemployment and hardship for the poor. Even so, Venezuela's head start was such that when Chávez was elected, it had a per capita income in the region that was second only to Argentina's.

Another common explanation for Chávez's rise holds that it was driven by voters' reaction against economic inequality, which was driven in turn by pervasive corruption. But when Chávez came to power, income was more evenly distributed in Venezuela than in any neighboring country. If inequality determined electoral outcomes, then a Chávez-like candidate would have been more probable in Brazil, Chile, or Colombia, where the gap between the well-off and everyone else was larger.

Venezuela may not have been collapsing in 1998, but it had been stagnating and, in some respects, backsliding, as oil prices slumped to just $11 per barrel, leading to a new round of austerity. Chávez was brilliant at mining the resulting discontent. His eloquent denunciations of inequality, exclusion, poverty, corruption, and the entrenched political elite struck a chord with struggling voters, who felt nostalgic for an earlier, more prosperous period. The inept and complacent traditional political and business elite who opposed Chávez never came close to matching his popular touch.

Venezuelans gambled on Chávez. What they got was not just an outsider bent on upending the status quo but also a Latin American leftist icon who soon had followers all around the world. Chávez became both a spoiler and the star attraction at global summits, as well as a leader of the burgeoning global wave of anti-American sentiment sparked by U.S. President George W. Bush's invasion of Iraq. At home, shaped by his career in the military, Chávez had a penchant for centralizing power and a profound intolerance of dissent. He set out to neuter not just opposition politicians but also political allies who dared question his policies. His collaborators quickly saw which way the wind was blowing: policy debates disappeared, and the government pursued a radical agenda with little forethought and no real scrutiny.

A 2001 presidential decree on land reform, which Chávez handed down with no consultation or debate, was a taste of things to come. It broke up large commercial farms and turned them over to peasant cooperatives that lacked the technical know-how, management skills, or access to capital to produce at scale. Food production collapsed. And in sector after sector, the Chávez government enacted similarly self-defeating policies. It expropriated foreign-owned oil ventures withoutcompensation and gave them to political appointees who lacked the technical expertise to run them. It nationalized utilities and the main telecommunications operator, leaving Venezuela with chronic water and electricity shortages and some of the slowest Internet connection speeds in the world. It seized steel companies, causing production to fall from 480,000 metric tons per month before nationalization, in

2008, to effectively nothing today. Similar results followed the seizure of aluminum companies, mining firms, hotels, and airlines.

In one expropriated company after another, state administrators stripped assets and loaded payrolls with Chávez cronies. When they inevitably ran into financial problems, they appealed to the government, which was able to bail them out. By 2004, oil prices had spiked again, filling government coffers with petrodollars, which Chávez spent without constraints, controls, or accountability. On top of that were the easy loans from China, which was happy to extend credit to Venezuela in exchange for a guaranteed supply of crude oil. By importing whatever the hollowed-out Venezuelan economy failed to produce and borrowing to finance a consumption boom, Chávez was able to temporarily shield the public from the impact of his disastrous policies and to retain substantial popularity.

But not everyone was convinced. Oil industry workers were among the first to sound the alarm about Chávez's authoritarian tendencies. They went on strike in 2002 and 2003, demanding a new presidential election. In response to the protests, Chávez fired almost half of the work force in the state-run oil company and imposed an arcane currency-exchange-control regime. The system morphed into a cesspool of corruption, as regime cronies realized that arbitraging between the state-authorized exchange rate and the black market could yield fortunes overnight. This arbitrage racket created an extraordinarily wealthy elite of government-connected kleptocrats. As this budding kleptocracy perfected the art of siphoning off oil proceeds into its own pockets, Venezuelan store shelves grew bare.

It was all painfully predictable—and widely predicted. But the louder local and international experts sounded the alarm, the more the government clung to its agenda. To Chávez, dire warnings from technocrats were a sign that the revolution was on the right track.

Passing the Torch

In 2011, Chávez was diagnosed with cancer. Top oncologists in Brazil and the United States offered to treat him. But he opted instead to search for a cure in Cuba, the country he trusted not only to treat him but also to be discreet about his condition. As his illness progressed, his dependence on Havana deepened, and the mystery about the real state of his health grew. On December 8, 2012, an ailing Chávez made one final television appearance to ask Venezuelans to make Maduro, then vice president, his successor. For the next three months, Venezuela was governed spectrally and by remote control: decrees emanated from Havana bearing Chávez's signature, but no one saw him, and speculation was rife that he had already died. When Chávez's death was finally announced, on March 5, 2013, the only thing that was clear amid the atmosphere of secrecy and concealment was that Venezuela's next leader would carry on the tradition of Cuban influence.

Chávez had long looked to Cuba as a blueprint for revolution, and he turned to Cuban President Fidel Castro for advice at critical junctures. In return, Venezuela sent oil: energy aid to Cuba (in the form of 115,000 barrels a day sold at a deep discount) was worth nearly $1 billion a year to Havana. The relationship between Cuba and Venezuela became more than an alliance. It has been, as Chávez himself once put it, "a merger of two revolutions." (Unusually, the senior partner in the alliance is poorer and smaller than the junior partner—but so much more competent that it dominates the relationship.) Cuba is careful to keep its footprint light: it conducts most of its consultations in Havana rather than Caracas.

It did not escape anyone's attention that the leader Chávez annointed to succeed him had devoted his life to the cause of Cuban communism. As a teenager, Maduro joined a fringe pro-Cuban Marxist party in Caracas. In his 20s, instead of going to university, he sought training in Havana's school for international cadres to become a professional revolutionary. As Chávez's foreign minister from 2006 to 2013, he had seldom called attention to himself: only his unfailing loyalty to Chávez, and to Cuba, propelled his ascent to the top. Under his leadership, Cuba's influence in Venezuela has become pervasive. He has stacked key government posts with activists trained in Cuban organizations, and Cubans have come to occupy sensitive roles within the Venezuelan regime. The daily intelligence briefs Maduro consumes, for instance, are produced not by Venezuelans but by Cuban intelligence officers.

With Cuban guidance, Maduro has deeply curtailed economic freedoms and erased all remaining traces of liberalism from the country's politics and institutions. He has continued and expanded Chávez's practice of jailing, exiling, or banning from political life opposition leaders who became too popular or hard to co-opt. Julio Borges, a key opposition leader, fled into exile to avoid being jailed, and Leopoldo López, the opposition's most charismatic leader, has been moved back and forth between a military prison and house arrest. Over 100 political prisoners linger in jails, and reports of torture are common. Periodic elections have become farcical, and the government has stripped the opposition-controlled National Assembly of all powers. Maduro has deepened Venezuela's alliances with a number of anti-American and anti-Western regimes, turning to Russia for weapons, cybersecurity, and expertise in oil production; to China for financing and infrastructure; to Belarus for homebuilding; and to Iran for car production.

As Maduro broke the last remaining links in Venezuela's traditional alliances with Washington and other Latin American democracies, he lost access to sound economic advice. He dismissed the consensus of economists from across the political spectrum:

although they warned about inflation, Maduro chose to rely on the advice of Cuba and fringe Marxist policy advisers who assured him that there would be no consequences to making up budget shortfalls with freshly minted money. Inevitably, a devastating bout of hyperinflation ensued.

A toxic combination of Cuban influence, runaway corruption, the dismantling of democratic checks and balances, and sheer incompetence has kept Venezuela locked into catastrophic economic policies. As monthly inflation rates top three digits, the government improvises policy responses that are bound to make the situation even worse.

Anatomy of a Collapse

Nearly all oil-producing liberal democracies, such as Norway, the United Kingdom, and the United States, were democracies before they became oil producers. Autocracies that have found oil, such as Angola, Brunei, Iran, and Russia, have been unable to make the leap to liberal democracy. For four decades, Venezuela seemed to have miraculously beat these odds—it democratized and liberalized in 1958, decades after finding oil.

But the roots of Venezuelan liberal democracy turned out to be shallow. Two decades of bad economics decimated the popularity of the traditional political parties, and a charismatic demagogue, riding the wave of an oil boom, stepped into the breach. Under these unusual conditions, he was able to sweep away the whole structure of democratic checks and balances in just a few years.

When the decade-long oil price boom ended in 2014, Venezuela lost not just the oil revenue on which Chávez's popularity and international influence had depended but also access to foreign credit markets. This left the country with a massive debt overhang: the loans taken out during the oil boom still had to be serviced, although from a much-reduced income stream. Venezuela ended up with politics that are typical of autocracies that discover oil: a predatory, extractive oligarchy that ignores regular people as long they stay quiet and that violently suppresses them when they protest.

The resulting crisis is morphing into the worst humanitarian disaster in memory in the Western Hemisphere. Exact figures for Venezuela's GDP collapse are notoriously difficult to come by, but economists estimate that it is comparable to the 40 percent contraction of Syria's GDP since 2012, following the outbreak of its devastating civil war. Hyperinflation has reached one million percent per year, pushing 61 percent of Venezuelans to live in extreme poverty, with 89 percent of those surveyed saying they do not have the money to buy enough food for their families and 64 percent reporting they have lost an average of 11 kilograms (about 24 pounds) in body weight due to hunger. About ten percent of the population— 2.6 million Venezuelans—have fled to neighboring countries.

The Venezuelan state has mostly given up on providing public services such as health care, education, and even policing; heavy-handed, repressive violence is the final thing left that Venezuelans can rely on the public sector to consistently deliver. In the face of mass protests in 2014 and 2017, the government responded with thousands of arrests, brutal beatings and torture, and the killing of over 130 protesters.

Meanwhile, criminal business is increasingly conducted not in defiance of the state, or even simply in cahoots with the state, but directly through it. Drug trafficking has emerged alongside oil production and currency arbitrage as a key source of profits to those close to the ruling elite, with high-ranking officials and members of the president's family facing narcotics charges in the United States. A small connected elite has also stolen national assets to a unprecedented degree. In August, a series of regime-connected businessmen were indicted in U.S. federal courts for attempting to launder over $1.2 billion in illegally obtained funds—just one of a dizzying array of illegal scams that are part of the looting of Venezuela. The entire southeastern quadrant of the country has become an exploitative illegal mining camp, where desperate people displaced from cities by hunger try their luck in unsafe mines run by criminal gangs under military protection. All over the country, prison gangs, working in partnership with government security forces, run lucrative extortion rackets that make them the de facto civil authority. The offices of the Treasury, the central bank, and the national oil company have become laboratories where complicated financial crimes are hatched. As Venezuela's economy has collapsed, the lines separating the state from criminal enterprises have all but disappeared.

The Venezuelan Dilemma

Whenever U.S. President Donald Trump meets with a Latin American leader, he insists that the region do something about the Venezuelan crisis. Trump has prodded his own national security team for "strong" alternatives, at one point stating that there are "many options" for Venezuela and that he is "not going to rule out the military option." Republican Senator Marco Rubio of Florida has similarly flirted with a military response. Secretary of Defense James Mattis, however, has echoed a common sentiment of the U.S. security apparatus by publicly stating, "The Venezuelan crisis is not a military matter." All of Venezuela's neighboring countries have also voiced their opposition to an armed attack on Venezuela.

And rightly so. Trump's fantasies of military invasion are deeply misguided and extremely dangerous. Although a U.S.-led military assault would likely have no problem overthrowing Maduro in short order, what comes next could be far worse, as the Iraqis and the Libyans know only too well: when outside powers overthrow autocrats sitting atop failing states, open-ended chaos is much more likely to follow than stability—let alone democracy.

Nonetheless, the United States will continue to face pressure to find some way of arresting Venezuela's collapse. Each initiative undertaken so far has served only to highlight that there is, in reality, little the United States can do. During the Obama administration, U.S. diplomats attempted to engage the regime directly. But negotiations proved futile. Maduro used internationally mediated talks to neutralize massive street protests: protest leaders would call off demonstrations during the talks, but Chavista negotiators would only stonewall, parceling out minor concessions designed to divide their opponents while they themselves prepared for the next wave of repression. The United States and Venezuela's neighbors seem to have finally grasped that, as things stand, negotiations only play into Maduro's hands.

Some have suggested using harsh economic sanctions to pressure Maduro to step down. The United States has tried this. It passed several rounds of sanctions, under both the Obama and Trump administrations, to prevent the regime from issuing new debt and to hamper the financial operation of the state-owned oil company. Together with Canada and the EU, Washington has also put in place sanctions against specific regime officials, freezing their assets abroad and imposing travel restrictions. But such measures are redundant: if the task is to destroy the Venezuelan economy, no set of sanctions will be as effective as the regime itself. The same is true for an oil blockade: oil production is already in a free fall.

Washington can sharpen its policy on the margins. For one thing, it needs to put more emphasis on a Cuban track: little can be achieved without Havana's help, meaning that Venezuela needs to be front and center in every contact Washington and its allies have with Havana. The United States can cast a wider net in countering corruption, preventing not just crooked officials but also their frontmen and families from enjoying the fruits of corruption, drug trafficking, and embezzlement. It could also work to turn the existing U.S. arms embargo into a global one. The Maduro regime must be constrained in its authoritarian intent with policies that communicate clearly to its cronies that continuing to aid the regime will leave them isolated in Venezuela and that turning on the regime is, therefore, the only way out. Yet the prospects of such a strategy succeeding are dim.

After a long period of dithering, the other Latin American countries are finally grasping that Venezuela's instability will inevitably spill across their borders. As the center-left "pink wave" of the early years of this century recedes, a new cohort of more conservative leaders in Argentina, Brazil, Chile, Colombia, and Peru has tipped the regional balance against Venezuela's dictatorship, but the lack of actionable options bedevils them, as well. Traditional diplomacy hasn't worked and has even backfired. But so has pressure. For example, in 2017, Latin American countries threatened to suspend Venezuela's membership in the Organization of American States. The regime responded by withdrawing from the organization unilaterally, displaying just how little it cares about traditional diplomatic pressure.

Venezuela's exasperated neighbors are increasingly seeing the crisis through the prism of the refugee problem it has created; they are anxious to stem the flow of malnourished people fleeing Venezuela and placing new strains on their social programs. As a populist backlash builds against the influx of Venezuelan refugees, some Latin American countries appear tempted to slam the door shut—a temptation they must resist, as it would be a historic mistake that would only worsen the crisis. The reality is that Latin American countries have no idea what to do about Venezuela. There may be nothing they can do, save accepting refugees, which will at least help alleviate the suffering of the Venezuelan people.

Power to the People

Today, the regime is so solidly entrenched that a change of faces is much more likely than a change of system. Perhaps Maduro will be pushed out by a slightly less incompetent leader who is able to render Cuban hegemony in Venezuela more sustainable. Such an outcome would merely mean a more stable foreign-dominated petro-kleptocracy, not a return to democracy. And even if opposition forces—or a U.S.-led armed attack—somehow managed to replace Maduro with an entirely new government, the agenda would be daunting. A successor regime would need to reduce the enormous role the military plays in all areas of the public sector. It would have to start from scratch in restoring basic services in health care, education, and law enforcement. It would have to rebuild the oil industry and stimulate growth in other economic sectors. It would need to get rid of the drug dealers, prison racketeers, predatory miners, wealthy criminal financiers, and extortionists who have latched on to every part of the state. And it would have to make all these changes in the context of a toxic, anarchic political environment and a grave economic crisis.

Given the scale of these obstacles, Venezuela is likely to remain unstable for a long time to come. The immediate challenge for its citizens and their leaders, as well as for the international community, is to contain the impact of the nation's decline. For all the misery they have experienced, the Venezuelan people have never stopped struggling against misrule. As of this summer, Venezuelans were still staging hundreds of protests each month. Most of them are local, grass-roots affairs with little political leadership, but they show a people with the will to fight for themselves.

Is that enough to nudge the country away from its current, grim path? Probably not. Hopelessness is driving more and more Venezuelans to fantasize about a Trump-led military intervention, which would offer a fervently desired deus ex machina for a long-suffering people. But this amounts to an ill-advised revenge fantasy, not a serious strategy.

Rather than a military invasion, Venezuelans' best hope is to ensure that the flickering embers of protest and social dissent are not extinguished and that resistance to dictatorship is sustained. Desperate though the prospect may seem, this tradition of protest could one day lay the foundations for the recovery of civic institutions and democratic practices. It won't be simple, and it won't be quick. Bringing a state back from the brink of failure never is.

Reading 6.3

How Che Guevara Taught Cuba to Confront COVID-19

Don Fitz

Beginning in December 1951, Ernesto "Che" Guevara took a 9-month break from medical school to travel by motorcycle through Argentina, Chile, Peru, Colombia, and Venezuela. One of his goals was gaining practical experience with leprosy. On the night of his 24th birthday, Che was at La Colonia de San Pablo in Peru swimming across the river to join the lepers. He walked among 600 lepers in jungle huts looking after themselves in their own way.

Che would not have been satisfied to just study and sympathize with them—he wanted to *be* with them and understand their existence. Being in contact with people who were poor and hungry while they were sick transformed Che. He envisioned a new medicine, with doctors who would serve the greatest number of people with preventive care and public awareness of hygiene. A few years later, Che joined Fidel Castro's 26th of July Movement as a doctor and was among the 81 men aboard the *Granma* as it landed in Cuba on December 2, 1956.

Cuban doctors head to Italy to battle coronavirus, *Physicians Weekly*, Mar 23, 2020.

Revolutionary Medicine

After the January 1, 1959, victory that overthrew Fulgencio Batista, the new Cuban constitution included Che's dream of free medical care for all as a human right. An understanding of the failings of disconnected social systems led the revolutionary government to build hospitals and clinics in underserved parts of the island at the same time that it began addressing crises of literacy, racism, poverty, and housing. Cuba overhauled its clinics both in 1964 and again in 1974 to better link communities and patients. By 1984, Cuba had introduced doctor-nurse teams who lived in the neighborhoods where they had offices (*consultorios*).

The United States became ever more bellicose, so in 1960 Cubans organized Committees for Defense of the Revolution to defend the country. The committees prepared to move the elderly, disabled, sick, and mentally ill to higher ground if a hurricane approached, thus intertwining domestic health care and foreign affairs, a connection that has persisted throughout Cuba's history.

As Cuba's medical revolution was based on extending medical care beyond the major cities and into the rural communities that needed it the most, it was a short step to extend that assistance to other nations. The revolutionary government sent doctors to Chile after a 1960 earthquake and a medical brigade in 1963 to Algeria, which was fighting for independence from France. These actions set the stage for the country's international medical aid, which grew during the decades and now includes helping treat the COVID-19 pandemic.

In the late 1980s and early '90s, two disasters threatened the very existence of the country. The first victim of AIDS died in 1986. In December 1991, the Soviet Union collapsed, ending its $5 billion annual subsidy, disrupting international commerce, and sending the Cuban economy into a free fall that exacerbated the AIDS epidemic. A perfect storm for AIDS infection appeared on the horizon. The HIV infection rate for the Caribbean region was second only to southern Africa, where a third of a million Cubans had recently been during the Angolan wars. The embargo on the island reduced the availability of drugs (including those for HIV/AIDS), made existing pharmaceuticals outrageously expensive, and disrupted the financial infrastructures used for drug purchases. Desperately needing funds, Cuba opened the floodgate of tourism, bringing an increase in sex exchanged for money.

The government drastically reduced services in all areas except two: education and health care. Its research institutes developed Cuba's own diagnostic test for HIV by 1987. Over 12 million tests were completed by 1993. By 1990, when gay people had become the island's primary HIV victims, homophobia was officially challenged in schools. Condoms were provided for free at doctor's offices, and, despite the expense, so were antiretroviral drugs.

Cuba's united and well-planned effort to cope with HIV/AIDS paid off. In the early 1990s, at the same time that Cuba had 200 AIDS cases, New York City (with about the same population) had 43,000 cases.[1] Despite having only a small fraction of the wealth and resources of the United States, Cuba had overcome the devastating effects of the U.S. blockade and had implemented an AIDS program superior to that of the country seeking to destroy it. During this special period, Cubans experienced longer lives and lower infant mortality rates in comparison to the United States. Cuba inspired healers throughout the world to believe that a country with a coherent and caring medical system can thrive, even against tremendous odds.

COVID-19 Hits Cuba

Overcoming the HIV/AIDS and special period crises prepared Cuba for COVID-19. Aware of the intensity of the pandemic, Cuba knew that it had two inseparable responsibilities: to take care of its own with a comprehensive program and to share its capabilities internationally.

The government immediately carried out a task that proved very difficult in a market-driven economy—altering the equipment of nationalized factories (which usually made school uniforms) to manufacture masks. These provided an ample supply for Cuba by the middle of April 2020, while the United States, with its enormous productive capacity, was still suffering a shortage.

Discussions at the highest levels of the Cuban Ministry of Public Health drew up the national policy. There would need to be massive testing to determine who had been infected. Infected persons would need to be quarantined while ensuring that they had food and other necessities. Contact tracing would be used to determine who else might be exposed. Medical staff would need to go door to door to check on the health of every citizen. *Consultorio* staff would give special attention to everyone in the neighborhood who might be high risk.

By March 2, Cuba had instituted the Novel Coronavirus Plan for Prevention and Control.[2] Within four days, it expanded the plan to include taking the temperature of and possibly isolating infected incoming travelers. These occurred before Cuba's first confirmed COVID-19 diagnosis on March 11. Cuba had its first confirmed COVID-19 fatality by March 22, when there were 35 confirmed cases, almost 1,000 patients being observed in hospitals, and over 30,000 people under surveillance at home. The next day it banned the entry of nonresident foreigners, which took a deep bite into the country's tourism revenue.[3]

That was the day that Cuba's Civil Defense went on alert to respond rapidly to COVID-19 and the Havana Defense Council decided that there was a serious problem in the city's Vedado district, famous for being the largest home to nontourist foreign visitors who were more likely to have been exposed to the virus. By April 3, the district was closed. As Merriam Ansara witnessed, "anyone with a need to enter or leave must prove that they have been tested and are free of COVID-19." The Civil Defense made sure stores were supplied and all vulnerable people received regular medical checks.[4]

Vedado had eight confirmed cases, a lot for a small area. Cuban health officials wanted the virus to remain at the "local spread" stage, when it can be traced while going from one person to another. They sought to prevent it from entering the "community spread" stage, when tracing is not possible because it is moving out of control. As U.S. health professionals begged for personal protective equipment (PPE) and testing in the United States was so sparse that people had to *ask* to be tested (rather than health workers testing contacts of infected patients), Cuba had enough rapid test kits to trace contacts of persons who had contracted the virus.

During late March and early April, Cuban hospitals were also changing work patterns to minimize contagion. Havana doctors went into Salvador Allende Hospital for 15 days, staying overnight within an area designated for medical staff. Then they moved to an area separate from patients where they lived for another 15 days and were tested before returning home. They stayed at home without leaving for another 15 days and were tested before resuming practice. This 45 day period of isolation prevented medical staff from bringing disease to the community via their daily trips to and from work.

The medical system extends from the *consultorio* to every family in Cuba. Third-, fourth-, and fifth-year medical students are assigned by *consultorio* doctors to go to specific homes each day. Their tasks include obtaining survey data from residents or making extra visits to the elderly, infants, and those with respiratory problems. These visits gather preventive medicine data that is then taken into account by those in the highest decision-making positions of the country. When students bring their data, doctors use a red pen to mark hot spots where extra care is necessary. Neighborhood doctors meet regularly at clinics to talk about what each doctor is doing, what they are discovering, what new procedures the Cuban Ministry of Public Health is adopting, and how the intense work is affecting medical staff.

In this way, every Cuban citizen and every health care worker, from those at neighborhood doctor offices to those at the most esteemed research institutes, plays a part in determining health policy. Cuba currently has 89,000 doctors, 84,000 nurses, and 9,000 students scheduled to graduate from medical studies in 2020. The Cuban people would not tolerate the head of the country ignoring medical advice, spouting nonsense, and determining policy based on what would be most profitable for corporations.

The Cuban government approved free distribution of the homeopathic medicine PrevengHo-Vir to residents of Havana and Pinar del Rio province.[5] Susana Hurlich was one of many receiving it. On April 8, Dr. Yaisen, one of three doctors at the *consultorio* two blocks from her home, came to the door with a small bottle of PrevengHo-Vir and explained how to use it. Instructions warn that it reinforces the immune system but is not a substitute for Interferon Alpha 2B, nor is it a vaccine. Hurlich believes that something important "about

Cuba's medical system is that rather than being two-tiered, as is often the case in other countries, with 'classical medicine' on the one hand and 'alternative medicine' on the other, Cuba has ONE health system that includes it all. When you study to become a doctor, you also learn about homeopathic medicine in all its forms."[6]

Global Solidarity in the Time of COVID-19

A powerful model: Perhaps the most critical component of Cuba's medical internationalism during the COVID-19 crisis has been using its decades of experience to create an example of how a country can confront the virus with a compassionate and competent plan. Public health officials around the world were inspired by Cuba's actions.

Transfer of knowledge: When viruses that cause Ebola, mainly found in sub-Saharan Africa, increased dramatically in fall 2014, much of the world panicked. Soon, over 20,000 people were infected, more than 8,000 had died, and worries mounted that the death toll could reach into hundreds of thousands. The United States provided military support; other countries promised money. Cuba was the first nation to respond with what was most needed: it sent 103 nurse and 62 doctor volunteers to Sierra Leone. Since many governments did not know how to respond to the disease, Cuba trained volunteers from other nations at Havana's Pedro Kourí Institute of Tropical Medicine. In total, Cuba taught 13,000 Africans, 66,000 Latin Americans, and 620 Caribbeans how to treat Ebola without themselves becoming infected. Sharing understanding on how to organize a health system is the highest level of knowledge transfer.

Venezuela has attempted to replicate fundamental aspects of the Cuban health model on a national level, which has served Venezuela well in combating COVID-19. In 2018, residents of Altos de Lidice organized seven communal councils, including one for community health. A resident made space in his home available to the Communal Healthcare System initiative so that Dr. Gutierrez could have an office. He coordinates data collections to identify at-risk residents and visits all residents in their homes to explain how to avoid infection by COVID-19. Nurse del Valle Marquez is a Chavista who helped implement the Barrio Adentro when the first Cuban doctors arrived. She remembers that residents had never seen a doctor inside their community, but when the Cubans arrived "we opened our doors to the doctors, they lived with us, they ate with us, and they worked among us."[7]

Stories like this permeate Venezuela. As a result of building a Cuban-type system, *teleSUR* reported that by April 11, 2020, the Venezuelan government had conducted 181,335 early polymerase chain reaction tests in time to have the lowest infection rate in Latin America. Venezuela had only six infections per million citizens while neighboring Brazil had 104 infections per million.[8]

When Rafael Correa was president of Ecuador, over 1,000 Cuban doctors formed the backbone of its health care system. Lenin Moreno was elected in 2017 and Cuban doctors were soon expelled, leaving public medicine in chaos. Moreno followed International Monetary Fund recommendations to slash Ecuador's health budget by 36%, leaving it without health care professionals, without PPE, and, above all, without a coherent health care system. While Venezuela and Cuba had 27 COVID-19 deaths, Ecuador's largest city, Guayaquil, had an estimated death toll of 7,600.[9]

International medical response: Cuban medicine is perhaps best known for its internationalism. A clear example is the devastating earthquake that rocked Haiti in 2010. Cuba sent medical staff who lived among Haitians and stayed months or years after the earthquake. U.S. doctors, however, did not sleep where Haitian victims huddled. They instead returned to luxury hotels at night and departed after a few weeks. John Kirk coined the term *disaster tourism* to describe the way that many rich countries respond to medical crises in poor countries.

The commitment that Cuban medical staff show internationally is a continuation of the effort made by the country's health care system in spending three decades finding the best way to strengthen bonds between caregiving professionals and those they serve. By 2008, Cuba had sent over 120,000 health care professionals to 154 countries, its doctors had cared for over 70 million people in the world, and almost 2 million people owed their lives to Cuban medical services in their country.

The Associated Press reported that when COVID-19 spread throughout the world, Cuba had 37,000 medical workers in 67 countries. It soon deployed additional doctors to Suriname, Jamaica, Dominica, Belize, Saint Vincent and the Grenadines, Saint Kitts and Nevis, Venezuela, and Nicaragua.[10] On April 16, *Granma* reported that "21 brigades of healthcare professionals have been deployed to join national and local efforts in 20 countries."[11] The same day, Cuba sent two hundred health personnel to Qatar.[12]

As northern Italy became the epicenter of COVID-19 cases, one of its hardest hit cities was Crema in the Lombardy region. The emergency room at its hospital was filled to capacity. On March 26, Cuba sent fifty-two doctors and nurses who set up a field hospital with three intensive care unit beds and thirty-two other beds with oxygen. A smaller and poorer Caribbean nation was one of the few aiding a major European power. Cuba's intervention took its toll. By April 17, thirty of its medical professionals who went abroad tested positive for COVID-19.[13]

Bringing the world to Cuba: The flip side of Cuba sending medical staff across the globe is the people it has brought to the island—both students and patients. When Cuban doctors were in the Republic of the Congo in 1966, they saw young people studying independently under streetlights at night and arranged for them to come to Havana. They brought in even more African students during the Angolan wars of 1975–88 and then brought large numbers of Latin American students to study medicine following Hurricanes Mitch and Georges. The number of students coming to Cuba to study expanded even more in 1999 when it opened classes at the Latin American School of Medicine (ELAM). By 2020, ELAM had trained thirty thousand doctors from over one hundred countries.

Cuba also has a history of bringing foreign patients for treatment. After the 1986 nuclear meltdown at Chernobyl, twenty-five thousand patients, mostly children, came to the island for treatment, with some staying for months or years. Cuba opened its doors, hospital beds, and a youth summer camp.

On March 12, nearly fifty crew members and passengers on the British cruise ship *MS Braemar* either had COVID-19 or were showing symptoms as the ship approached the Bahamas, a British Commonwealth nation. Since the *Braemar* flew the Bahamian flag as a Commonwealth vessel, there should have been no problem disembarking those aboard for treatment and return to the United Kingdom. But the Bahamian Ministry of Transport declared that the cruise ship would "not be permitted to dock at any port in the Bahamas and no persons will be permitted to disembark the vessel."[14] During the next five days, the United States, Barbados (another Commonwealth nation), and several other Caribbean countries turned it away. On March 18, Cuba became the only country to allow the *Braemar's* over one thousand crew members and passengers to dock. Treatment at Cuban hospitals was offered to those who felt too sick to fly. Most went by bus to José Martí International Airport for flights back to the United Kingdom. Before leaving, *Braemar* crew members displayed a banner reading "I love you Cuba!"[15] Passenger Anthea Guthrie posted on her Facebook page: "They have made us not only feel tolerated, but actually welcome."[16]

Medicine for all: In 1981, there was a particularly bad outbreak of the mosquito-borne dengue fever, which hits the island every few years. At the time, many first learned of the very high level of Cuba's research institutes that created Interferon Alpha 2B to successfully treat dengue. As Helen Yaffe points out, "Cuba's interferon has shown its efficacy and safety in the therapy of viral diseases including Hepatitis B and C, shingles, HIV-AIDS, and dengue."[17] It accomplished this by preventing complications that could worsen a patient's condition and result in death. The efficacy of the drug persisted for decades and, in 2020, it became vitally important as a potential cure for COVID-19. What also survived was Cuba's eagerness to develop a multiplicity of drugs and share them with other nations.

Cuba has sought to work cooperatively toward drug development with countries such as China, Venezuela, and Brazil. Collaboration with Brazil resulted in meningitis vaccines at a cost of 95¢ rather than $15 to $20 per dose. Finally, Cuba teaches other countries to produce medications themselves so they do not have to rely on purchasing them from richer countries.

In order to effectively cope with disease, drugs are frequently sought for three goals: *tests* to determine those infected; *treatments* to help ward off or cure problems; and *vaccines* to prevent infections. As soon as polymerase chain reaction rapid tests were available, Cuba began using them widely throughout the island. Cuba developed both Interferon Alpha 2B (a recombinant protein) and PrevengHo-Vir (a homeopathic medication). *TeleSUR* reported that by March 27, over forty-five countries had requested Cuba's Interferon in order to control and then get rid of the virus.[18]

Cuba's Center for Genetic Engineering and Biotechnology is seeking to create a vaccine against COVID-19. Its Director of Biomedical Research, Dr. Gerardo Guillén, confirmed that his team is collaborating with Chinese researchers in Yongzhou, Hunan province, to create a vaccine to stimulate the immune system and one that can be taken through the nose, which is the route of COVID-19 transmission. Whatever Cuba develops, it is certain that it will be shared with other countries at low cost, unlike U.S. medications that are patented at taxpayers' expense so that private pharmaceutical giants can price gouge those who need the medication.

Countries that have not learned how to share: Cuban solidarity missions show a genuine concern that often seems to be lacking in the health care systems of other countries. Medical associations in Venezuela, Brazil, and other countries are often hostile to Cuban doctors. Yet, they cannot find enough of their own doctors to travel in dangerous conditions or go to poor and rural areas, by donkey or canoe if necessary, as Cuban doctors do.

When in Peru in 2010, I visited the Pisco *policlínico*. Its Cuban director, Leopoldo García Mejías, explained that then-president Alan García did not want additional Cuban doctors and that they had to keep quiet in order to remain in Peru. Cuba is well aware that it has to adjust each medical mission to accommodate the political climate.

There is at least one exception to Cuban doctors remaining in a country according to the whims of the political leadership. Cuba began providing medical attention in Honduras in 1998. During the first eighteen months of Cuba's efforts in Honduras, the country's infant mortality rate dropped from 80.3 to 30.9 deaths per 1,000 live births. Political moods changed and, in 2005, Honduran Health Minister Merlin Fernández decided to kick Cuban doctors out. However, this led to so much opposition that the government changed course and allowed the Cubans to stay.

A disastrous and noteworthy example of when a country refused an offer of Cuban aid is in the aftermath of Hurricane Katrina. After the hurricane hit in 2005, 1,586 Cuban health care professionals were prepared to go to New Orleans. President George W. Bush, however, rejected the offer, acting as if it would be better for U.S. citizens to die rather than admit the quality of Cuban aid.

Though the U.S. government does not take kindly to students studying at ELAM, they are still able to apply what they learn when they come home. In 1988, Kathryn Hall-Trujillo of Albuquerque, New Mexico, founded the Birthing Project USA, which trains advocates to work with African-American women and connect with them through the first year of the infant's life. She is grateful for the Birthing Project's partnership with Cuba and the support that many ELAM students have given. In 2018, she told me: "We are a coming home place for ELAM students—they see working with us as a way to put into practice what they learned at ELAM."

Cuban doctor Julio López Benítez recalled in 2017 that when the country revamped its clinics in 1974, the old clinic model was one of patients going to clinics, but the new model was of clinics going to patients. Similarly, as ELAM graduate Dr. Melissa Barber looked at her South Bronx neighborhood during COVID-19, she realized that while most of the United States told people to go to agencies, what people need is a community approach that recruits organizers to go to the people. Dr. Barber is working in a coalition with South Bronx Unite, the Mott Haven Mamas, and many local tenant associations. As in Cuba, they are trying to identify those in the community who are vulnerable, including "the elderly, people who have infants and small children, homebound people, people that have multiple morbidities and are really susceptible to a virus like this one."[19]

As they discover who needs help, they seek resources to help them, such as groceries, PPE, medications, and treatment. In short, the approach of the coalition is to go to homes to ensure that people do not fall through the cracks. In contrast, U.S. national policy is for each state and each municipality to do what it feels like doing, which means that instead of having a few cracks that a few people fall through, there are enormous chasms with large groups careening over the edge. What countries with market economies need are actions like those in the South Bronx and Cuba carried out on a national scale.

This was what Che Guevara envisioned in 1951. Decades before COVID-19 jumped from person to person, Che's imagination went from doctor to doctor. Or perhaps many shared their own visions so widely that, after 1959, Cuba brought revolutionary medicine anywhere it could. Obviously, Che did not design the intricate inner workings of Cuba's current medical system. But he was followed by healers who wove additional designs into a fabric that now unfolds across the continents. At certain times in history, thousands or millions of people see similar images of a different future. If their ideas spread broadly enough during the hour that social structures are disintegrating, then a revolutionary idea can become a material force in building a new world.

Notes

1. Nancy Scheper-Hughes, "AIDS, Public Policy, and Human Rights in Cuba," *Lancet* 342, no. 8877 (1993), 965–67.
2. Pascual Serrano, "Cuba en Tiempos de Coronavirus," *cuartopoder*, March 21, 2020.

3. Helen Yaffe, "Cuban Medical Science in the Service of Humanity," *CounterPunch*, April 10, 2020.

4. Merriam Ansara, "John Lennon in Quarantine: A Letter From Havana," *CounterPunch*, April 9, 2020.

5. Heidy Ramírez Vázquez, "Medicamento Homeopático a Ciudadanos en Cuba," *Infomed al Día*, April 12, 2020.

6. Susana Hurlich, "Door by Door the Cuban Government Delivers Immune Boosting Medicine to the People," *Resumen-English*, April 9, 2020.

7. Cira Pascual Marquina, "A Caracas Commune Prepares for the Coronavirus Crisis: Four Voices from the Altos de Lidice Communal Healthcare System," *Venezuela Analysis*, April 11, 2020.

8. "Venezuela Has the Lowest Contagion Rate in Latin America," *teleSUR*, April 14, 2020.

9. Alan MacLeod, "Bodies in the Streets: IMF Imposed Measures Have Left Ecuador Unable to Cope with Coronavirus," *MintPress News*, April 13, 2020.

10. "Cuban Docs Fighting Coronavirus Around World, Defying US," *Associated Press*, April 3, 2020.

11. Ministry of Foreign A airs Statement, "The COVID-19 Pandemic Makes Clear the Need to Cooperate Despite Political Differences," *Granma*, April 16, 2020.

12. Ángel Guerra Cabrera, "Cuba: El Interferón Salva Vidas," *La Jornada*, April 16, 2020.

13. Farooque Chowdhury, "Undaunted Cuba Defies the Empire and Extends Hands of Solidarity to Continents," *Countercurrents*, April 17, 2020.

14. Peter Kornbluh, "Cuba's Welcome to a Covid-19-Stricken Cruise Ship Reflects a Long Pattern of Global Humanitarian Commitment," *Nation*, March 21, 2020.

15. Amy Goodman with Peter Kornbluh, "'Humanitarian Solidarity': Even Under U.S. Sanctions, Cuba Sends Doctor Brigade to Italy and More," *Democracy Now!*, March 24, 2020.

16. Kornbluh, "Cuba's Welcome to a Covid-19-Stricken Cruise Ship."

17. Helen Yaffe, "Cuba's Contribution to Combating COVID-19," *Links International Journal of Socialist Renewal*, March 14, 2020.

18. Over 45 Countries Ask Cuba for Interferon to Treat Covid-19," *teleSUR*, March 27, 2020.

19. John Tarleton, "Cuban-Trained Doctor Helps Mobilize Pandemic Response in Her South Bronx Community," *Indypendent*, April 11, 2020.

Index

CPSIA information can be obtained
at www.ICGtesting.com
Printed in the USA
FSHW022103281220
77216FS